FAMILIES IN LATER LIFE:
EMERGING THEMES AND CHALLENGES

FAMILIES IN LATER LIFE: EMERGING THEMES AND CHALLENGES

LILIANA SOUSA
EDITOR

Nova Science Publishers, Inc.
New York

For permission to use material from this book please contact us:
Telephone 631-231-7269; Fax 631-231-8175
Web Site: http://www.novapublishers.com

NOTICE TO THE READER

LIBRARY OF CONGRESS CATALOGING-IN-PUBLICATION DATA

Families in later life : emerging themes and challenges / editor, Liliana Sousa.
    p. cm.
Includes index.
ISBN 978-1-60692-328-3 (hardcover)
1. Older people--Family relationships. 2. Family. I. Sousa, Lillian.
HQ1061.F346 2009
306.87084'6--dc22
                  2008046761

Published by Nova Science Publishers, Inc. ◑ *New York*

CONTENTS

PREFACE

This book aims to help provide an understanding of the relationship between the elderly generation and the multigenerational families they belong to through an analysis of family and individual development in later life and a study of the structural and functional complexion of the multigenerational family (the basic unit of analysis). The increase of life expectancy and the consequent later ageing of the population is making Western families undergo considerable changes. The demographic ageing of societies is increasing the number of living generations and decreasing the number of living relatives within these generations. These ageing societies are also seeing a changing of some traditional life-transitions, such as individuals delaying economic independence from parents, marriage or long-term cohabitation, as well as parenting. Themes discussed in this book are: 1. multigenerational families are now commonplace in the western countries; 2. legacies and inheritance are an important theme for the integrity of families in later lives (since the increase of welfare-states, the economic importance of inheritance decreases); 3. a substantial proportion of elderly persons and their families live in poverty, having to deal with the diminishing of their sensoral and physical capacities, as well as lower income and higher medical expenses; 4. families have to combine the caregiving of elderly relatives with the caretaking of their own children and a professional career; 5. counseling becomes an important factor for older adults since many families issue then arise.

Editorial - Families play a major role in shaping our lives at all points in the life cycle. The family is as important in later life as it is at any other stage in life. However, there is still a relative scarcity of literature on families in later life, in comparison with the significant literature on the early stages of the family life cycle. In fact, most research and literature on ageing has concentrated either on the elderly person or the family carer, i.e., on considering the family as revolving around or dedicated to the elderly.

As old age expands, the number of elderly families increases and social changes take place, new themes are emerging. The purpose of this book is to provide an understanding of the topics that are emerging as life expectancy increases, specifically within the field of family relations and including new structures and normative/developmental challenges.

This book aims to provide a normative and developmental view of family relations in later life and to challenge negative stereotypes of old people, families in later life and the ageing process. These negative stereotypes have been highly influential in reinforcing the view of old age as a phase in life that should be shunned or denied. It is our purpose to understand families in later life as a normative phase in the life cycle which involves an emotional starting and ending point, the former marked by a chronological age and the latter by physical closure (death).

This introduction aims to summarise the main topics arising out of research into ageing families and to highlight emerging themes and challenges, particularly those relating to the normative process of family and individual ageing.

Chapter 1 - The multigenerational family is flourishing nowadays, mainly as a result of increased life expectancy, meaning there is a greater probability that individuals will spend a longer period of time in the family development phase known as *"families in later life"* (Carter & McGoldrick, 2005). However, few theoretical perspectives consider the challenges and rewards of multigenerational family relationships in later life (e.g. Silverstein & Bengtson, 1997; King & Wynne, 2004).

In general, research in family relationships and individual development has been treated separately. Ryff and Seltzer (1995: 95) argue that "studies of individual development in adulthood and the later years show only oblique links with family life" and "the extensive literature on family relations extends across different age groups and life periods, and yet (…) shows limited connection to theories of, and findings about, individual development".

Moreover, common sense conveys the image of elderly people as incapable, dependent, vulnerable and depressed (Sousa & Cerqueira, 2006). Research, however, has revealed the important roles they play within the family, such as substituting parents in caring for grandchildren (Hader, 1965). Although significant, these functions always seem to assume a secondary role within the family scenario. The elderly generation only appear to be useful when they substitute the younger generations or provide support that the latter ones are too busy to manage. A question mark therefore remains over the role of the oldest generation within the multigenerational family: is it just an appendix to the family that can be called upon to replace a more vital organ in times of difficulty or does it have a unique and irreplaceable role to play in the functioning of the multigenerational family system?

This chapter aims to help provide an understanding of the relationship between the elderly generation and the multigenerational families they belong to through an analysis of family and individual development in later life and a study of the structural and functional complexion of the multigenerational family (the basic unit of analysis).

The following pages will cover: a) the importance of studying the multigenerational family in the present moment; b) a structural characterization of the multigenerational family (a heuristic tool for understanding the extended family dynamics that enables its differentiation from other family and social systems); c) issues involving family and individual development in later life that enable a better understanding regarding the experience of the elderly generations; d) a description of the fundamental functions in the multigenerational family and a characterization of the family members who perform them; e) an analysis of the relationship between the structural and functional dimensions of multigenerational families and the individual and family development tasks in the later stages of life, as a means of grasping a better understanding of the relationship between the elderly person and his/her multigenerational family.

Chapter 2 - Material inheritance (the creation and transmission of a material legacy from one generation to another) is not only a matter of economics. In addition to serving an economic purpose, the transmission of material property also has emotional implications in terms of family relationships: it may facilitate continuity or create conflict and separation.

In this chapter the authors present an exploratory study of elderly Portuguese donors (aged over 74), with the aim of exploring more deeply the role played by material inheritance in the construction of family integrity (achieving meaning, connection and continuity within the multigenerational family). The results show that material inheritance: i) constitutes a normative challenge for later life families, combining instrumental, relational and emotional/symbolic dimensions; ii) plays a part in constructing family integrity through the balanced management of material property and care; iii) involves basic family skills such as adaptability, filial maturity, open communication and joint problem solving.

From this perspective, material inheritance represents an *window* on family dynamics and processes in the final phase of life and an opportunity for families and professionals to maximise or recreate the skills and transactional patterns associated with the construction of (individual and family) integrity.

Chapter 3 - Counseling older adults with family issues addresses problems of older adults within their primary interpersonal context, the family. Although it is still a rare topic and practice, it is, however, an important response to challenges faced by older adults in later life.

With the purpose of making a review of the current state of knowledge in this field and in order to reflect on some aspects that have not yet been the object of many studies, this chapter combines theory and research with case examples, emphasizing the practical clinical decisions faced when working with older people in either individual or institutional settings. It addresses issues relevant to counseling with older people and aims to be useful not only to those readers who are involved in the provision of psychological services but also to those who are interested in the challenges and concerns faced by older people.

It closes with the importance of using empowerment and forgiveness when the older patient is confronted with the need to deal with complex family situations. It also stresses the need to do more research in the field.

Chapter 4 - Elderly men on ageing families constitute a recent focus of research. Since gender and families in later life have been mostly studied in view of women's experiences, scientific reflections addressing older men's family roles, their sense of maleness and the relationships they establish with relatives remained scarce and demanding greater awareness. This chapter focuses on issues involving older men and late-life masculinities, and aims to make contributions to the ongoing debate on gender and ageing by reframing traditional research themes as that of caregiving relationships. At the outset, it takes a glance at older men's gendered lives, exploring the seemingly incompatibility of "old men" and "masculinity", and focus on the way the salience of gender ideology is revealed in specific live events as retirement, widowhood and caring for a dependent family member. Secondly, allowing for this last experience's relevance in contemporary ageing families, the chapter presents some findings from a qualitative study that looks carefully at the features that characterize the willingness of a group of men aged 65 and over to assume the "non-traditional" caregiving role and the masculinity negotiations underneath its enactment. As spouse carers differ from other family caregivers on many dimensions, particularly on the extent to which caring for an ill partner may be a "normative" part of the marriage contract and entail necessary tasks for sustaining the quality of the relationship (maintaining the independence as a couple), the significance ascribed to the experience within the marital dynamics is emphasised.

Chapter 5 - Caring for an elderly dependent relative has been described mainly as a burden or a stressful experience which has a significant impact on the health of family carers and other aspects of their lives. Over the past two decades, researchers have examined the effects of several types of intervention designed to reduce the stress and burden associated with the caring role. The findings, however, are varied and inconsistent and no single intervention has been completely successful in responding to all the needs and problems of carers. The relative failure of intervention outcomes can frequently be attributed to the methodological weakness of intervention research studies. This chapter provides a summary of the interventions designed to reduce the stress and burden for carers and an overview of their (in)effectiveness. It emphasises the need to consider other reasons beyond methodological issues in order to understand the mixed picture provided by research findings. It also underlines the need to move beyond the burden paradigm emphasised in the idea of the "biomedicalization of caregiving".

Chapter 6 - Significant increases in life expectancy over the last decades, with the consequent increase in the number of people suffering from chronic illnesses, started to raise new concerns regarding the elderly. At the same time, demographic and lifestyle changes contribute to a lower availability of the family to provide care. Thus, measures to improve the quality of life of elderly people are now a major priority in main research and governmental programs. Here we report the findings from a study with a sample of the Portuguese population, from the interior centre town of Viseu, which is situated in a transition area between the coast and the interior, and between north and south, and which is characterised by large asymmetries and inequalities. The study aimed to investigate the characteristics of chronic illnesses, quality of life, functional dependence in daily activities and family support in this population. Elderly people were subdivided in two samples: those still living at home (either by themselves or with family members) and those institutionalized. Statistical analyses compared the main aspects of interest between the two groups and these are discussed in detail. In general, it can be concluded that the characteristics of this sample are comparable to those observed in other studies. Loneliness, low retirement pensions, family rejection and social exclusion are the most significant factors compromising the quality of life of the elderly from this region. Measures to deal with the significant ageing of the population and its consequences worldwide must take into account the need for independence and social support for a longer period of time, and the financial and personal costs of caregiving.

Chapter 7 - The intention of this book is to introduce new themes that may enable theoretical frameworks for families in later life to be constructed or redefined. It seeks to go beyond ageism, so to create a view that does not focus only on health problems, functional and mental decline and family caregiving. Adopting a normative perspective, means to construct a way of thinking about families in later life that creates a sense of purpose, diminishes the fear of ageing, and enables us to view later life as another phase in life. This goal may be ambitious, but the authors would like to sow the seeds that will lead to the rediscovery of ageing.

In this final chapter the authors hope to contribute towards extending our understanding of one of the few theoretical frameworks that offers a normative and developmental perspective on families in later life: family integrity (King & Wynne, 2004). Whereas there is a vast amount of literature on the early stages of the family life cycle, relatively few theoretical contributions cover family processes in later life (King & Wynne, 2004). Therefore, "a normal life course perspective of family development and ageing is needed, emphasising the potential for growth and meaning as much as negative aspects of change" (Walsh, 2005: 310). This study has been developed in order to deepen our understanding of the process of constructing family integrity, as opposed to disconnection or alienation.

In: Families in Later Life: Emerging Themes and Challenges
Editor: Liliana Sousa

ISBN 978-1-60692-328-3
© 2009 Nova Science Publishers, Inc.

Editorial

NEW THEMES ON AGEING FAMILIES

Liliana Sousa

SUMMARY

Families play a major role in shaping our lives at all points in the life cycle. The family is as important in later life as it is at any other stage in life. However, there is still a relative scarcity of literature on families in later life, in comparison with the significant literature on the early stages of the family life cycle. In fact, most research and literature on ageing has concentrated either on the elderly person or the family carer, i.e., on considering the family as revolving around or dedicated to the elderly.

As old age expands, the number of elderly families increases and social changes take place, new themes are emerging. The purpose of this book is to provide an understanding of the topics that are emerging as life expectancy increases, specifically within the field of family relations and including new structures and normative/developmental challenges.

This book aims to provide a normative and developmental view of family relations in later life and to challenge negative stereotypes of old people, families in later life and the ageing process. These negative stereotypes have been highly influential in reinforcing the view of old age as a phase in life that should be shunned or denied. It is our purpose to understand families in later life as a normative phase in the life cycle which involves an emotional starting and ending point, the former marked by a chronological age and the latter by physical closure (death).

This introduction aims to summarise the main topics arising out of research into ageing families and to highlight emerging themes and challenges, particularly those relating to the normative process of family and individual ageing.

1. RESEARCH ON FAMILIES IN LATER LIFE

In 1989, Denise Flori published an article in the Journal of Marital and Family Therapy entitled "The prevalence of later life family concerns in marriage and family therapy journal literature (1976-1985)". This analysis aimed to assess the amount of attention devoted to problems associated with ageing within a family context. The author argued that the increased number of older adults and multigenerational families should be reflected in an increased focus on later family life issues. However, her main findings indicated that neither journal

(Family Process and the Journal of Marital and Family Therapy) covered later life family issues to any appreciable degree. It concluded that elderly people in marital and family relationships represented a new area of development in family therapy.

In 2006, Van Amburg *et al.* published an article, also in the Journal of Marital and Family Therapy, entitled "Ageing and family therapy: prevalence of ageing issues and later family life concerns in marital and family therapy literature (1986-1993)". Following Flori's findings, the authors decided to analyse developments in themes linking older adults and families. They conducted a content analysis of 873 articles published in the Journal of Marital and Family Therapy, Family Process, Family Systems Medicine, and the Journal of Family Psychology between 1986 and 1993. Only 3.2% (n=28) of those articles specifically focussed on ageing issues and later life family concerns. The most common topics were adult child/older parent relationships, the problems of caregiving and parent/adult child conflict, spousal caregiving, depression in older people within the context of caregiving and grandparent/grandchild relationships. A variety of theoretical approaches were adopted by the authors of the 28 ageing-focused articles: transgenerational (the most common), family life cycle, strategic, experiential, behavioural, and constructivism (the least frequent).

The authors outlined the following picture of the gerontological issues that emerged:

- As gerontological content is sparsely represented in family therapy literature, "the family therapy community is still engaged in coming of age".
- The most common problems leading families to resort to therapy occurred within the context of adult child/older parent relationships (e.g., caregiving and/or conflicts).
- Although the problems discussed in the 28 ageing-focused articles were diverse, many of the issues facing older adults, such as the transition to retirement, widowhood, sibling relationships in later life, sexual dysfunction, or long-lasting marriages, were noticeably absent.

2. RESEARCH ON FAMILIES IN LATER LIFE (2000-2008)

To supplement these findings and bring them up to date, we also decided to analyse the content of articles focusing on families in later life. This was considered a means of understanding the most common, as well as the emerging or neglected, research topics and a method of outlining paths for research into families in later life.

We selected six journals on the basis of their aims, field (family studies and gerontology) and impact factor. Three journals dedicated to family studies with higher impact factors (ISI Web of Knowledge) were selected: Family Process (impact factor, 2006 = 0.935); Family Relations (impact factor, 2006 = 0.731) and the Journal of Family Psychology (impact factor, 2006 = 1.833). Another three journals covering the topic of gerontology were then selected: The Gerontologist (impact factor, 2006 = 1.965); Age and Ageing (impact factor, 2006 = 1.919) and the Journals of Gerontology Series B – Psychological Sciences and Social Sciences (impact factor, 2006 = 1.720).

Key words were selected for the search on the basis of our objectives and some previous content review. Key words for the family studies journals were elderly, later life, ageing, old people and the aged, whilst the key words for the journals on gerontology were family, marital, siblings, grandparent, parent, child, filial. A search was carried out of articles published between 2000 and 2008 in which the key word featured in the title, abstract and/or key-word listing. The topics for analysis were defined in advance on the basis of the topics contained in the six journals (Table 1) and the articles were classified by the author of this chapter.

Table 1. Research topics on families in later life

1. **Diversity**: ethnicity, social class and sexual orientation.
2. **Social problems and social challenges**: poverty, immigration, combat veterans, minority groups, the homeless.
3. **Individual developmental**: social, physical, psychological and emotional development; sexuality; life-span; life cycle; life course; generativity; identity.
4. **Social policy and economy**: social support systems; family and individual benefits; policies; the health system and insurance; family policy.
5. **Family intervention**: therapy; family therapy; clinical; counselling; psycho-educational; community intervention; support groups; formal support; family-focused prevention programs.
6. **Social interactions**: attitudes; ageism; interpersonal relations; social networks; community interactions; informal support; social adaptation.
7. **Educational gerontology**: formal and informal education.
8. **Health status**: functionality; routine activities; depression; chronic diseases; impairments; cognitive functioning; dementia.
9. **Gerontotechnology**: use of technology with the elderly and their families.
10. **Research methods development**: psychometric tests; models testing; scales development; methodological and statistical advances; assessment.
11. **Family and other systems:** families in relation to other formal and informal systems.
11.1 **Health care**: primary care; palliative care; rehabilitation; clinical and/or geriatric medicine; nursing; hospitalization; medical information; assessment; case management.
11.2 **Institutionalization**: residential care; nursing homes; old peoples' homes; long-term placement.
11.3. **Other systems**: education; employment; social welfare; friends and neighbours.
11.4. **Community care**: support services; adult day services; community-based services; long-term home care.
12. **Family process**: the family as a system; family relations; living arrangements; life stages.
13. **Marital process**: marital interaction.
14. **Parental process**: parent-child relationships.
15. **Grandparenting**: grandparent-grandchildren interaction.
16. **Sibling process**: sibling relationships.
17. **Families in transition:** separation, divorce and single parenting; remarriage and the stepfamily; adoption; death and dying, grief and bereavement.
18. **Family violence and abuse**: abuse of the elderly.
19. **Family caregiving**: carers to the elderly.
20. **Spirituality**/religion
21. **Gender**: influence of gender and specificities.

Main Topics

In the initial selection, 368 articles were identified although 45 were excluded since family issues (such as marital status) were only considered as socio-demographic variables. A total of 323 articles were identified (Table 2): 41.8% - The Gerontologist; 35.3% - Journals of Gerontology Series B – Psychological Sciences and Social Sciences; 10.5% - Family Relations; 7.7% - Age and Ageing; 3.7% - Journal of Family Psychology; 0.9% - Family Process. Most of the articles (84.8%) were published in the gerontological journals, with just 15.1% appearing in the family studies journals. As was the case with Flori (1989) and Van Amburg et al. (2006), our results underlined the scant attention devoted to families in later life by the family studies journals. Van Amburg et al. (2006) justified similar results (a scarcity of literature) of the basis of the type of journals included in the study (possibly the number of ageing-focused articles is lower than in other family therapy or more gerontologically focused journals). This explanation was not reinforced by our results. In fact, we investigated other family studies journals and found only 49 articles relating to families in later life. Furthermore, the authors suggest that this topic is probably more developed in gerontological journals and we did, in fact, find 273 articles in those publications. However, they represented around 13.6% of all the articles published by the three journals used in this content analysis. It seems that research on the family is devoted more to other stages of the family life cycle, whilst research on gerontological issues does not focus on family processes. Therefore, families in later life do not receive enough attention from researchers.

We found no consistent trend relating to the year of publication (Table 2), given that more or less the same number of articles was published each year.

Table 2. Articles on families in later life by journal and year of publication

Year	Journal						Total
	Age and Ageing	Geronto -logist	Journals of Gerontology	Family Process	Family Relations	Journal of Family Psychology	
2000	1	13	10	2	5	0	**31**
2001	4	16	13	0	4	1	**38**
2002	2	13	13	0	5	2	**35**
2003	2	23	15	0	2	2	**44**
2004	3	12	15	1	3	0	**34**
2005	4	20	18	0	3	0	**45**
2006	7	19	18	0	10	2	**56**
2007	2	19	12	0	1	4	**38**
2008*	0	0	0	0	1	1	**2**
Total	25	135	114	3	34	12	**323**
Total of articles published	732	628	653	333	365	506	**3217**
% of articles on families in later life	3.4%	21.5%	17.5%	0.9%	9.3%	2.4%	**10,04%**

* This analysis took place in March 2008, when normally just one issue of each journal had been published.

Table 3. Classification of the articles on the topics

Topics	Family Process	Family Relations	Journal of Family Psychology	Age and Ageing	Gerontologist	Journals of Gerontology	Total
1. Diversity				1	5	3	9
2. Social problems		2	1		25	33	61
3. Individual developmental		7		1	6	17	31
4. Social policy		1			8	2	11
5. Family intervention	2	7		1	28	1	39
6. Social interaction	2	4			13	25	44
7. Educational gerontology		3					3
8. Health status		8	2	21	69	53	153
9. Gerontotechnology		1			6		7
10. Research		1		2	13	3	19
11. Family and other systems							
11.1 Health care		6		8	15	2	31
11.2 Institutionalization				1	19	8	28
11.3 Other systems		2			5	1	8
11.4 Community care				2	14	4	20
12. Family	2	7	3		19	26	57
13. Marital		7	2	1	21	30	61
14. Parental		9	3		11	23	46
15. Grandparenting		6	3		5	7	21
17. Families in transition		1	1	1	13	15	31
18. Family abuse		1			2		3
19. Family caregiving		13	1	10	93	40	157
20. Spirituality		2	1		1	1	5
21. Gender issues		1	2		11	30	44

The articles were classified into several categories/topics (Table 3). Each article was classified in terms of the different topics involved in the study, although the articles, in fact, usually crossed over into different subject areas, such as family carers, gender and kinship.

The results revealed two major topics:

- Health status (47.4%). These articles refer the health problems of elderly people and/or family carers (other family members are occasionally mentioned).
- Family caregiving (48.6%). The articles mention factors associated with the family carer, usually, stress, burden, dynamics and carer selection.

The subsequent most frequently cited topics clearly had a much lower weighting:

- Social problems (18.9%) (e.g. social diversity or vulnerability).
- Marital process (18.9%) (e.g. spousal caregiving or marital satisfaction).

Table 4. Classification of articles on research topics by year of publication

Topics	2000	2001	2002	2003	2004	2005	2006	2007	2008	Total
1. Diversity	1	1		2		1	2	2		9
2. Social problems	6	6	8	10	3	12	8	8		61
3. Individual developmental	4	5	3	6	3	5	2	2	1	31
4. Social policy		1	2	1	3	2	1		1	11
5. Family intervention	2	1	3	11	7	2	5	7	1	39
6. Social interaction	5	5	4	8	5	7	6	4	0	44
7. Educational gerontology				2			1			3
8. Health status	12	19	19	20	16	26	26	15		153
9. Gerontotechnology			1	2	1	1	2			7
10. Research			3	6	2	4	3	1		19
11. Family and other systems										
11.1 Health care	4	2	2	4	6	4	3	6		31
11.2 Institutionalization	2	3	5		2	8	5	3		28
11.3. Other systems			4	2			1	1		8
11.4 Community care		5	2	2	2	3	3	3		20
12. Family	4	4	7	10	5	10	10	6	1	57
13. Marital	9	8	4	4	11	9	8	8		61
14. Parental	6	7	4	4	3	5	10	6	1	46
15. Grandparenting	3	2	5	2	2	2	2	2	1	21
17. Families in transition	7	6	5	2		4	5	2		31
18. Family abuse					1	1		1		3
19. Family caregiving	15	23	20	24	14	17	23	20	1	157
20. Spirituality	1	1	1			1		1		5
21. Gender	10	8	3	4	4	3	8	4		44
Total	31	38	35	44	34	45	56	38	2	323

In addition, no articles could be categorized under one of the previously defined topics: sibling processes. Categorization of the articles by year of publication indicated consistency (Table 4).

Finally, commonalities (the number of times a topic is associated with another topic in the some article) were calculated (Table 5). The data revealed that health status and family caregiving are often associated (95 articles), and are also commonly associated with several other topics, in particular marital processes.

Table 5. Commonalities: shared topics

Topics	2	3	4	5	6	7	8	9	10	11.1	11.2	11.3	11.4	12	13	14	15	17	18	19	20	21
1. Diversity	4	1	2	1	1		4			2	1	1	1	2	2			1	1	4	4	4
2. Social problems		8	2	7	11	2	15		1	2	2	2	6	14	8	10	3	3	2	26	1	11
3. Individual developmental			1	4	4	2	11				2	2	4	4	11	7	5	5	1	6	1	7
4. Social policy				2	2		3		2	1	1	1			2					7	1	1
5. Family intervention					4	2	19	3	3	3	1	3	3	4	2	2	1	2	2	27	1	1
6. Social interaction						2	14	1		1		1	7	7	7	3	2			19		5
7. Educational gerontology							1	1														
8. Health status								5	10	17	17	2	8	12	34	8	4	12		95		12
9. Gerontotechnology											1									7		
10. Research										3	4	3	4							1		1
11.1 Health care												2	9	8	2		1	1		16		1
11.2 Institutionalization												2	8	2	1	2	1	3		19		1
11.3 Other systems													1	2						4		
11.4 Community care														2	2		1	1		14		
12. Family															1	12	8	1		15		7
13. Marital																8	3	11		16	2	19
14. Parental																		5		20		13
15. Grandparenting																		1		5	5	5
17. Families in transition																				10	3	4
18. Family abuse																						
19. Family caregiving																						18
20. Spirituality																						
21. Gender issues																						

2.1. Diversity

Diversity included articles on ethnicity (for instance, African American, Chinese, Latin or tribal communities), sexual orientation (gay, lesbian and bisexual) and social class. These articles were commonly associated with health problems (chronic disease, dementia, dependence) and family caregiving (availability, beliefs, and effects).

Five articles focussed on positive and/or normative aspects: family strengths and the wisdom of the elderly as a challenge to elder abuse in tribal communities (Holkup *et al.*, 2007); well-being in older Mexican American couples (Peek *et al.*, 2006); the influence of family obligations and relationships on retirement decisions (Szinovacz, DeViney & Davey' 2001); experiences and realities of gay and lesbian seniors and their families in accessing health and social services in the community (Brotman, Ryan & Cormier, 2003); social support for lesbians, gays and bisexuals (Grossman, D'Augelli & Hershberger, 2000).

2.2. Social Problems and Challenges

Articles under the heading of social problems included immigration, adversity, poverty, homelessness and combat veterans. Most of these research subjects were included in the family caregiving process and/or were related to the health status of the elderly and/or the family carer.

With regard to the issue of immigration, for example, Wong, Yoo and Stewart (2006) studied the changing meaning of family support amongst older Chinese and Korean immigrants. The participants discussed changing views on family social support and the need to integrate both American and Chinese or Korean culture, leading to biculturalism. Three distinct perspectives on the family emerged: i) participants felt they had become peripheral family members, ii) parents were no longer authority figures in families, and iii) participants were more independent.

In relation to the theme of adversity, Wickrama, Conger and Abraham (2005) examined the intergenerational transmission of adversity through mental disorder and physical illness. The findings demonstrated key mediating pathways in the intergenerational transmission of social adversity and the importance of improving both socioeconomic and health resources. On the issue of poverty, McGarry and Schoeni (2005) investigated poverty in widow(er)s and stressed that elderly widows are three times more likely to live in poverty than older married people. Crane *et al.* (2005) explored the causes of homelessness in later life. The results showed that two-thirds of the participants had never been homeless before and that most subjects became homeless through a combination of personal problems and incapacities, gaps in welfare policy and inadequate delivery of services. Combat veterans received also attention. Rose *et al.* (2007) argued that quality care for frail elderly people should include the family and be evaluated in terms of patient-centred, family-focused care. Coleman & Podolskij (2007) studied the loss and recovery of identity in the life histories of Soviet World War II veterans.

Despite these specific issues, the articles usually focussed on, or included as a supplementary issue, the process of family caregiving (usually adult children carers) or else focussed specifically on stress and burden in family carers and included some discussion of interventions.

2.3. Individual Development

In general, the articles classified under this category highlighted the following themes: i) ageing and health-related problems (such as cognitive impairment, incontinence, disability, health-seeking behaviors); ii) ageing and social impacts (such as the sense of usefulness, loss of significant others, loneliness); iii) ageing and psychological changes (such as changes in personality traits, end of life decisions, well-being and life satisfaction); iv) ageing and changes in family processes (such as marital quality, the transition to retirement and family relationships, parent–child relationships). Gender emerged as a transversal topic, usually focusing on women. Some articles involved a developmental perspective on the process of family caregiving, such as the evolving dynamics of caregiving (since caregiving may last for more than 10 years) and preparation for future care needs. Roberto and Jarrott (2008) explored the topic of carers and life-span, identifying several developmental themes within research into late-life caregiving including individual well-being, relational effects and caregiver growth. Some alternative topics also emerged; for example, Colvin et al. (2004) studied the impact of gaining a child through birth, adoption, or marriage from a life-span perspective.

The King and Wynne (2004) article on family integrity offered an important framework for the study of families in later life from a normative and developmental perspective. The authors argued that, in contrast to the rich and abundant literature on the early stages of the family life cycle, there are relatively few theoretical accounts of family developmental processes in later life. The concept of "family integrity" represents the ultimate, positive outcome of the older adult's developmental striving toward meaning, connection, and continuity within his/her multigenerational family.

2.4. Social Policy and Economics

Social policy received less attention, probably because social policies tend to be centred on the individual rather than the family or because they feature more in the sociology, economics or policy journals. Nevertheless, it is worth noting a certain inconsistency: whereas almost all states, societies and communities demand family support for elderly people, little attention is paid to social policies that support families in caregiving. Additionally, family caregiving is a recent topic on the political agenda and states (especially in southern Europe) emphasize family responsibility for elderly relatives.

Articles on this topic included issues such as pensions, health insurance, the satisfaction of elderly people with the social support system, the balance of long-term care costs as opposed to family home care, and social support for families, also taking minority groups and family benefits into account.

Feinberg and Newman (2004) described the initial experiences of 10 states (in the USA) in providing support services to family or informal carers of elderly adults and adults with disabilities. The authors argued that viewing family carers as a client population was a paradigm shift for many state officials.

2.5. Family Intervention

Articles on family intervention focussed mainly on the health problems of elderly people and their carers, as well as on the different types of intervention used to support them. Essentially the following types of intervention may be identified: i) carer-centred intervention (stress, anger, burden and depression management; improvements in quality of life and self-efficacy, training and education, increasing the use of respite services, the impact on the family carer of interventions centred on the elderly person); ii) family-centred intervention (prevention and mitigation of abuse of the elderly); iii) dual interventions involving family caregivers and care receivers; iv) dual interventions involving staff from institutions and family members. It was possible to identify several intervention/support models: community programs (formal and/or informal), internet-based social support networks, psycho-educational and psychosocial models, skills training and support groups. Sörensen, Pinquart and Duberstein (2002) have published the results of a meta-analysis on caregiver intervention studies in which the authors aimed to determine the effectiveness of interventions for family carers of older adults. The findings revealed that: i) combined interventions produced significant improvements to the carer burden, depression, subjective well-being, perceived caregiver satisfaction, ability/knowledge, and care receiver symptoms; ii) intervention had a greater effect on increasing carer ability/knowledge than on the carer burden and depression; iii) psycho-educational and psychotherapeutic interventions showed the most consistent short-term effects; iv) intervention had less effect for carers of dementia sufferers than for other groups.

We would like to highlight two issues that appear to reveal new themes in families in later life:

a) Caregiver compassion. Schulz et al. (2007) aim to stimulate discussion and research into patient suffering and caregiver compassion. The authors consider those two constructs as central to an understanding of the family caregiving process.

b) Ageism in family and marital therapy. Ivey, Wieling and Harris (2000) point out the impact of ageism on therapy with elderly couples and families in later life, highlighting some neglected key aspects, namely sexuality and intimacy.

2.6. Social Interaction

Articles on social interaction referred mainly to social networks of elderly people and/or family carers. Studies of social networks of elderly people tended to characterise the members (family, friends, neighbours, formal elements) and describe the functions of the social network (usually material, instrumental and emotional support). Some specific topics emerged: network type and mortality risk in later life, the presence of a spouse and frequency of interaction with others, social network typologies and mental health, cognitive decline, depression and isolation, social network differences in terms of gender, age and socioeconomic status, interactions across the life span. These topics were developed in relation to different populations such as immigrants, ethnic groups, widows, elderly dependents, gays, lesbians and bisexuals.

The emerging new themes appear to be: i) volunteer participation as a means of recovering from spousal bereavement in later life (Li, 2007), showing that people who experienced spousal loss reported a greater likelihood of pursuing volunteer roles, not immediately, but a few years after the death of their spouse; ii) network types amongst the elderly and the relationship between network type and morale (Litwin, 2001), in which the findings suggest that respondents in diverse or friendship networks reported the highest morale whilst those in exclusively family or restricted networks had the lowest. Whereas the first article points to the positive social integration of elderly people even after a significant loss, the second focuses on developmental and normative processes in later life.

The articles also emphasised the family carer network: spouse and adult child networks, social support systems (informal, church, and formal), social support and perceived burden, rewards. Family support, responsibility and interaction involving the elderly were studied in situations in which the elderly relative was in long-term care.

Hong *et al.* (2001) studied a topic that is frequently neglected, namely older women with a mentally retarded adult child, examining the psychological consequences of changes in social support during later years.

2.7. Educational Gerontology

Only three articles were categorized under the topic of educational gerontology. This issue is quite well-developed and there is a journal specifically dedicated to the topic (Educational Gerontology). Educational gerontology may focus more on individual issues and less on family issues.

Two articles came from Ballard and Morris (2003 a, b). The authors reported on a needs assessment for mid-life and older adults relating to family life education. The findings emphasised that the highest rated topics were nutrition and health, fitness and exercise, and the positive aspects of ageing. They subsequently reviewed the theory and practice of education with midlife and older adult populations in order to understand preferences for instructional strategies and techniques and the factors influencing attendance, participation and satisfaction with programs. Price and Whitney (2006) conducted a comprehensive review of educational resources specific to family gerontology in order to increase awareness of family gerontology and encourage the advance of this interdisciplinary field.

2.8. Health Status

Articles covered a wide range of health problems affecting different family members (particularly elderly individuals, carers or spouses) and family subsystems (for instance, marital or parental). In general, the articles focussed on the health problems of the elderly and their effects, impact or associations with health problems in family members (mainly the family carer) or subsystems (mainly the marital system).

Most of the health problems of the elderly are age-related and include a wide range of physical and mental disturbances, namely cognitive decline, diabetes, vision impairment, Alzheimer's disease, dementia, cognitive impairment, depression, mental health, Parkinson's disease, hearing loss and fecal incontinence. Other health problems may also occur, such as asthma, malnutrition, cancer, pain or strokes. Certain treatments, such as surgery and rehabilitation, were studied in terms of their impact on the family.

These health problems tended to be associated with health problems in other family members, particularly the family carer, namely (perceived) health status, psychiatric morbidity, sleep disturbances, emotional distress, burden, health behaviours, anxiety, depression and stress. In addition, other indicators of family and individual functioning were covered, namely participation in leisure activities, perception of quality of family relations, marital satisfaction, social participation, well-being, quality of life, self-esteem, life satisfaction, self-efficacy, ability/knowledge and daily functioning.

The family carer was the family member most frequently discussed. Some studies reported on family carers in general whilst others distinguished between spouses and children and/or between genders. The positive impact of family caregiving seems to an increasingly popular research area and includes personal growth, social involvement, self-esteem, ability and knowledge. In relation to family carers, the issues of grief and bereavement were covered in relation, for example, to progressive deterioration in cases of dementia.

The marital subsystem also featured as a subject in the articles, usually in relation to the impact of a spouse's health problem on their partner, i.e., marital processes/quality and health problems (in particular, depression) and spouses as caregivers (mainly female carers). Studies on the role of marital quality highlighted other issues which still require further investigation. For example, Brown, Bulanda and Lee (2005) examined the significance of non-marital cohabitation, with findings that suggested that cohabiters report more depressive symptoms, on average, than married couples.

As a transitional process in the life cycle, widowhood received some attention, mainly in terms of the associated health problems: i) Fry (2001) studied the relationship between the self-efficacy beliefs of the widowed and their ratings of perceived health-related quality of life, life satisfaction, and self-esteem; ii) van Gelder *et al.* (2006) investigated the association between marital status and living situation. Couples in long-term marriages received limited attention: Yorgason *et al.* (2006) studied long-term marriage and daily health-related relationship stressors.

Parental issues were rarely covered and usually associated with caregiving. Single parenthood emerged in one article: Avison & Davies (2005) studied the effects of single parenthood on parental health. Grandparenting was not a common topic although some articles emphasised the role played by grandparents in caring for their grandchildren and the impact on their health (for example, Hughes *et al.*, 2007).

The family as a system was rarely considered. Various studies investigated family history and its influence on health problems, although some did focus on family adaptation and communication. Some aspects of intergenerational transmission and relations were also addressed. For example, Wickrama, Conger and Abraham (2005) investigated processes accounting for the transmission of socioeconomic deprivation from one generation to the next through mental disorder and physical illness.

Some studies focussed on intervention, almost always of the type designed to improve carer health and well-being or dual interventions centred on the caregiver and care recipient. In addition, some studies concentrated on the development of scales, usually to assess the situation of carers, (such as burden, self-efficacy and grief).

Three topics emerged in just one article: genetic testing, childlessness and ethics. Roberts (2000) surveyed the children and siblings of patients with Alzheimer's disease with regard to potential predictive testing options for the disorder. Zhang & Hayward (2001) studied the effects of childlessness on loneliness and depression in elderly people. O'Keeffe (2001) studied resuscitation guidelines, emphasizing ethical considerations.

2.9. Gerontotechnology

There were seven articles on gerontotechnology, all focussing on family caregiving, five of which were also associated with health problems. The articles mainly described the use of various technologies to support family carers, such as internet-based or telephone-based support, video-conferencing and multimedia.

2.10. Research Development and Methods

In terms of research, most of the articles focused on the development of scales to assess various family carer difficulties, such as problems, preferences, burden, grief, task management, stress, strain, and self-efficacy. Scales were also based on dual assessment, for example, the provision and reception of care and satisfaction with formal care. Certain ethical issues were highlighted, such as the protection of patient privacy when compiling research data and the techniques used to recruit and retain participants in research. Mitrani *et al.* (2005) adapted the Structural Family Systems rating to assess interaction patterns in families of dementia carers. This article focussed on the family as a system rather than the more common approach of focussing on the family carer alone.

2.11. The Family and other Systems

This topic was divided into three subcategories: families and health care, families and institutionalisation, and families and other systems, including employment and social welfare. This separation allowed for an understanding of family interactions with the more important systems in later life.

Articles on health care mainly covered research associated with family involvement or family responsibility towards elderly relatives in long or short-term care, usually in nursing homes. Within this area, family carers tended to receive special attention, particularly in terms of understanding how caregiving changes from being based in the community to long-term care. Keefe and Fancey (2000) categorized family responsibilities as "indirect", involving overseeing care, or "'direct", involving performing specific tasks. Another topic concentrated on the availability of carers to support elderly relatives in institutionalised care, specifically outlining intervention strategies for professionals to involve carers. Collaboration between the family (usually the carer) and institution staff was also emphasized in terms of communications, relationships and partnerships.

A less substantial amount of research centred on primary care, highlighting the issues of medical information, medication and health education. Some articles also referred to the quality of services, with a view to improving quality of life and efficient use of resources on the part of older adults. Brotman, Ryan and Cormier (2003) referred to the health and social needs of elderly gays and lesbians.

Articles under the topic of institutionalisation reported on research aimed at understanding family involvement, and visiting, as well as strategies to improve visiting and involvement, predictors and reasons for placement and family member and resident satisfaction with institutions.

Articles on other systems referred to: i) employment, in particular how carers perform multiple roles and reconcile their careers with caring; ii) support provided by social systems for families and elderly people; iii) adult day care services and the reasons determining the use of this type of support.

2.12. Community Care

Home care was associated mainly with family caregiving and, in particular, the impact of the caregiving role on the carer. In general, the caregiving role is assumed by a spouse or adult child, in both cases usually a woman. The marital relationship was the family bond most frequently studied. Additionally, some articles addressed the issue of the impact of adult day care services, attitudes toward these services and factors influencing the use of the services.

2.13. Family Processes

Articles emphasised family support for elderly relatives, whether within the community or in an institutionalised setting. Another relevant topic was intergenerational relationships and how they change and assume multiple roles during the life course, in association with family satisfaction. In addition, intergenerational transmission (the family legacy) was highlighted in different fields, namely health, the role of the carer and deprivation. Some articles addressed the topic of the home environment and/or living arrangements

Two articles covered family theory: i) King and Wynne (2004) developed the concept of family integrity in later life; ii) Roberto, Blieszner and Allen (2006) examined the extent to which theory has been used in empirical studies of families in later life and identified the main types of theoretical frameworks.

Family processes were often associated with social problems, i.e., how family interaction and dysfunction leads to social exclusion. Crane *et al.* (2005), for example, addressed the causes of homelessness, a topic frequently neglected in later life.

2.14. Marital Processes

Articles on marital interaction mainly covered: i) the quality of marital relations throughout the course of life (the influence of conflict and forgiveness); ii) the effects of health/age related changes in later life (such as cognitive impairment or chronic disease); ii) the effects of social changes, such as retirement or children leaving home. Depression was the most commonly studied health problem within the theme of marital relationships. Another main issue was spousal caregiving, in terms of rewards and costs, satisfaction, grief and growth, stress, burden and dynamics. The consequences of widowhood was also a common topic, involving its effect on social participation, economic security (poverty), psychological well-being and recovery from bereavement.

Four articles addressed topics that were not covered in any other articles: i) Teaster, Roberto and Dugar (2006) developed a study on violence in couples, arguing that although reports of intimate partner violence decrease with age, a significant number of ageing women experience this; ii) Pudrovska, Schieman and Carr (2006) highlighted singlehood in older adults, examining whether divorced, widowed, and never-married older adults differ in their experiences of *single strain*, an indicator of chronic stressors associated with being unmarried; iii) Brown, Lee and Bulanda (2006) concentrated on the experience of *cohabitation*, or living together unmarried in an intimate, heterosexual union; iv) Johnson & Favreault (2004) analysed single mothers and poverty in later life, and the fact that many single mothers are likely to face particular economic challenges in old age as they have often had limited employment histories and cannot rely on husbands for financial support.

2.15. Parental Processes

Articles addressing parental relationships centred mainly on the adult child caregiving role in terms of cost and rewards, grief and growth, changes in social networks, stress, dynamics, balancing caregiving with other roles, the quality of parental bonding and caregiving. Other issues were also considered, such as parental bonding and quality of relationships, ambivalence, reciprocity, the effects of retirement, contacts and co-residence. Some articles emphasised relationships between older mothers and their children, particularly daughters (support, favouritism and transmission).

Peters, Hooker and Zvonkovic (2006) referred to older parents' ambivalent perceptions of their relationships with their adult children. Two predominant sources of ambivalence emerged: i) children being busy, so that parents were dissatisfied with the frequency and quality of time spent together; ii) ambivalent parental perceptions of children's romantic partners and parenting styles. Lehr and Jinkuk (2005) and Lehr (2002) addressed a specific issue: parents caring for mentally handicapped adult children. Ganong and Coleman (2006) examined beliefs about the responsibilities of the adult child to an older stepparent or parent who has remarried later in life. Zhang and Hayward (2001) studied the negative effects of childlessness on psychological well-being.

2.16. Grandparenting

The main topic concerned grandparents as carers or individuals involved in bringing up grandchildren. Articles explored the circumstances leading to this situation and the impact on the health and psychological well-being of grandparents. The topic of grandchildren acting as carers to their grandparents was also addressed. Additionally, various articles covered grandparent-grandchild relationships, namely (loss of) contact, satisfaction, closeness, the impact of divorce and remarriage and intergenerational transmission.

2.17. Families in Transition

The main issue addressed was death and dying, in particular spousal loss but also caregiver adjustment after the death of the care receiver and/or adjustment to the process of dying (trajectories or transitions in caregiving). Kwak & Haley (2005), for example, reviewed literature on racial or ethnic diversity and end-of-life decision making. Other issues or family transitions included divorce and remarriage, step parents, single parenting and cohabitation.

2.18. Family Violence and Abuse

Only three articles covered the issue of family violence and abuse: i) Iecovich (2005) studied family abuse and neglect of the elderly in Israel; ii) Holkup *et al.* (2007) drew attention to interventions targeted at elder abuse in tribal communities; iii) Mosqueda *et al.* (2004) presented a model for the integration of social and medical services in order to improve support for mistreated elderly people. This was a difficult research area, which could probably be investigated under the topic of "research methods" in order to facilitate further development.

2.19. Family Caregiving

Family caregiving included articles on grandparents caring for grandchildren and parents caring for mentally handicapped children but concentrated mainly on the care of older relatives within the family. When faced with changes in physical health, cognition, and daily functioning, older adults most frequently rely on family members for all kinds of support. As carers are usually adult children and spouses, this does not, in effect, constitute actual family care, and is centred on primary care. The research indicated that secondary carers do exist (family members, friends, neighbours), but they do not play a full role. The literature also covered caregiving in relation to various health problems, although most articles referred to dementia and more specifically Alzheimer's disease.

The articles cited various topics included in the care of elderly relatives within the family, namely caregiving trajectories, family legacy, distribution of caregiving tasks within the family, gender, family conflict, caregiver strain, costs and rewards, burden, stress, caregiving and other roles, health, mobility, behaviour management, mental health, social networks, coping, depression, distress and the use of adult day care services. Carer involvement/support in institutional settings and staff and family collaboration were also examined. Support for family carers was another issue, involving social support, family interventions, improved care and psychosocial and psycho-educational programs. The articles focussed less frequently on caregiver and care recipient relationships (suffering and compassion).

Mitrani *et al.* (2006) introduced a wider framework: family functioning in the stress process of caregivers, including family functioning within the stress-process model of caregiver distress as an intervening variable in the relationship between objective burden and distress. It is also important to highlight the topics less commonly associated with family caregiving that may be viewed as new research areas, namely educational gerontology, spirituality and religion.

2.20. Spirituality and Religion

This topic emerged in five articles: i) Braun (2000) discussed the book "Spiritual Resiliency in Older Women" by Ramsey and Blieszner; ii) Fry (2001) examined the contribution of key existential factors in predicting the psychological well-being of older adults following spousal loss; iii) Krause *et al.* (2002) examined whether three dimensions of religion (private religious practices, religious coping and belief in the afterlife) buffer the effect of the death of a significant other; iv) Ballard & Morris (2005) studied religious belief factors influencing older adult attendance on family life education programmes; v) Fincham *et al.* (2007) studied the longitudinal relations between forgiveness and conflict resolution in marriage.

2.21. Gender

The influence of gender was considered in many articles involving, for example, differences in marital satisfaction, adapting to widowhood, social networks and quality of life. However, many studies focussed on women, covering aspects such as mother and daughter relationships and relationships with grandmothers. Only one article focused on men: Campbell and Martin-Matthews (2003) studied the gendered nature of men's filial care. Most of the articles crossed into caregiving and gender issues, namely distribution of tasks and differences in burden, stress and/or depression.

2.22. Single Topics

Certain subjects emerged in a much smaller number of articles (only one or two) and it was therefore difficult to highlight them in an analysis by category. These single topics were material possession, driving, childlessness and men as a research focus.

Material Possessions

Marx, Solomon & Miller (2004) examined the "final gift exchange" process in which older adults give away cherished possessions in return for lasting appreciation. The process of disposing of personal possessions emerges as associated with three salient dimensions (family, economy, and self), allowing the authors to create a heuristic describing ideal-type gift exchange scenarios by categorizing objects as valued or not valued by family and the economy, as well as being an important aspect of the gift giver's material self. The main findings suggest that a lack of shared definitions of the meaning and value of objects create dilemmas in disposing of personal objects, particularly those connected to a person's material self.

Ekerdt *et al.* (2004) described the activities that older people undertake in order to reduce the volume of their possessions when moving to smaller residences. People take pleasure in arrangements that see their possessions used, cared for, and valued as they had done, thus fulfilling a responsibility to their belongings. The authors consider that disbandment is an acute episode in a more general, lifelong process of possession management; it is an encounter with things that are meaningful to the self which, as it unfolds, also creates new meanings for these things.

Material possessions also receive attention in some marketing and psychology journals, particularly in relation to family purchasing processes in later life. Other authors (e.g. Harper, 2004) point out the importance of material possessions in crucial aspects of the lives of families in later life, such as inheritances and assistance for older people no longer able to manage their finances.

Driving

Fonda, Wallace and Herzog (2001) studied changes in driving patterns (driving cessation and reduction), their negative consequences for depressive symptoms in older people and whether these consequences are mitigated through the existence of a spouse who drives. It appears that driving cessation or reduction is important to the elderly person as an individual and to the family, particularly since new transport arrangements have to be organized.

Men at the Centre of Research

Many articles highlight gender issues, but place women at the centre of research (for example, mother-child relationships). In this content analysis, only one article put men as the centre of research. *Campbell and Martin-Matthews (2003), in an article entitled* "the gendered nature of men's filial care", investigated socio-demographic and family structure factors that predicted men's involvement in the different gendered dimensions of filial caregiving, namely traditionally male, gender neutral, and traditionally female care.

Childlessness

Zhang and Hayward (2001) argued that the rapid growth in the size of the childless elderly population has prompted concerns about the negative effects of childlessness on psychological well-being. The study examined the effects of childlessness on aspects of the psychological well-being of elderly people: loneliness and depression. The results showed that: i) childlessness per se did not significantly increase the prevalence of loneliness and depression in old age for married, divorced, widowed, and never-married elderly persons; ii) divorced, widowed, and never-married men who were childless had significantly higher rates of loneliness compared to women in comparable circumstances; iii) divorced and widowed men who were childless also had significantly higher rates of depression than divorced and widowed women.

2.23. Articles versus Books

The relatively small number of articles on families in later life published in gerontology and family studies journals led us to examine books on this subject more closely. This analysis is not as accurate as the former and consists only of a review of books published by certain publishers (SAGE, Taylor & Francis, Routledge, Wiley, Lawrence Erlabaum Associates, Nova Science Publishers) during the last 15 years (1993-2008). However, even an overview of the books reveals a much richer literature and many unique and emerging topics. Although the books again focus mainly on family caregiving and health problems in elderly people and/or family carers, a wider range of subjects are highlighted. Some of the emerging themes include:

- Sexuality and intimacy.
- Marriage in later life: long-term marriages, stepfamilies, divorce and remarriage.
- Sibling relationships in later life.
- Inheritances and gift giving.
- Multigenerational/intergenerational families.
- Theoretical frameworks for families in later life.
- Elder abuse.
- Homelessness.
- Kinship relationships over the lifespan.

It appears that the literature on families in later life is mainly published in books and probably (since our review of the books was not exhaustive) based more on theoretical analysis than research data. In any case, the subjects of the books give a good idea of emerging later life themes.

3. FAMILIES IN LATER LIFE: TOWARDS NORMATIVE AND DEVELOPMENTAL CHALLENGES

Gerontological research has focused mainly on the development of elderly people and the role that families play in their lives, particularly in terms of family caregiving (focusing on elderly dependents). Equally, literature on family psychology is starting to pay more attention to families in later life, even though it often centres on the relationship between older parents and their adult children. The focus has therefore been on elderly individuals, ignoring family relations and other close connections, and family issues have generally emerged as concentrating on dependent elderly people and the family carer.

This was most probably the best direction for research to take, since the rapid ageing of the population demanded that serious attention was paid to needs and characteristics and that practices were quickly developed to respond to these needs: i) rapid demographic ageing demanded that there should be a focus on the individual process of ageing and the care required by the most needy elderly people; ii) family caregiving constitutes the first available support for every individual, particularly those who are dependent (including the elderly). Additionally, family studies have also had to focus on the more significant social situations, such as children and their families.

Inadvertently, this research focus has reinforced negative images of old people: the development process reveals some of their limitations, even when balanced by their wisdom and experience of life; family caregiving concentrates on dependent elderly people, highlighting their difficulties and fragilities; family abandonment has been highlighted, since some elderly people live alone or are badly cared for. Research seems to be promoting some unintentional adverse effects and needs to reflect on certain questions, namely:

- Is research promoting negative images of ageing?
- How is research promoting ageism?
- How is ageism influencing research?

At a time when the life expectancy at birth is over 70 years in developed countries and the topics that are most relevant to the ageing process and care of the elderly are receiving a great deal of research interest, it is time to look towards normative and developmental family processes in later years of life and their richness. Families in later life constitute another stage in life and, as in any other stage, the construction of well-being is fundamental.

As in the case of their younger counterparts, families in later life experience both change and continuity. In addition to *retirement, grandparenthood,* and changing *intergenerational relationships,* in later life family members experience marital transitions, the onset of health problems and changes in marital satisfaction and sexuality, as well as emerging care needs affecting older family members. Race, ethnicity, class, country of origin, age, and sexual orientation combine to further increase the diversity of experience within the family in later life.

4. THE NEW THEMES IN THIS BOOK

The many topics highlighted in this content analysis provide several indications of themes that can be developed. In addition, some individual topics have emerged which highlight challenges to research. Moreover, several areas of research seem to be in their initial stages and need further attention: gays, lesbians and bisexuals; homelessness, elder abuse and neglect; spirituality (including topics such as compassion, forgiveness, reciprocity, altruism, acceptance and harmony) and religion; the help provided by the elderly to adult children. Additionally there is a need for theoretical frameworks that are specifically adapted to families in later life, since those used for families in later life are normally an extension or an application of other models developed for other stages of life. This would appear to be a useful approach but needs to be extended to incorporate the specific features of families in later life. Finally, there is a huge lack of a positive focus on ageing, involving aspects such as maturity, life experience, and wisdom at the level of family processes. This book is therefore an attempt to respond to these challenges.

Part I. Developmental and Normative Processes in Later Life

This section presents research that contributes towards the construction of specific theoretical frameworks highlighting developmental and normative processes in later life, whilst also incorporating certain topics that have emerged as in need of further development:

Chapter 1 – The multigenerational family and the elderly: a mutual or parasitical symbiotic relationship? This chapter aims to provide an understanding of the relationship between the elderly generation and the multigenerational families through an analysis of family and individual development in later life and a study of the structural and functional complexion of the multigenerational family (the basic unit of analysis).

Chapter 2 – Legacies and material inheritance: constructing family integrity in later life. Family integrity constitutes a developmental process in later life which is influenced by the creation and transmission of legacies and inheritances. This chapter aims to contribute to a deep knowledge on the influence of material inheritance in the construction of family integrity. It presents a psychological perspective on material inheritance and discusses family and individual competencies which are relevant to the process of family integrity.

Chapter 3 - Counselling older adults with family issues: forgiving and empowering. In this chapter we aim to give a general view of the topic of helping older adults faced with family problems. Aging together, in a family perspective, implies many times working personal, communicational and intergenerational issues. Counselling older adults can be one of the possible answers in the promotion of personal and family flourishement and integrity. This intervention may be based on forgiveness and necessarily passes through empowerment of the elderly and his/her family members.

Part II. Reframing Traditional Research Themes for Families in Later Life

Certain topics are common research areas, but usually highlight only the negative aspects of ageing. In this section, we therefore try to offer a new dimension to the usual topics within a more normative and developmental context.

- Chapter 4- Elderly men on ageing families. This chapter's main objective is to make contributions to the ongoing debate on gender and ageing by focusing on the issues involving older men and late-life masculinities. It explores the socio-cultural pervasiveness of ageism in the contemporary discourses on older men and the challenging roles they face within families in later life, particularly caregiving within long-lived marriage relationships.

- Chapter 5 - Reinventing family caregiving: a challenge to theory and practice. Over the past 30 years caregiving has been conceptualized mainly as a stressful event. Consequently an increasing number of research intervention studies have been designed to relieve this burden, although the findings are confusing and conflicting and the effectiveness of interventions has been questioned. Within this context, this chapter discusses some explanations for the modest success of interventions and problematises the biomedical paradigm underlying family caregiving research and practice.

- Chapter 6 - Quality of life, family role and chronic illness in elderly people institutionalized and living at home. In this chapter a study on a sample of the elderly Portuguese population is reported, focusing characteristics of chronic illnesses, quality of life, functional dependence in daily activities and family support in this population. The majority of the elderly people involved in the study report a positive assessment of their quality of life. However, factors such as loneliness, low retirement pensions, family rejection and social exclusion pose significant threats to this quality of life and should be taken into serious consideration in governmental and EU measures regarding elderly people.

Part III. Overview: Constructing Family Integrity in Later Life

This overview attempts to draw up guidelines for normative and developmental processes in families in later life.

REFERENCES

Avison, W. & Davies, L. (2005). Family structure, gender, and health in the context of the life course. *The Journals of Gerontology Series B: Psychological Sciences and Social Sciences*, 60: S113-S116.

Ballard, S. & Morris, M. (2003a). The family life education needs of midlife and older adults. *Family Relations*, 52 (2): 129-136.

Morris, M. & Ballard, S. (2003b). Instructional techniques and environmental considerations in family life education programming for midlife and older adults. *Family Relations*, 52 (2): 167-173.

Ballard, S. & Morris, M. (2005). Factors influencing midlife and older adults' attendance in family life education programs. *Family Relations*, 54 (3): 461-472.

Braun, B. (2000). Spiritual resiliency in older women: models of strengths for challenges through the life span. *Family Relations*, 49 (3): 353-353.

Brotman, S.; Ryan, B. & Cormier, R. (2003). The health and social service needs of gay and lesbian elders and their families in Canada. *Gerontologist*, 43: 192-202.

Brown, S.; Bulanda, J. & Lee, G. (2005). The significance of non-marital cohabitation: marital status and mental health benefits among middle-aged and older adults. *The Journals of Gerontology Series B: Psychological Sciences and Social Sciences*, 60: S21-S29.

Brown, S.; Lee, G. & Bulanda, J. (2006). Cohabitation among older adults: a national portrait. *The Journals of Gerontology Series B: Psychological Sciences and Social Sciences*, 61: S71-S79.

Campbell, L. & Martin-Matthews, A. (2003). The gendered nature of men's filial care. *The Journals of Gerontology Series B: Psychological Sciences and Social Sciences*, 58: S350-S358

Coleman, P. & Podolskij, A. (2007). Identity loss and recovery in the life stories of Soviet World War II veterans. *Gerontologist*, 47: 52-60.

Colvin, J.; Chenoweth, L.; Bold, M. & Harding, C. (2004). Caregivers of older adults: advantages and disadvantages of Internet-based social support. *Family Relations*, 53 (1): 49-60.

Crane, M.; Byrne, K.; Fu, R.; Lipmann, B.; Mirabelli, F.; Rota-Bartelink, A.; Ryan, M.; Shea, R.; Watt, H. & Warnes, A. (2005). The causes of homelessness in later life. *The Journals of Gerontology Series B: Psychological Sciences and Social Sciences*, 60: S152-S159.

Ekerdt, D.; Sergeant, J.; Dingel, M. & Bowen, M. (2004). Household disbandment in later life. *The Journals of Gerontology Series B: Psychological Sciences and Social Sciences*, 59: S265-S273.

Feinberg, L. & Newman, S. (2004). A study of 10 States since passage of the National Family Caregiver Support Program: policies, perceptions, and program development. *Gerontologist*, 44: 760-769.

Fincham, F.; Beach, S. & Davilla, J. (2007). Longitudinal relations between forgiveness and conflict resolution in marriage. *Journal of Family Psychology*, 21(3) 542-545.

Flori, D. (1989). The prevalence of later life family concerns in the marriage and family therapy journal literature (1976-1985): a content analysis. *Journal of Marital and Family Therapy*, 15, 289-297.

Fonda, S.; Wallace, R. & Herzog, R. (2001). Changes in driving patterns and worsening depressive symptoms among older adults. *The Journals of Gerontology Series B: Psychological Sciences and Social Sciences*, 56: S343-S351.

Fry, P. (2001). The unique contribution of key existential factors to the prediction of psychological well-being of older adults following spousal loss. *Gerontologist*, 41: 69-81.

Ganong, L. & Coleman, M. (2006). Obligations to stepparents acquired in later life: relationship quality and acuity of needs. *The Journals of Gerontology Series B: Psychological Sciences and Social Sciences*, 61: S80-S88.

Grossman, A.; D'Augelli, A. & Hershberger, S. (2000). Social support networks of lesbian, gay, and bisexual adults 60 years of age and older. *The Journals of Gerontology Series B: Psychological Sciences and Social Sciences*, 55:P171-P179.

Harper, S. (2004). Families in Ageing Societies. A Multi-Disciplinary Approach. Oxford: Oxford Institute of Aging.

Holkup, P.; Salois, E.; Tripp-Reimer, T. & Weinert, C. (2007). Drawing on wisdom from the past: an elder abuse intervention with tribal communities. *Gerontologist*, 47: 248-254.

Hong, J.; Seltzer, M. & Krauss, M. (2001). Change in social support and psychological well-being: a longitudinal study of aging mothers of adults with mental retardation. *Family Relations*, 50 (2): 154-163.

Hughes, M.; Waite, L.; LaPierre, T. & Luo, Y. (2007). All in the family: the impact of caring for grandchildren on grandparents' health. *The Journals of Gerontology Series B: Psychological Sciences and Social Sciences*, 62: S108-S119.

Iecovich, E. (2005) Elder abuse and neglect in Israel: a comparison between the general elderly population and elderly new immigrants. *Family Relations*, 54 (3): 436-447.

Ivey, D.; Wieling, E. & Harris, S. (2000). Save the young – the elderly have lived their lives: ageism in marriage and family therapy. *Family Process*, 39 (2): 163-176.

Johnson, R. & Favreault, M. (2004). Economic status in later life among women who raised children outside of marriage. *The Journals of Gerontology Series B: Psychological Sciences and Social Sciences*, 59: S315-S323.

Keefe, J. & Fancey, P. (2000). The care continues: responsibility for elderly relatives and after admission to a long term care facility. *Family Relations*, 49 (3): 235-244.

King, D. & Wynne, L. (2004): The emergence of "family integrity" in later life. *Family Process*, 43 (1): 7-21.

Krause, N.; Liang, J.; Shaw, B.; Sugisawa, H.; Kim, H-H & Sugihara, Y. (2002). Religion, death of a loved one, and hypertension among older adults in Japan. *The Journals of Gerontology Series B: Psychological Sciences and Social Sciences*, 57: S96-S107.

Kwak, J. & Haley, W. (2005). Current research findings on end-of-life decision making among racially or ethnically diverse groups. *Gerontologist*, 45: 634-641.

Lehr, E. (2002). Mothers and fathers of adults with mental retardation: feelings of intergenerational closeness. *Family Relations*, 51 (2): 156-165.

Lehr, E. & Jinkuk, H. (2005). Older caregiving parents: division of household labor, marital satisfaction and caregiver burden. *Family Relations*, 54 (3): 448-460.

Li, Y. (2007). Recovering from spousal bereavement in later life: does volunteer participation play a role? *The Journals of Gerontology Series B: Psychological Sciences and Social Sciences*, 62: S257-S266.

Litwin, R. (2001). Social network type and morale in old age. *Gerontologist*, 41: 516-524.

Marx, J.; Solomon, J. & Miller, L. (2004). Gift wrapping ourselves: the final gift exchange. *The Journals of Gerontology Series B: Psychological Sciences and Social Sciences*, 59: S274-S280.

McGarry, K. & Schoeni, R. (2005). Widow(er) poverty and out-of-pocket medical expenditures near the end of life. *The Journals of Gerontology Series B: Psychological Sciences and Social Sciences*, 60: S160-S168.

Mitrani, V.; Lewis, J.; Feaster, D.; Czaja, S.; Eisdorfer, C.; Schulz, R. & Szapocznik, J. (2005). The role of family functioning in the stress process of dementia caregivers: a structural family framework. *Gerontologist*, 46: 97-105.

Mosqueda, L.; Burnight, K.; Liao, S. & Kemp, B. (2004). Advancing the field of elder mistreatment: a new model for integration of social and medical services. *Gerontologist*, 44: 703-708.

O'Keeffe, S. (2001). Development and implementation of resuscitation guidelines: a personal experience. Age Ageing, 30: 19-25.

Peek, M.; Stimpson, J.; Townsend, A. & Markides, K. (2006). Well-being in older Mexican American spouses. *Gerontologist*, 46: 258-265.

Peters, C.; Hooker, K. & Zvonkovic, A. (2006). Older Parents' perceptions of ambivalence with their children. *Family Relations*, 55 (5): 539-551.

Price, C. & Whitney (2006). Resources for advancing family gerontology education. *Family Relations*, 55 (5): 649-662.

Pudrovska, T.; Schieman, S. & Carr, D. (2006). Strains of singlehood in later life: do race and gender matter? *The Journals of Gerontology Series B: Psychological Sciences and Social Sciences*, 61: S315-S322.

Roberto, K. & Jarrott, S. (2008). Family caregivers of older adults: a life span perspective. *Family Relations*, 57 (1): 100-111.

Roberto, K. Blieszner, R. & Allen, K. (2006). Theorizing in family gerontology: new opportunities for research and practice. *Family Relations*, 55 (5): 513-525.

Roberts, J. (2000). Anticipating response to predictive genetic testing for Alzheimer's disease: a survey of first-degree relatives. *Gerontologist*, 40: 43-52.

Rose, J.; Bowman, K.; O'Toole, E.; Abbott, K.; Love, T.; Thomas, C. & Dawson, N. (2007). Caregiver objective burden and assessments of patient-centred, family-focused care for frail elderly veterans. *Gerontologist*, 47: 21-33.

Schulz, R.; Hebert, R.; Dew, M.; Brown, S.; Scheier, M.; Beach, S.; Czaja, S.; Martire, L.; Coon, D.; Langa, K.; Gitlin, L.; Stevens, A. & Nichols, L. (2007). Patient suffering and caregiver compassion: new opportunities for research, practice, and policy. *Gerontologist*, 47: 4-13.

Sörensen, S.; Pinquart, M. & Duberstein, P. (2002). How effective are interventions with caregivers? An updated meta-analysis. *Gerontologist*, 42: 356-372.

Szinovacz, M.; DeViney, S. & Davey, A. (2001). Influences of family obligations and relationships on retirement. Variations by gender, race, and marital status. *The Journals of Gerontology Series B: Psychological Sciences and Social Sciences*, 56: S20-S27.

Teaster, P.; Roberto, K. & Dugar, T. (2006). Intimate partner violence of rural aging women. *Family Relations*, 55 (5): 636-648.

Van Amburg, S.; Barber, C. & Zimmerman, T. (2006). Aging and family therapy: Prevalence of aging issues and later family life concerns in marital and family therapy literature (1986-1993). *Journal of Marital and Family Therapy*, 22 (2), 195–203.

Van Gelder, B.; Tijhuis, M.; Kalmijn, S.; Giampaoli, S.; Nissinen, A. & Kromhout, N. (2006). Marital status and living situation during a 5-year period are associated with a subsequent 10-year cognitive decline in older men: the FINE study. *The Journals of Gerontology Series B: Psychological Sciences and Social* Sciences, 61: P213-P219.

Wickrama, K.; Conger, R. & Abraham, W. (2005). Early adversity and later health: the intergenerational transmission of adversity through mental disorder and physical illness. *The Journals of Gerontology Series B: Psychological Sciences and Social Sciences*, 60: S125-S129.

Wong, S.; Yoo, G. & Stewart, A. (2006). The changing meaning of family support among older Chinese and Korean immigrants. *The Journals of Gerontology Series B: Psychological Sciences and Social Sciences*, 61: S4-S9.

Yorgason, J.; Almeida, D.; Neupert, S.; Spiro, A. & Lesa, H. (2006). A dyadic examination of daily health symptoms and emotional well-being in late-life couples. *Family Relations*, 55 (5): 613-624.

Zhang, Z. & Hayward, M. (2001). Childlessness and the psychological well-being of older persons. *The Journals of Gerontology Series B: Psychological Sciences and Social Sciences*, 56: S311-S320.

In: Families in Later Life: Emerging Themes and Challenges   ISBN 978-1-60692-328-3
Editor: Liliana Sousa   © 2009 Nova Science Publishers, Inc.

Chapter 1

THE MULTIGENERATIONAL FAMILY AND THE ELDERLY: A MUTUAL OR PARASITICAL SYMBIOTIC RELATIONSHIP?[*]

Henrique Vicente and Liliana Sousa

SUMMARY

The multigenerational family is flourishing nowadays, mainly as a result of increased life expectancy, meaning there is a greater probability that individuals will spend a longer period of time in the family development phase known as *"families in later life"* (Carter & McGoldrick, 2005). However, few theoretical perspectives consider the challenges and rewards of multigenerational family relationships in later life (e.g. Silverstein & Bengtson, 1997; King & Wynne, 2004).

In general, research in family relationships and individual development has been treated separately. Ryff and Seltzer (1995: 95) argue that "studies of individual development in adulthood and the later years show only oblique links with family life" and "the extensive literature on family relations extends across different age groups and life periods, and yet (…) shows limited connection to theories of, and findings about, individual development".

Moreover, common sense conveys the image of elderly people as incapable, dependent, vulnerable and depressed (Sousa & Cerqueira, 2006). Research, however, has revealed the important roles they play within the family, such as substituting parents in caring for grandchildren (Hader, 1965). Although significant, these functions always seem to assume a secondary role within the family scenario. The elderly generation only appear to be useful when they substitute the younger generations or provide support that the latter ones are too busy to manage. A question mark therefore remains over the role of the oldest generation within the multigenerational family: is it just an appendix to the family that can be called upon to replace a more vital organ in times of difficulty or does it have a unique and irreplaceable role to play in the functioning of the multigenerational family system?

This chapter aims to help provide an understanding of the relationship between the elderly generation and the multigenerational families they belong to through an analysis of family and individual development in later life and a study of the structural and functional complexion of the multigenerational family (the basic unit of analysis).

The following pages will cover: a) the importance of studying the multigenerational family in the present moment; b) a structural characterization of the multigenerational family (a heuristic tool for understanding the extended family dynamics that enables its differentiation from other family and social systems); c) issues involving family and individual development in later life that enable a better understanding regarding the experience of the elderly generations; d) a description of the fundamental functions in the multigenerational family and a characterization of the family members who perform them; e) an analysis of the relationship between the structural and functional dimensions of multigenerational families and the individual and family development tasks in the later stages of life, as a means of grasping a better understanding of the relationship between the elderly person and his/her multigenerational family.

Keywords: Multigenerational Family; Family Development; Individual Development; Generation; Multigenerational Family Structure; Multigenerational Family Functions

INTRODUCTION

Challenges to the Study of Families in Later Life: Pursuing a Development Model

It is expected that the diversity, complexity and importance of family relationships in later life will increase in the near future (Walsh, 2005). Therefore it's necessary to organise development models for the family which take into account the potential for growth and the changes that take place during this period and also include elements that are relevant and meaningful to the elderly generation, such as wisdom and integrative understanding.

Walsh (2005: 323) notes that theory and research have been biased by a fundamental gap: "they fail to include values and meanings that are salient to elders". Placing emphasis on the therapeutic domain, the author warns that problems involving elderly members of the family may be masked by complaints or symptoms in other parts of the family system. In fact, little or no attention is paid to current relationships within the extended family in most family therapy offices. It seems that the reification of the nuclear family model within the clinical setting has marginalized the extended family and consequently compromised our understanding of family systems.

In 1970, Spark and Brody were already considering "elderly" families and intergenerational relationships as the "clinical frontier" for family therapy. They believed that elderly members of the family could play an important role in family dynamics and that their

---

* Work financed by the Foundation for Science and Technology of the Ministry of Science, Technology and Higher Education through a research grant under POCI 2010 – Advanced Training in Science – Measure IV.3 (reference SFRH/BD/23545/2005)

inclusion in the treatment of "young" families could become an excellent preventive measure against cyclical repetitions of pathological relational patterns. The authors appealed to their colleagues, family therapists, to extend to the elderly their shared beliefs in the potential for change and growth, in the competencies and capabilities they generally attributed to "younger" families in their everyday practice Their appeal included one aspect that was otherwise rarely mentioned: the fact that whilst the family environment is important in the lives of elderly people, elderly people are also important in family life.

Defining the Multigenerational Family

The terms *"multigenerational family"* and *"extended family"* are often used indiscriminately to describe the subject of this chapter. This alone may lead into serious misunderstandings which should be promptly clarified, since these terms are used with at least two distinct meanings, namely:

- A *living arrangement* containing three or more generations, which may or may not include collateral groups. In other words, a group of people connected by family ties who live together, made up of several generations (as opposed to the nuclear family which is composed of two generations – parents and children – living together). The term *"multigenerational family"* is frequently used for conveying this notion (e.g. DeLeire & Kalil, 2001; Ruggles, 2003)
- A *relational experience* involving a group of people who are kin related in some way, regardless of how they are organised in terms of living arrangements. In other words, a social system made of various independent but interacting (nuclear and/or multigenerational) family units. The term *"extended family"* commonly refers to this concept (e.g. Carter & McGoldrick, 2005; Papalia, Sterns, Feldman, & Camp, 2002).

In this chapter the second terminology is used: the *"multigenerational family"* as a relational experience. It's a fact that the term *"extended family"* could be used to describe the relational experience whereas the term *"multigenerational family"* would therefore be reserved to describe habitation units consisting of more than two generations, but the former does not encapsulate the intergenerational dimension which characterizes present-day family relationships. According to this perspective, if the term *"multigenerational family"* is used to describe a living arrangement, a family nucleus, we become bereft of adequate terms to describe the family system to which this nucleus belongs, which is heavily defined by intergenerationality and is contained within, but differentiated from, the *"community"* system.

Moreover, the definition of the *"multigenerational family"* as a relational experience conforms to the argument put forward by Bedford and Blieszner (2000), i.e., that a more inclusive description of the family system is needed in order to integrate elderly people into family studies. We therefore present the following terminological proposal:

- *"Multigenerational family"* – describes a system within a hierarchical system model which lies midway between the *"nuclear family"* and the *"community"* (similar to what Carter and McGoldrick (2005) term the *"extended family"*).

- *"Multigenerational family nucleus"* – identifies living arrangements involving more than two generations or collateral family members (similar to what Litwin (1995) terms the *"multigenerational household"*).

This terminology is used throughout the chapter, except in quotations or citations from other authors where the corresponding term from the nomenclature above has been inserted in square brackets.

Abandoning the Myth of Family Abandonment

In the 1970s there was a renewed interest in how families relate to their eldest generations, as some sociologists began to debate "the presumed collapse of social ties" and the "death of family solidarity" (Attias-Donfut & Rozenkier, 1996: 51). However there is current evidence to suggest that families continue to play an important role in the lives of their individual members (Harper, 2005).

Research has contradicted the myth of elderly abandonment by their families, although it still persists in many discourses. It would obviously be naive to think that all families provide the best care for their elderly members. *"Not all parent-child relationships in old age are happy"* stated Troll in 1982, whilst also emphasizing the importance of intergenerational relationships. Nevertheless, it would be wrong to state that families nowadays abandon their elderly members, since relationships involving support and mutual responsibility are long-lasting (Spark & Brody, 1970).

The idea of the dismembering of the extended family system and the breakup of relationships between members of multigenerational families has also been questioned and the idyllic image of families in the old days living in multigenerational habitation units extensively debated. Ariès (1973/1988: 10) does not believe it likely that the "extended family [*multigenerational family nucleus*] has ever existed […], except in times of insecurity in which the lineage was obliged to substitute the public authorities, and in certain economic and legal circumstances". The French historian adds that this assumption is based on cultural context, with the proviso that this type of family may have existed in the Mediterranean region (including Portugal) as it was an area in which the legal right to bequeath all property to one child favoured cohabitation. Through an iconographic analysis Ariès traced the origins of contemporary family feelings to the Middle Ages, but he also stated that images or representations featuring more than two generations were extremely rare. Over the course of recorded history, the nuclear family seems to have been the preferred form of family organisation, only giving rise to other forms when political, social and economic circumstances thus dictated.

Historical perspectives on the extended family of the past have probably been influenced by the experiences, apprehensions and preconceptions of the present. In discussing man's first incursions into the historical sciences, Freud (1910/2007) noted that it was inevitable that this early history should have been an expression of present beliefs and wishes rather than a true image of the past, for many things had been dropped from the nation's memory, whilst others were distorted. For example, various authors who were anxious to find explanations for the presumed collapse of the extended family identified industrialization as the driving force behind the nuclearisation of the family. However Segalen (1986/1999) notes that, far from "nuclearising" the family, the first phases of industrialisation were actually supported by the cohabiting extended family, since it was able to provide a certain amount of basic services in the absence of any social protection structures (for a more extensive review of the myths surrounding relationships between generations and the presumed existence of a "golden age" of family and old age in the past, we recommend the work edited by Hareven in 1996).

(De)segregating the Nuclear Family

In recent decades the effects of modernisation on the family have been explored, highlighting the debate on family links/disconnection from other social systems (such as neighbours and the community). Sussman (1988) in *"The isolated nuclear family: Fact or fiction?"* of 1959, concluded that the correct answer was "fiction", since family ties, in particular those forged between generations, have a decisive influence on essential family processes. The family has undergone marked changes associated with the vicissitudes of ongoing modernisation and urbanisation. However, the nuclear family is not an isolated atom in the social scenario but is "integrated within a network of mutual assistance and activity which can be described as an interdependent kin family system" (Sussman, 1988: 8).

Despite these facts, the idea remained that the extended family was only important to: a) the working class or lower income class; b) those who still lived close to each other or remained immovable when most families journeyed away in search of a better life. However, Bell (1968) states that for middle class families the extended family remains a "functional social entity", highlighting relationships between children/spouses and parents/in-laws as essential links in the distribution of resources from the older generation to the younger.

The multigenerational family is, therefore, a system in its own right and a common arrangement when considered in experiential and relational terms and when we avoid restricting our spectrum of observation to the nuclear family (Relvas, 1996/2004). It is essential that it should be social sciences analyse, particularly in terms of the interactive aspects of the subsystems it contains, since the system has its own idiosyncratic characteristics that are only revealed when this type of family constitutes the basic unit of analysis.

1. THE MULTIGENERATIONAL FAMILY SYSTEM AND THE ELDERLY GENERATION

As we have seen, nowadays the multigenerational family still appears to be a relevant object of study and it is therefore important to consider the literature on this system in relation to elderly generations.

The central importance of the family system in the later phases of life is unquestionable, with spouses, siblings and children constituting an important resource in the social adaptation of elderly people (e.g. Suggs, 1985; Okabayashi, Liang, Krause, Akiyama, & Sugisawa, 2004). However, the role of the more distant relatives has not been subjected to extensive study (Lang, 2005). Parallel to this, the elderly generations appear to play an important role in the life of their families: grandparents, for example, may serve as a stabilising factor in relationships between parents and children (Botcheva & Feldman, 2002) or be responsible for bringing up grandchildren when parents are unable to do so (Goodman & Silverstein, 2001; Poehlmann, 2003).

Moreover, an increasingly large amount of data attests to the importance of the extended family context in the life of all family members (including elderly people). For example, in a study of adolescents whose parents had died of AIDS in New York, it was found that 89% of the replacement carers were female members of the extended family (Rotherham-Borus *et al.*, 2002). In another study on the impact of infant cancer on fathers, it was found that support from the extended family was necessary in order to enable parents to maintain a positive attitude (Brody & Simmons, 2007).

To sum up, research shows the mutual and reciprocal importance of the younger and older generations. It also bears witness to the fact that "distant" kin relationships may play a key role. Some authors put forward the theory that in western countries as a whole (in which the more individualistic trends and more pessimistic predictions for the future of the family can be found), relationships with family members outside the nuclear family will become increasingly important (Mulder, 2007).

This data underlines the importance of the "multigenerational family", which includes: inter- and intra- generational relationships and interaction between collateral lineages of family members.

One of the most common patterns of current family relationships is the "modified-extended family" (Litwak, 1960). This is a system composed of a set of nuclear families which maintain strong links, despite living in separate homes. This structure enables the combined norms regarding independent households and family "sharing and caring" to be maintained or, in other words, strong affective ties, visits and contacts by telephone, together with various forms of mutual support (Beck & Beck, 1989).

Despite the fact that the preference for nuclear families has made this the prevailing family unit, multigenerational family units or those composed of several generations are actually more common than might be expected. Beck and Beck (1989) verified that a minority of white middle-aged women have, at some point in their lives, lived in extended units and that this is actually the norm for black middle-aged women, given that almost two-thirds have lived in households shared with members of the extended family for at least part of their middle years. Given these results, the authors postulated the existence of an "intermittent-extended family" which occurs when the "modified-extended family" is faced with a crisis, thus underlining the dynamic and flexible nature of the family.

Lang (2005), using data from the *Berlin Aging Study* (BASE), verified that the more distant family members are important to the majority of elderly people since they constitute an important social resource in old age. Despite this, elderly people tend to maintain active relationships with only half of the members of their families, i.e., a large number of family ties do not feature in their network of relationships. These ties may persist in "hidden mode" and may be activated in times of need. Extended family networks may be perceived as structures which provide opportunities for interpersonal contact, and as a consequence it is important to distinguish between two different concepts (Lang, 2005: 65):

- *Kinship Availability*, the size of the family network actually available to the individual, or the number of relatives structurally available ("the objective structure of kinship networks").

- *Kinship Activation*, the level to which active personal relationships are maintained between relatives independently of functional transactions, associated with a reduction in the risk of isolation ("the individual's subjective use or realization of the available kinship network").

In his study Lang (2005) finds data that supports the hypothesis that the elderly don't select their social partners with the sole purpose of satisfying instrumental support needs, but also as a means of maximizing significant emotional experiences, highlighting the subjective dimension inherent to the relationship between elders and their multigenerational families. By including distant relatives in their social networks, elderly people have access to a source of experiences involving continuity and long-term commitments, indicating that this aspect may be an important predictor of the level of social adaptation in later life.

Research focussing on the social networks of elderly people with the goal of exploring and understanding their interpersonal context has also highlighted the role of relationships with the extended family in later life, which has proven to be vitally important given the losses that must also be faced at this time of life. According to Sluzki (1996/2002), the evolution of the social networks of individuals in later life is governed by three coexisting factors which have cumulative effects:

- The social network shrinks, since the number of members is reduced by death, migration or debilitation;
- Opportunities for renewing the social network and the motivation to do so gradually diminish;
- Network maintenance becomes more difficult due to the amounts of energy this requires.

Despite their undeniable contribution towards understanding family experiences in later life, all the studies cited have one factor in common: a sectoral or splintered approach towards the study of the multigenerational family which involves breaking it down into component parts that become the target of the research. In order to understand the relationship between elderly people and the multigenerational family, it is important to understand from the outset the idiosyncrasies of this system which distinguish it from other systems.

2. THE STRUCTURE OF THE MULTIGENERATIONAL FAMILY

The conceptual tools used to understand and study the multigenerational family must be distinct from those used for the nuclear family and/or couples (Vicente & Sousa, 2007). The majority of studies on multigenerational and intergenerational themes focus on a relationship within the family system, such as the elderly person and the family carer (e.g. Figueiredo, 2007), mothers and adult daughters (e.g. Schwarz, 2006) or grandparents and grandchildren (e.g. Neugarten & Weinstein, 1968; Kornhaber & Woodward, 1981).

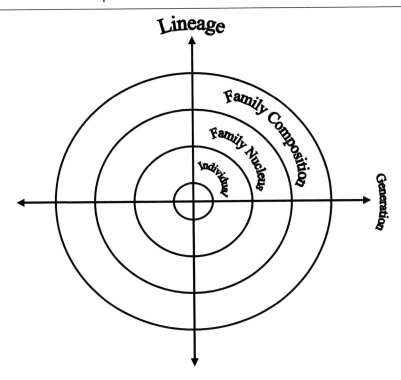

Source: Vicente & Sousa (2007: 153).

Figure 1. Subsystems of the multigenerational family.

The multigenerational family is a systemic whole and therefore the analysis of its component parts can only reveal a small part of its complexity. It is necessary to analyse it as a whole and hence a model must be provided for understanding its structure. With this aim in mind, Vicente and Sousa (2007) carried out genogram interviews (based on McGoldrick & Gerson, 1987) with members of the intermediate generations of 25 multigenerational families (in this study, families containing four living generations).

Hierarchical and subsystem organisation is a key property of systems, without which nothing more than random grouping or chaos would exist. Thus it is important to recognise family subsystems and understand how they relate to each other. It is important to bear in mind that a (sub)system consists of four components (Durand, 1979/1992):

- The *boundaries* (separating the system from the surrounding environment);
- The *members* (identification and classification of the members who constitute an integral part of a system or subsystem);
- The *network of relationships, transport and communications* (vehicles for conveying materials and information);
- The *reservoirs* (stores of materials, energy and information).

On the basis of an extensive review of the relevant literature and the content analysis of the interviews, Vicente and Sousa (2007) identified five subsystems in the multigenerational family: individual, generation, lineage, family nucleus and family composition (Figure 1).

The *individual subsystem* is composed of each of the individual family members who also have functions and roles in other social (sub)systems. This sense of multiple belonging creates a dynamism that has an important impact on their development and behaviour in each of these contexts (Alarcão, 2000). The roles accumulated by contemporary women in the family and in the employment market are an excellent example of the critical dynamics of dual functioning, which may or may not create conflict.

The *generational subsystem* is composed of individuals from the same generation within a given family, who are usually similar in age and share multiple life experiences (Fine & Norris, 1989). The generation is a central concept in intergenerational relationships studies (Rossi & Rossi, 1990), although it is frequently confused with the concept of *cohort* (a group of individuals of similar ages who share common historical experiences). A generation is defined by a family relationship, whereas a cohort is defined by interaction with historic events which affect the life course and development of a group.

The *lineage subsystem* is defined as the vertical association within the family of individuals of different ages from different generations with particular and distinct social and cultural experiences. It is defined by a blood relationship and a common genetic heritage, involving individuals who share ancestor or descendant bonds. Relationships between members of the same family lineage are always intergenerational, in contrast to the exclusively intra-generational relationships of members of the same generational subsystem. In a study about social networks of elderly people living in France, Attias-Donfut and Rozenkier (1996) concluded that these revolved more around intergenerational relationships, i.e., tended to be long-term relationships sometimes developed early in life, involving several complex emotions such as gratitude and resentment, obligation and need, and implicit and explicit expectations.

The *family nucleus* consists of a specific number of individuals who live together, whether connected by family ties (of blood or marriage) or not, and generally corresponds to the family unit. Sometimes the unit includes members who do not have family ties, such as a foreign student living with the family for a period of time. Relationships and family support are closely linked to the composition of the family nucleus (Lowenstein, 1999). Living arrangements do not only constitute a physical environment but are also a point of encounter, a forum, a setting which provides opportunities for mutual help and support. Nowadays the most common arrangement in multigenerational families is for the older generations to live alone or with their spouses: the so-called "elderly households" (Lowenstein, 1999). Family units consisting of members from various generations tend only to occur in moments of need (Wall, 2005). These multigenerational family nuclei create physical intergenerational proximity, i.e., the elimination of the geographical distance that separates the generations, and the waning of boundaries between generational subsystems.

Family compositions are constituted by association (e.g. due to geographical proximity), alliances (e.g. to muster the provision of care or support) or coalition (e.g. founded on or derived from conflicts between family members) involving two or more family nuclei. Some compositions appear to be family factions or different teams playing autonomously and independently under the same banner, and generally impose duplication (or multiplication) of multigenerational family roles within the extended family context.

Any assessment and understanding of multigenerational families demands that attention is paid to these different systemic levels as well as an analysis of their implications on family dynamics and responses to problems (normative or otherwise). Parallel to this, it is to be expected that specific functions and tasks emerge within a system which is distinctively complex from others, such as the multigenerational family (see Section 4).

3. FAMILY AND INDIVIDUAL DEVELOPMENT

In order to understand the familial experiences of the older generations it is important to bear in mind three fundamental issues: the development of the individual, the family and society. In brief, the opportunities and obstacles which emerge in a particular phase of life are reflected in the tasks and capacities inherent to the development of the individual who, in turn, is part of a family which has its own specific form of development. Experiences both as an individual and as a family member are influenced and structured socioculturally by a set of norms, expectations and perceptions held by society in relation to its members (Hagestad & Burton, 1986). Three different kinds of time are thus involved: individual, family and historical (Sousa, Figueiredo, & Cerqueira, 2004).

As the title of this section clearly suggests, we have sought to investigate the links between the first two, since they are the most relevant to our area of work, leaving the challenge open for those who wish to supplement the work presented here in terms of its broader social and historical dimensions.

King and Wynne (2004) note the scarcity of theoretical proposals for family development processes in the second half of life. However, older generations and their families face multiple tasks, challenges and conflicts that are just as rich and complex as those of the younger generations. Their resolution or appropriate and positive integration also facilitates developmental progress, as opposed to stagnation or regression in cases of failure. Retirement, becoming a grandparent, chronic illness, family care and support, and widowhood represent some of the most frequently cited challenges (Walsh, 2005).

In relation to family development, this final phase or stage is conventionally referred to as "families in later life". According to Carter and McGoldrick (2005: 2), the key to this phase lies in accepting changes: "the shifting generational roles". The authors define a series of second-order changes in family status required to proceed developmentally: a) maintaining the individual's and/or couple's functioning and interests in face of physical decline and exploring new familial and social role options; b) supporting the middle generations in order to enable them to assume a more central role; c) making room in the system for the wisdom and experience of old age, thus supporting the elder generation without overburdening them; d) dealing with the death of spouses, siblings and other peers and preparing for one's own death. It should be noted we have highlighted this model since all the other developmental phases identified by Carter and McGoldrick (2005) involve tasks which imply interaction with systems outside the nuclear family, namely with other generations and lineages.

Regarding individual development, it is important to emphasise the contribution made by those who sought to equate the entire spectrum of human life as an open field for potential growth that is not merely restricted to the early phases of life. Erikson (1950/1976), in a progressive effort in relation to the prevailing development theories of its time, which focused almost exclusively on childhood and adolescence, extended the horizons of developmental studies, proposing an epigenetic model covering the entire life of the individual, thereby becoming a pioneer in the study of the psychological development of elderly generations. He stated that the elderly face the task of finding meaning in life and constructing a sense of ego integrity as opposed to despair, and of reviewing and integrating their life, accepting losses and preparing for death. Erikson (1950/1976: 268-269) summarised this final balance as "the acceptance of our own unique life cycle as something that had to happen and does not allow substitution ... healthy children will not fear life if their elders have integrity enough not to fear death". Erikson's sharp statement highlights the way in which the development of the different generations is interlinked. It also supports the notion that the author considered the developmental aspects of two distinct generations within the same family to be inseparable, just as family development is inseparable from the growth of its individual members.

Erikson's studies had an enormous impact on the way in which the human and social sciences came to view the life cycle. The concepts put forward in his theories were taken up by various researchers, namely Vaillant who, in 2002, completed an empirical testing of Erikson's theories using a substantial database from the *"Harvard Study of Human Development"*, the most ambitious and extensive longitudinal study ever devised on this theme. With the results of this study in his hand, Vaillant began by discarding the term "developmental stage" used by Erikson, in favour of the term "developmental task" as proposed by Havinghurst, arguing that, when applied to adult development, the word "stage" could only be used metaphorically as adult tasks are sometimes carried out non-sequentially. In other words, the boundaries between the developmental phases in adulthood are more fluid and flexible than, for example, Piaget's stages of cognitive development. In effect, Erikson conceptualised the development of the adult as a dynamic and ongoing process rather than a linear progression through a series of separate stages or phases. Vaillant (2002) also made some personal contributions to the original theory, adding two tasks to the original eight defined by Erikson, namely *"career consolidation"*, standing between the *"intimacy"* task of young adulthood and the *"generativity"* task of middle age, and the *"keeper of the meaning"*, which precedes the final task of *"integrity"*.

The work of Vaillant (2002) implies that individual development in old age, such as becoming the keeper of the meaning or the search for a sense of integrity, is of vital importance to healthy family development. As the author observes: *"only the old can make the past come alive for the next generation"* (Vaillant, 2002: 146). Spira and Wall (2006) also emphasised the importance of the narrative capital of grandparents in the construction of adolescent identity. The same authors cite Margaret Mead who, in 1970, affirmed that grandparents, as the living repositories of family and social change, can help their adolescent grandchildren to understand themselves better, providing them with direct bridges to the past and a sense of continuity and confidence in facing future challenges. The link between family and individual development in the later phases of life, which was frail in Erikson's original conceptualisation (Ryff & Seltzer, 1995), gained substance in later research. A study by Reese and Murray (1996), for example, concluded that the opportunity to influence great-grandchildren increases the possibility that the great-grandparents will find meaning and transcendence in their lives.

Family and individual development are inseparable, although the way in which they are connected is not totally clear. In an effort to understand the relationship between family processes and individual development, King & Wynne (2004) associated the construction of ego identity with a broader process of meaning construction and with relational development within the family system: the "family integrity" (similar to the concept of ego integrity) (see Chapter 2 and Overview). "Family integrity" would be the *"ultimate, positive outcome of an older adult's developmental striving toward meaning, connection, and continuity within his or her multigenerational family"* (2004: 7).

Family integrity depends on three competences within the family system: (a) the transformation of relationships over time; (b) the resolution or acceptance of past losses or family conflicts; (c) the shared creation of meaning by passing on individual and family legacies in the form of stories or rituals shared over generations. There is therefore a strong normative pressure for the elderly individual to be a part of the multigenerational family, since this might bring meaning and value to their life. As this phase of life is characterized by greater wisdom and the ability to express impartial concerns within a broader social sphere which includes (but is not restricted to) the extended family, the elderly are not the only ones who gain from the process of meaning construction and from relational development, since the whole family is also affected.

4. FUNCTIONS AND ROLES WITHIN THE MULTIGENERATIONAL FAMILY

In addition to providing a structural conceptualization of the multigenerational family and a contextualization of the elder generational subsystem in terms of family and individual development, it is also important to study essential functions whose exercise is required in the multigenerational family system to assure its maintenance and development. In other words, we need to understand what the extended family essentially needs in order to exist and operate, so that conclusions can later be reached regarding its relationship with its oldest members. We therefore begin by identifying the idiosyncratic characteristics of the multigenerational family system with the aim of subsequently presenting hypotheses for the family functions within the system that are crucial to its survival (Table 1).

Table 1. The multigenerational family: characteristics and functions

Specific characteristics	Function
Large number of subsystems (usually families with many members distributed amongst many nuclei; coexistence of multiple generations and lineages).	Linking subsystems
Long and complex historical trajectory (combining the history of individuals, nuclear families, family compositions, lineages and the generations they contain).	Preserving family memories
Coexistence of individuals and nuclear families in practically all phases of family and individual development (each with specific tasks and challenges).	Support for the various subsystems

In addition to matching the distinctive characteristics of the multigenerational family, these functions also appear to hold correspondence with the challenges which all systems have to face (Durand, 1979/1992: 26):

1) "Establishing well coordinated behaviour" (maintaining ties and communications through links between subsystems).

2) "Finding adequate responses to disturbances originating in the surrounding environment" (when added to disturbances originating from within the system, this represents the support function for the various subsystems).

3) "Learning new behaviour" (as memory is indispensible to learning, this attests to the importance of preserving family memories in the evolution of the extended family system).

Any system requires specific mechanisms to enable it to survive, which are associated with its distinctive characteristics. Within this context, Vicente and Sousa (2008) carried out research that enabled them to extend their understanding of these functions and of the people who undertake them more often, therefore assuming a socially recognized role. The roles were named: 1) *"keeper of family memories"*; 2) *"connecting link in the family"*; 3) *"family first aider"* (the decision for the last role label was made to specifically focus on the person within the family set-up who was first approached for help in a crisis, as opposed to the long term family carer).

The study of these functions and of the individuals who carry them out within the family unit, together with an assessment of the multigenerational family as a whole, is important in understanding how family life contributes towards, and is influenced by, individual development (Ryff & Seltzer, 1995).

We now present a summary of the main results of the study.

The Keeper of Family Memories

The role of *"keeper of family memories"* belongs to the older members of the family or, in other words, the oldest generation. This goes hand in hand with the process of constructing family integrity (King & Wynne, 2004), typical of "families in later life", which involves creating a legacy on the basis of stories and rituals shared amongst generations, and with Vaillant's (2002) proposal for the inclusion of the "keeper of the meaning" stage, although the latter refers to a broader social sphere which includes, but is not restricted to, the family. It is a function essentially undertaken by women, and by a larger number of widows when compared to other functions. This may indicate a role associated with gender, but a simpler explanation may be found in the fundamental difference between the average life expectancies of men and women, i.e., in the fact that men simply do not live long enough to undertake this role more often.

The "keeper of family memories" basically has the job of creating and preserving memories or, in other terms, is associated with preserving and maintaining narrative/historical elements, moral values and/or material objects. Their basic functions may be better understood with the metaphor of the archivist. The individuals who carry out this task know the life stories of ancestors who are no longer alive, often draw up family trees and gather and collect photographs and objects (such as schoolbooks or clothes) *"for posterity"*.

Sometimes memory and conservation are complemented with transmission, involving the act of bequeathing something to someone in the family i.e., the inter- and/or intra-generational transfer of elements that have been preserved or maintained. The transmission dimension of this function implies breaking down barriers between generational subsystems and opening up lines of intergenerational communication so that information and/or materials can flow from the reservoirs of the oldest generation to the other generations. This function is often inherited i.e., the function of transmitting and bequeathing is, in itself, inherited. As a rule, the former "keeper of family memories" delivers the (material and non-material) items to a member of the next generation who has shown an interest and curiosity in them. These inherited functions represent and convey a sense of continuity and integrity in extended family relationships.

Transmission is one of the themes most frequently covered in the sphere of intergenerational relations studies (Fine & Norris, 1989). When elderly people "*tell stories about the old days*" they are not only finding meanings for their lives but also providing a means for the younger generations to reinterpret stories in the light of their own experiences, interests and cultural context, i.e., it involves a dialogical enterprise (Tschuggnall & Welzer, 2002). Both parties involved seem to benefit from transmission: the givers extend their own *self* onto the next generations (Price, Arnould, & Curasi, 2000) and the recipients acquire elements that help them develop their own identity (Spira & Wall, 2007). Moreover, the whole to which both parties belong, the multigenerational family, also gains from this relationship, since it sees that its history is preserved, which in turn strengthens its identity and individuality as a social system and assures continuity.

The Connecting Link in the Family

The functions of the *"connecting link in the family"* typically belong to middle-aged people (50 to 60 years old) who are part of the intermediate generation (G2)[1]. Perrig-Chiello and Sturzenneger (2001) consider that the middle-aged generation is a "hinge generation" in which there is a change of focus from supporting then letting go of children, who have become more independent, to caring for parents, who have become less independent. At the same time, important challenges are negotiated in other spheres, such as professional life.

This function is mainly exercised by women. Studies on social relations and filial maturity in middle age suggest that men have a more pragmatic attitude towards supporting the family, whilst women have more sociophilic tendencies. Women therefore have more contact with their parents and friends while men tend to focus on the marital relationship. Troll (1982) explains this in terms of the fact that men usually marry younger women and therefore are less likely to survive them due to differences in life expectancy. In addition, men have more opportunities to re-marry following widowhood or divorce. Perrig-Chiello and Sturzenneger (2001) believe that this difference is due to the traditional female role of assuming responsibility for social matters inside and outside the family.

Serving as the "connecting link in the family" involves, above all, making and maintaining connections and is very close to the associational dimension of intergenerational solidarity (Silverstein & Bengtson, 1997). In practical terms, this function translates into promoting family meetings (e.g. organising celebrations such as dinners or birthday parties)

---

[1] The generations are identified by a similar nomenclature to that used in other sociological studies (e.g. Rossi & Rossi, 1990), consisting of the letter "G" followed by a number: G1 represents the oldest generation and G4 the youngest.

and opening up communications between subsystems (e.g. connections between estranged members of the family), fostering family unity and inter- and intra-generational solidarity, and facilitating frequent social contact and shared activities. The amount of time available, financial and economic resources and the geographical location of households are socio-demographic factors which appear to affect how this function is exercised. In terms of personal characteristics or features, they are conciliatory and judicious people who tend to seek out contacts in their social environment.

The Family First Aider

As with the "connecting link in the family", the functions of the *"family first aider"* tend to be carried out by middle aged individuals (50 to 60 years old) who belong to the intermediate generation (G2), although they may be a little younger. This data conforms to Erikson's theory of development and the concept of *"generativity"*. Also on a sociodemographic level, a more equal distribution between sexes is evident in the more "pragmatic" role of "family first aider", 46% of whom are male.

In comparison with the other roles, the *"family first aider"* tends to be married. In studying the effects of care and multigenerational support, Loomis and Booth (1995) found no data to support the hypothesis regarding the existence of a generation of overburdened middle-aged adults. One of the explanations put forward concerns the hypothetical existence of a selective effect in families, in which those most capable of assuming responsibility for providing support do so on their own initiative. In this study, and in keeping with this hypothesis, it was found that individuals with "stronger" marriages tended to assume multigenerational responsibilities.

Professional activity emerges as one of the most significant factors in the exercise of this function, since the knowledge acquired and social network developed in this environment are fundamental to harnessing support for the family system. They are people who have the time, despite their professional obligations, and the economic resources to provide financial support for the family.

The interviews equate the exercise of this function with providing "family support" and with what may be termed promoting the functional dimension of intergenerational and intra-generational solidarity and exchanges of financial and instrumental support (Silverstein & Bengtson, 1997). The association of this role with intervention in moments of crisis was rarely mentioned. That is to say, the identification of one member of the family as the "guiding light" in cases of need is not associated with any difference in the length of time the support may last. However, this person varies according to which section of the family the individual in need belongs to (i.e., to which "family composition" she/he belongs) and according to the type of support required (e.g. instrumental, financial, emotional or advisory support).

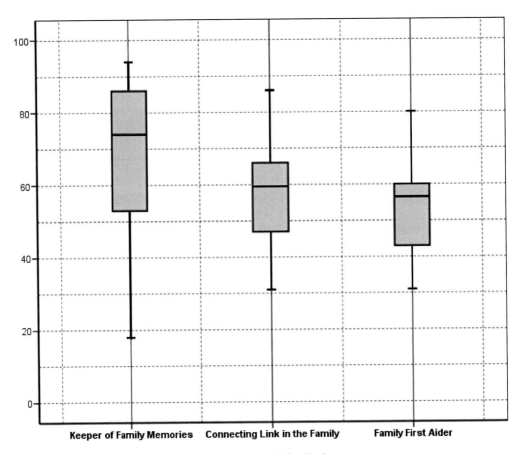

Graph 1. Distribution of roles in the multigenerational family by age group.

Hughes and Waite (2005) state that the tasks and interactions in the exercise of family roles demand physical, emotional and cognitive investments from those who assume them. However, these same roles also offer rewards and support which individuals may use as resources. In fact, it appears important to balance *needs* and *resources*, both of which constitute conceptual tools for identifying the mechanisms by which families influence the well-being and health of their members. The demands which a multigenerational family makes on its members in order to maintain itself as a functional system which "feeds" its members may be distributed amongst the different individuals and generations, who have access to different resources. Graph 1 shows the age group distribution for subjects identified in terms of the roles they play in multigenerational families through a *box-and-whisker plot* which offers a visual image of the existing relationship between age progression / individual development and the assumption of different roles within the multigenerational family.

CONCLUSION: THE MULTIGENERATIONAL FAMILY AND THE ELDERLY: A MUTUAL OR PARASITICAL SYMBIOTIC RELATIONSHIP?

Literature on family relationships attests to the significance and importance of the multigenerational family. Family members are required to carry out certain tasks and respond to challenges and crises in order to maintain this system. The different generations therefore end up *receiving* specific roles and no generation is *exempt*. As Attias-Donfut and Rozenkier (1996: 52) state: "*in the circle of exchange, each generation serves simultaneously as helper and recipient*".

The most significant changes in the later phases of family and individual development affect the type of support provided: the older generations function as the keepers of family memories and the intermediate generations as the connecting link in the family or the family first aider.

The emphasis here is placed on the different types of support exchanged, rather than on the inversion or reversal of support provided. The skills and competences of each generation justify the type of support that is offered. In addition, in the systemic framework adopted no single type of support appears to be more important than another in terms of the functioning of the multigenerational family system. On the contrary, they appear to be complementary.

The intermediate generations: a) due to the individual development phase in which they position themselves, take on functions that require more dexterity, as they are physically stronger; b) assume the role of providing financial and instrumental support, as well as linking the family to other social systems, since they are professionally active and involved in broad, heterogeneous social networks; c) assume responsibility for maintaining links within the multigenerational family and for providing it with support and care since, in terms of identity, they are experiencing the "stagnation vs. generativity" conflict (Erikson, 1950/1976).

The older generation is entrusted with preserving and transmitting family memories and with providing a meaning to family experiences in its relations with past, present and future. This function is consonant or harmonized with their skills and competencies and the challenges they face in this particular phase of life. Their long experience of life and understanding of past and present family relationships, which they possess in relative abundance and which other generations lack, is essential in preserving memories of the family system. Approaching the complexity of family relationships as a result of divorce and remarriage, Settles (1988: 51) refers, albeit briefly and superficially, to this role in the contemporary family: "*the family chronicler who can keep the story straight and tell the great-grandchildren how the blended family all came about will have an important function*".

We believe that we are now able to respond to the question contained in the title of this chapter. In biological terms, symbiotic relationships between organisms may be categorised as: a) mutual, when both interacting species benefit from the association; b) commensal, when one of the species in the arrangement benefits from the relationship and the other is neither harmed nor helped; c) parasitical, when one of the species benefits from the relationship and the other is harmed. They may also be categorised in terms of their importance to the organisms involved: a) obligatory, when they are essential to the survival of at least one of the organisms involved; b) optional, when they are beneficial but not strictly necessary to the survival of the organisms.

Literature on the intergenerational subject has a tendency to value the benefits which the older generation obtains from belonging to and interacting with the larger "organism" which is the multigenerational family. Parallel to this, common sense tends to portray the exchanges and benefits involving the elderly generation and the multigenerational family as a parasitical relationship or, to put it differently, a situation in which the elderly emerge as mere consumers of family resources (for example, family care, which is covered extensively in literature on this subject).

The data we present here on functions within the multigenerational family that are essential to its "survival" as a system, reveals a distinct framework. The relationship between elderly generations and the multigenerational family emerges as a mutual rather than a parasitical symbiotic relationship: the function of the keeper of family memories (keeping, preserving and transmitting aspects of the history and identity of the multigenerational family) appears to be closely associated with the elderly. If we bear in mind the specific nature of the individual development of the elderly person and the conflicts that can arise at this time of life, we can easily recognise the benefits for the elderly of belonging to a multigenerational family and from assuming this role. The multigenerational family functions as the favoured setting for the final phases of individual development and also gains in terms of experience, spirit and status through the actions of elderly people. A theatre allegory might be put forward to illustrate the (sub)systems intertwining exposed here. A good match between the theatre stage (multigenerational family), the performance actors (different generations) and the play (human development), which influence and is influenced by idiosyncratic audiences (different societies and communities), if performed with a good sense of timing (historical factors), might confer rich rewards, physical and symbolical, to all involved.

The superimposition of individual and family development through the roles carried out within the multigenerational family may lead to a better understanding of the definition of successful ageing proposed by Vaillant (2002: 61): *"successful aging means giving to others joyously whenever one is able, receiving from others gratefully whenever one needs it, and being greedy enough to develop one's own self in between"*. It is a complex balance played out against the intersection of the different developmental paths and functions within the same family context. This would appear to support Ryff and Seltzer's (1995: 95-96) concept of reciprocal influences in which *"family life precedes individual development, and individual development precedes changes in family life, in a reciprocal pattern over time"*.

Other questions also emerge, the most obvious of which is to determine the roles played by the younger members of the multigenerational family. A body of literature is, in fact, emerging on the way in which the filial subsystem influences the parental subsystem (Ryff & Seltzer, 1995) and it remains to widen the field of observation to include the influences of the youngest members on the other subsystems and on the multigenerational family system. In addition, following on from the previous question, we believe that, given the complexity of the multigenerational family system, other distinctive and equally important functions will emerge in addition to those already identified here, which will require research.

We believe that these functions unfold as a *continuum* (Vicente & Sousa, 2008), ranging from those who most frequently carry them out and are recognised by the rest of the family (this study focussed on these people) to those who rarely engage in them. Many questions emerge from this spectrum conceptualization of the exercise of functions within the multigenerational family, such as the way in which quality of life is associated with particular functions within the multigenerational family and the development phase of the individual, the advantages and disadvantages of taking on a particular function outside the normal period in which it is carried out, the nuances that distinguish individuals in the same family who carry out the same functions and how these differences affect the functioning of the family.

The multigenerational family appears to be a very attractive area of study within the various social and human sciences, ranging from sociology to family psychology to developmental psychology, history and anthropology. This is due not only to its complexity, which we have only just begun to explore, but also to its current relevance in the light of the social and demographic trends that concern societies nowadays.

REFERENCES

Alarcão, M. (2000). *(des)Equilíbrios familiares*. Coimbra: Quarteto Editora.

Ariès, P. (1988). *A criança e a vida familiar no antigo regime*. (M. S. Pereira & A. L. Faria, Trans.). Lisbon: Relógio D'Água. (1st edition, 1973)

Attias-Donfut, C. & Rozenkier, A. (1996). The lineage-structured social networks of older people in France. In H. Litwin (ed.) *The social networks of older people. A cross-national analysis*. London: Praeger.

Beck, R. W. & Beck, S. H. (1989). The incidence of extended households among middle-aged black and white women. *Journal of Family Issues*, 10 (2), 147-168.

Bedford, V. H. & Blieszner, R. (2000). Older adults and their families. In D. H. Demo, Allen, K. R., & Fine, M. A. (eds.) *Handbook of family diversity*. Oxford: Oxford University Press.

Bell, C. (1968). Mobility and the middle class extended family. *Sociology*, 2, 173-184.

Botcheva, L. B. & Feldman, S. S. (2004). Grandparents as family stabilizers during economic hardship in Bulgaria. *International Journal of Psychology*, 39 (3), 157-168.

Brody, A. C. & Simmons, L. A. (2007). Family resilience during childhood cancer: The father's perspective. *Journal of Pediatric Oncology Nursing*, 24 (3), 152-165.

Carter, E. & McGoldrick, M. (2005). The expanded life cycle: Individual, family, and social perspectives. In E. Carter & M. McGoldrick (Eds.) *The expanded life cycle*. Boston: Allyn & Bacon.

DeLeire, T. & Kalil, A. (2001). Good things come in 3's: Single-parent multigenerational family structure and adolescent adjustment. Retrieved May 28, 2008, from http://harrisschool.uchicago.edu/About/publications/working-papers/

Demo, D. H., Allen, K. R., & Fine, M. A. (Eds.). (2000). *Handbook of family diversity*. Oxford: Oxford University Press.

Durand, D. (1992). *A sistémica*. Lisbon: Dinalivro. (1st edition, 1979).

Erikson, E. H. (1976). *Infância e Sociedade* (2nd ed.). (G. Amado, Trans.). Rio de Janeiro: Zahar Editores. (1st edition, 1950).

Figueiredo, D. (2007). *Cuidados familiares ao idoso dependente*. Lisbon: Climepsi Editores.

Fine, M. & Norris, J.E. (1989). Intergenerational relations and family therapy research: What we can learn from other disciplines. *Family Process*, 28 (3), 301-315.

Freud, S. (2007). *Uma recordação de infância de Leonardo da Vinci*. (M. J. Pereira, Trans.). Lisbon: Relógio D'Água. (1st edition, 1910)

Goodman, C. C. & Silverstein, M. (2001). Grandmothers who parent their grandchildren. *Journal of Family Issues*, 22 (5), 557-578.

Hader, M. (1965). The importance of grandparents in family life. *Family Process*, 4, 228-240.

Hagestad, G. O. & Burton, L. M. (1986). Grandparenthood, life context, and family development. *American Behavioral Scientist*, 29 (4), 471-484.

Hareven, T. K. (Ed.). (1996). *Aging and generational relations: Life-course and cross-cultural perspectives*. New York: Aldine de Gruyter.

Harper, S. (2005). The challenge for families of demographic ageing. In S. Harper (Ed.) *Families in ageing societies: A multi-disciplinary approach*. New York: Oxford University press, Inc.

Hughes, M. E. & Waite, L. J. (2005). The American family as a context for healthy ageing. In S. Harper (Ed.) *Families in ageing societies*. New York: Oxford University Press, Inc.

King, D. A. & Wynne, L. C. (2004). The emergence of "family integrity" in later life. *Family Process*, 43 (1), 7-21.

Kornhaber, A. & Woodward, K. (1981). *Grandparents/grandchildren, the vital connection*. New York: Anchor Press/Doubleday.

Lang, F. R. (2005). The availability and supportive functions of extended kinship ties in later life: Evidence from the Berlin ageing study. In S. Harper (Ed.) *Families in ageing societies: A multi-disciplinary approach*. New York: Oxford University press, Inc..

Litwak, E. (1960). Occupational mobility and extended family cohesion. *American Sociological Review*, 25, 385-394.

Litwin, H. (1995). *Uprooted in old age: Soviet Jews and their social networks in Israel*. London: Greenwood Press.

Loomis, L. S. & Booth, A. (1995). Multigenerational caregiving and well-being: The myth of the beleaguered sandwich generation. *Journal of Family Issues*, 16 (2), 131-148.

Lowenstein, A. (1999). Intergenerational family relations and social support. *Zeitschrift für Gerontologie und Geriatrie*, 32 (6): 398-406.

McGoldrick, M. & Gerson, R. (1987). *Genogramas en la evaluación familiar*. Barcelona: Gedisa Editorial.

Mulder, C. H. (2007). The family context and residential choice: A challenge for new research. *Population, Space and Place*, 13, 265-278.

Neugarten, B. & Weinstein, K. (1968). The changing American grandparent. *In* B. Neugarten (ed), *Middle age and aging*. London: University of Chicago Press.

Okabayashi, H., Liang, J., Krause, N., Akiyama, H., & Sugisawa, H. (2004). Mental health among older adults in Japan: Do sources of social support and negative interaction make a difference? *Social Science and Medicine*, 59, 2259-2270.

Papalia, D. E., Sterns, H. L., Feldman, R. D., & Camp, C. J. (2002). *Adult Development and Aging* (2nd ed.). New York: McGraw Hill.

Perrig-Chiello, P. & Sturzenneger, M. (2001). Social relations and filial maturity in middle-aged adults: contextual conditions and psychological determinants. *Zeitschrift für Gerontologie und Geriatrie*, 34, 21-27.

Poehlmann, J. (2003). An attachment perspective on grandparents raising their very young grandchildren: Implications for intervention and research. *Infant Mental Health Journal*, 24 (2), 149-173.

Price, L. L., Arnould, E. J., & Curasi, C. F. (2000). Older consumers' disposition of special possessions. *Journal of Consumer Research*, 27, 179-201.

Reese, C. G. & Murray, R. B. (1996). Transcendence: The meaning of great-grandmothering. *Archives of Psychiatric Nursing*, 10 (4), 245-251.

Relvas, A. P. (2004). *O ciclo vital da família: Perspectiva sistémica* (3rd ed.). Porto: Edições Afrontamento. (1st edition, 1996).

Rossi, A. & Rossi, P. (1990). *Of human bonding: Parent-child relations across the life course.* New York: Aldine de Gruyter.

Rotherham-Borus, M. J., Leonard, N. R., Lightfoot, M., Franzke, L. H., Tottenham, N., & Lee, S. (2002). Picking up the pieces: Caregivers of adolescents bereaved by parental AIDS. *Clinical Child Psychology and Psychiatry*, 7 (1), 115-124.

Ruggles, S. (2003). Multigenerational families in nineteenth century America. *Continuity and Change*, 18 (1), 139-165.

Ryff, C. D. & Seltzer, M. M. (1995). Family relations and individual development in adulthood and aging. In R. Blieszner & V. H. Bedford (eds.) *Handbook of aging and the family*. Westport, Connecticut: Greenwood Press.

Schwarz, B. (2006). Adult daughters' family structure and the association between reciprocity and relationship quality. *Journal of Family Issues*, 27 (2), 208-228.

Segalen, M. (1999). A revolução industrial: Do proletário ao burguês. In A. Burguière, C. Klapisch-Zuber, M. Segalen, & F. Zonabend (eds.) *História da Família*. Lisbon: Terramar. (1st edition, 1986)

Settles, B. H. (1988). Family as a many splendored concept. In S. K. Steinmetz (ed.) *Family and support systems across the life span*. New York: Plenum Press.

Silverstein, M. & Bengtson, V. L. (1997). Intergenerational solidarity and the structure of adult child-parent relationships in American families. *American Journal of Sociology*, 103, 429-460.

Sluzki, C. E. (2002). *La red social: Frontera de la practica sistemica* (3rd ed.). Barcelona: Gedisa Editorial. (1st edition, 1996)

Sousa, L. & Cerqueira, M. (2006). Influência do género nas imagens da velhice: Um estudo exploratório na população portuguesa. *Revista Kairós*, 9 (2), 69-86.

Sousa, L., Figueiredo, D. & Cerqueira, M. (2004). *Envelhecer em família*. Porto: Âmbar.

Spark, G. M. & Brody, E. M. (1970). The Aged Are Family Members. *Family Process*, 9, 195-210.

Spira, M. & Wall, J. (2006). Issues in multigenerational families: Adolescents' perceptions of grandparents' declining health. *Child and Adolescent Social Work Journal*, 23 (4), 390-406.

Suggs, P. K. (1985). Discriminators of mutual helping behaviour among older adults and their siblings. *Journal of Applied Gerontology*, 4 (2), 63-70.

Sussman, M. B. (1988). The isolated nuclear family: Fact or fiction. In S. K. Steinmetz (ed.) *Family and support systems across the life span*. New York: Plenum Press.

Troll, L. (1982). Family life in middle and old age: The generation gap. *The Annals of the American Academy*, 464, 38-46.

Tschuggnall, K. & Welzer, H. (2002). Rewriting memories: Family recollections of the national socialist past in Germany. *Culture & Psychology*, 8 (1), 130-145.

Vaillant, G. E. (2002). *Aging well: Surprising guideposts to a happier life from the landmark Harvard Study of Adult Development*. Boston: Little, Brown and Company.

Vicente, H. T. & Sousa, L. (2007). Família multigeracional: Estruturas típicas: Contributo para a avaliação do sistema familiar. *Psychologica*, 46, 143-166.

Vicente, H. T. & Sousa, L. (2008). Funções na família multigeracional: Contributo para a caracterização functional do sistema familiar multigeracional. (forthcoming)

Wall, K. (2005). Os grupos domésticos de co-residência. In K. Wall (org.) *Famílias em Portugal*. Lisboa: Imprensa de Ciências Sociais.

Walsh, F. (2005). Families in later life: Challenges and opportunities. In E. Carter & M. McGoldrick (Eds.) *The expanded life cycle: Individual, family, and social perspectives*. Boston: Allyn & Bacon.

In: Families in Later Life: Emerging Themes and Challenges   ISBN 978-1-60692-328-3
Editor: Liliana Sousa   © 2009 Nova Science Publishers, Inc.

Chapter 2

MATERIAL INHERITANCE: CONSTRUCTING FAMILY INTEGRITY IN LATER LIFE

Marta Patrão and Liliana Sousa

ABSTRACT

Material inheritance (the creation and transmission of a material legacy from one generation to another) is not only a matter of economics. In addition to serving an economic purpose, the transmission of material property also has emotional implications in terms of family relationships: it may facilitate continuity or create conflict and separation.

In this chapter we present an exploratory study of elderly Portuguese donors (aged over 74), with the aim of exploring more deeply the role played by material inheritance in the construction of family integrity (achieving meaning, connection and continuity within the multigenerational family). The results show that material inheritance: i) constitutes a normative challenge for later life families, combining instrumental, relational and emotional/symbolic dimensions; ii) plays a part in constructing family integrity through the balanced management of material property and care; iii) involves basic family skills such as adaptability, filial maturity, open communication and joint problem solving.

From this perspective, material inheritance represents an *window* on family dynamics and processes in the final phase of life and an opportunity for families and professionals to maximise or recreate the skills and transactional patterns associated with the construction of (individual and family) integrity.

Keywords: later life families, material inheritance, family integrity

INTRODUCTION

Material inheritance is an important theme for families in later life which becomes increasingly significant as the family confronts the (real or symbolic) loss of the older generation and, consequently, the natural succession of generations. It is a process which involves the passing on of material property from one generation to another within the family, generally from parents (donors) to their children (heirs), which is completed after the death of the oldest generation. This transmission is regulated by law, although the family assumes it as a task in the final phase of life, making use of (informal) transmission strategies. It is a normative experience (associated with a milestone in the life cycle) which all families experience, regardless of their social or cultural background and the economic value of their assets.

The passing down of material property from donor to heirs involves decisions regarding the management of assets (what to spend and save, how to deal with expenses and the increased need for care in the final stages of life) and how property is to be distributed amongst heirs: *when, to whom and how*. In addition to the economic aspects, these decisions involve the donor deciding how they will be remembered after death and how they want their valued personal possessions to be used. It therefore constitutes a relational experience associated with a life review, continuity of self and the preservation of identity (Csikszentmihalyi & Rochenberg-Halton, 1980). For the heirs who receive (or do not receive) property, it is frequently a sign of the love (or lack of love) and recognition of the donor. This symbolic aspect of material inheritance may awaken (old or new) rivalries between heirs, jealousy, and feelings of injustice and inequality. Conflict, in fact, constitutes one of the most significant aspects of the process of the transmission of a material inheritance within the family.

In pre-twentieth century times, material inheritance played a crucial role in family life. The passing down of material property from one generation to another constituted a guarantee of survival for the younger family members, who received the material assets they needed to establish themselves, whilst the older generations used the legacy strategically in exchange for care and protection. In contemporary society, following the development of the Welfare State, this economic strategy has been blunted. However, material transmission is still vital to family life since, notwithstanding economic needs, emotional needs still exist and there is still a need for continuity in the family. The material inheritance involves loyalties, family responsibilities and filial obligations, allows family history and rituals to be passed on and symbolizes the intergenerational transmission of power, trust, and love which may enhance or weaken family continuity (Sussman *et al.*, 1970).

Material inheritance is thus associated with themes that are essential to families in later life: financial wellbeing, harmony, death, continuity and family identity. Nevertheless it remains a topic that has not been explored extensively in literature on psychology and the family. This chapter aims to contribute towards extending our understanding of the function of inheritance in later life families and, in particular, the role it plays in the construction of family integrity (King & Wynne, 2004), a process which intervenes in the construction of meaning, connections and continuity in the multigenerational family at this stage in its life.

Through this study we hope to contribute towards extending knowledge of normative developmental processes in later life families, the challenges they face and the skills they use to deal with them. Material inheritance may represent a useful conceptual and intervention tool in relation to later life families, since it is a process that is common to all families and is associated with key elements in their development, such as the creation of meaning and continuity.

1. MATERIAL INHERITANCE IN THE LIVES OF FAMILIES IN LATER LIFE

Material inheritance in families has mainly been approached from a legal and economic perspective (Bernheim, Shleifer & Summers, 1985; Cox, 1987; McGarry, 1999). However, the emotional and relational aspects are gradually being taken into consideration, and it is recognised that they reveals aspects of the relationship between donors and heirs, for example through the kind of material property that is passed on, the way in which it is passed on, the people to whom it is given and how it is used (e.g. Sussman *et al.,* 1970; Kemp & Hunt, 2001).

1.1. Material Inheritance: Family Management

Material inheritance is regulated by law. This legal, social and cultural regulation ensures that social and family duties are fulfilled through inheritance, thus ensuring the continuity and survival of social and family systems (for example, the protection of minors). Since the introduction of the Civil Code (1864), Portuguese law has stipulated that property should be transmitted to descendants in equal amounts, regardless of gender or seniority. Additionally, the donor may bequeath one third of their assets to anyone they wish. The legal provisions in Portugal are different from the legislation in countries such as the United Kingdom and the USA which operate under a system of testamentary freedom enabling the donor to bequeath any amount of his/her property to anyone they wish (whether they are direct descendants or not).

A study of transmission patterns for material inheritance in various countries (and legal systems) has shown that even under the system of testamentary freedom people tend to respect the principles of genealogical equality (giving equal amounts to direct descendants). Parallel to this, transmission in *new forms* of family (e.g. following divorce and in remarried families) also shows a focus on the immediate family context, indicating that blood relations tend to take priority (Coleman & Ganong, 1998). This preference has been explained in terms of the survival of the system and the assurance of continuity (Webster, 2003), emphasizing the intrinsic desire to leave a material legacy i.e., the bequest motive of the donors (usually parents). The elderly tend to organise and construct the inheritance during their lifetime, reorganizing the management of material resources in order to safeguard it. Whilst it might be assumed that parent/child relationships constitute the strongest form of motivation, single people without direct descendants also value transmission and become involved in the creation of (material or symbolic) inheritances which they pass on to other family members, friends, the community or society. Similarly, having no affective involvement in a legacy (because there is no inheritance to leave or no one to leave it to) is associated with feelings of sadness (Rubinstein, 1996). Two hypotheses emerge in the literature to explain the reasons for leaving an inheritance: altruism (Becker, 1974) *versus* exchange (Bernheim, Shleifer & Summers, 1985)

The altruism model indicates that donors pass on their property to facilitate and improve living standards for their heirs (mainly their descendants), without expecting any form of compensation. It is an unconditional donation, which is more common in women who have higher incomes and levels of education (Kohli, 2003). The exchange model indicates that donors use their property to influence the behaviour of their heirs i.e., as a means of persuading them to provide or pay for care for them in old age. Bernheim, Shleifer & Summers (1985) tested the implications of this hypothesis and confirmed that the number of visits and the amount of time spent with these elderly donors increased in proportion to their income. In this context, donors tended to make conditional transmissions which are more common in single men with fewer financial resources and lower levels of education (Kohli, 2003). The exchange model suggests that transfers create and maintain family interdependence, creating social obligations and expectations of repayment (Cox, 1987). Reliable predictors for the provision of care in old age include the existence of material transmissions and the existence of an inheritance (Caputo, 2005).

However, it appears that the reasons for leaving a material inheritance fluctuate on a *continuum* between exchange (the conditional donation) and altruism (the unconditional donation), depending on various factors such as availability of assets or the quality of family relationships.

1.2. The Material Inheritance: Family Relationships

Inheritance (the construction and transfer of the material legacy) is a task that elderly people and later life families face and appears to be associated with the desire to prolong life and give it meaning, and to maintain a symbolic presence (after death) (Kane, 1996; Schaie & Willis, 2002; Hunter & Rowles, 2005). In addition, the disposal of special possessions may function as an element in the reconstruction of self, particularly when the distribution or donation of personal property serves as a ritual of transition within the life cycle (Marcoux, 2001).

The material inheritance represents a transfer from one generation to another and a focal point in family history in which vertical (e.g. family myths, emotional patterns passed down through the generations) and horizontal (e.g. predictable developmental stresses and unpredictable life events) stressors intersect (Carter & McGoldrick, 2005). Various decisions have to be made: *how, what, when and who to transfer the property to and how it will (or will not) be received.* In addition to the legal framework and the family's social background and history, these decisions also touch on family memory and the history and the nature of relationships between donors and heirs. Conflicts (past and present), triangles and alliances between family members frequently emerge in association with the material inheritance, arousing feelings and emotions of love, gratitude, anxiety, anger, satisfaction, blame, humiliation, pride or recognition (Kane, 1996). All these situations activate themes that are central to families in later life, such as the management of power, authority and (visible and invisible) loyalties and the balance between debit and credit (giving and receiving) (Prieur, 1999).

Lustbander (1996) suggests that for children the division and distribution of property may symbolise the affection, respect, trust or preferences of their parents. The different ways of passing on property to descendents (such as division into equal or unequal shares) may become a source of conflict between parents and children or between siblings (Prieur, 1999). Conflicts associated with inheritance tend to be prolonged, confined to the family and provoked by the unequal division of property or by violations of the rules of reciprocity and expectations (Sussman *et al.*, 1970; Stum, 2000; Kemp & Hunt, 2001).

Whilst acknowledging that the transfer of material goods (especially those with sentimental value) is a response to a developmental need in elderly members of the family which has implications for the quality of family relationships (Stum, 2000), literature does not clarify the role played by the material inheritance in this process. For instance, Price, Arnould & Curasi (2000) suggest that the role of special possessions in the creation of family legacies should be studied. Stum (2000) corroborates the need to further examine the connection between personal possessions and facilitating and validating role transitions amongst family members and how issues of control or power in family systems affect such transitions.

2. MATERIAL INHERITANCE AND FAMILY INTEGRITY: AN EXPLORATORY STUDY

King & Wynne (2004) introduced the concept of "family integrity[1]" as a normal developmental challenge for the elderly which is influenced by factors within the family system. Family integrity (versus disconnection and alienation) indicates that the older adult's striving toward ego integrity is inextricably bound up in the larger process of constructing meaning and relational development at the level of the family system (Table 1). With meaning, family members are better able to gain a sense of control and find order in chaos. The positive resolution of this process results in *"family integrity"*, as opposed to feelings of separation or alienation resulting from an absence of shared values, beliefs and feelings of family identity.

Family integrity depends on three competencies within the family system (Table 1): the transformation of relationships over time, the resolution or acceptance of disappointments, loss or past/present conflicts, and the creation of legacies based on histories or rituals shared over generations.

Material inheritance plays an important part in constructing family integrity (Patrão & Sousa, s/d), namely by:

- Empowering the consolidation of identity and integrity through the creation of a (material and/or spiritual) legacy.
- Implying the reorganisation of family relationships, power hierarchies and participation in family activities.
- Its relation to decisions on care for elderly parents and management of financial resources at this stage in family life.

---

[1] See Overview.

- Its great potential to create conflict in relationships (between the elder couple in question, parents and children and siblings) and the possible complications it may create in relation to family integrity.

Table 1. Family integrity

FAMILY INTEGRITY
Achieving meaning, connections and continuity within the multigenerational family, experienced as a deep sense of peace and/or satisfaction with past, present and future family relationships. Involves feelings of belonging and family bonds, emotional closeness and a mutual willingness to provide emotional and instrumental support (on the part of the elderly person and their family).
Observable family relational competencies
Transformation of relationships: maintenance of long-term commitment to family relationships and realignment of family relationships in order to deal with later life transitions: i) in the oldest generation the couple faces the re-invention of close bonds; ii) parents and children have to renegotiate power hierarchies and participation in family activities. Involves the establishment of mutually beneficial transactions for parents and children.
Resolution or acceptance of losses, disappointments or conflicts: in the face of personal and parental mortality it becomes imperative to: i) deal with old grievances, cut-offs or unmourned losses from the past; ii) handle present family problems or crisis situations (illness, financial difficulties). Requires an open communication style, willingness and strength to confront emotionally charged issues (both for older parents and children and grandchildren).
Creation of meaning and legacy: the coherent integration of personal life stories and family themes (creation of sustaining individual and family legacies), through: i) family story telling; ii) passing on of shared interests, life themes, values and material possessions; iii) participation in family activities and rituals. This process benefits both the elder members of the family, by maintaining their sense of purpose and respect in the family, and the younger generations, who inherit a family legacy (a model for their own aging process). Requires family cohesion and emotional closeness (greater interaction and sharing).

Based on King & Wynne, 2004.

Objectives

This study aims to understand the role of material inheritance in the construction of family integrity from the perspective of elderly people (aged over 74). The results have implications for interventions involving families, individuals and the community, mainly because they highlight certain family and individual competences which are challenged as part of this process. In addition, on a conceptual level, they lead to an understanding and knowledge of normative family processes in later life.

Methodology

In this study we used a semi-structured interview consisting of open questions which were presented in focus groups. The interview script was constructed on the basis of questions proposed by King and Wynne (2004) for use in discussing family integrity, to which other questions, designed to clarify the role played by material inheritance in this process, were added (Table 2).

Table 2. Interview

Introduction	In your opinion, based on your own experience or any other cases that you know of and can share with us …
Integrity	Which aspects of family life do you feel most satisfied and at peace with? And which aspects are you least satisfied and more troubled with? Specify aspects of (dis)satisfaction: i) financial relationships, ii) management of material resources.
Transformation of resolutions	How do family relationships change as people grow older? Specify: i) perceived transformation of financial relationships, ii) passing on of financial responsibilities; iii) participation in financial decisions and management of material property.
Resolution or acceptance of losses or conflicts	Which issues or problems will you be able to accept or resolve in this stage of your life? What may help you to accept or resolve these problems? Specify problems/issues related to: i) financial relationships, ii) material inheritance (past and present).
Creation of meaning and legacy	What would you like to share with or pass on to others (material and symbolic)? Why? Specify: i) material contents transmitted; ii) purposes of material transmission and iii) meanings attached.

Based on King and Wynne (2004).

In order to ensure that the information was relevant and varied, a non-random intentional sample was constructed, based on selected participants aged over 74 who were able to provide relevant information on this subject (privileged informants) and were comfortable with group discussions.

The focus groups were organised on the basis of gender (male/female) and residence (rural/urban), since these variables tend to affect material inheritance. For example, they are associated with the role of the donor within the family, the type of donation and the values attributed to material assets. Four groups were organised, each consisting of 5 participants: i) women from a rural environment; ii) women from an urban environment; iii) men from a rural environment; iv) men from an urban environment.

Literature states that the optimum number of participants for a focus group is 7 to 12 individuals, although it may be smaller if the discussion topics are sensitive and require greater intimacy (Piercy & Hertlein, 2005). In this study we opted for homogeneous groups of participants (female/male, rural/urban) and smaller numbers in the hope of maximising exploration of the subject matter and promoting feelings of security and willingness to participate, since the interview did cover sensitive and emotionally significant subjects.

The participants are also involved in another larger study on transmission of the material inheritance. The first author already knew them and contacted them to explain the aims of this study and the reason why they were being asked to take part in it. All those who were contacted agreed to collaborate and gave their informed consent in writing. A date was set for the interviews at this point.

The sample, which was divided into 4 groups, comprises 20 participants, aged between 75 - 94 years (Table 3).

Table 3. Sample

Groups	Gender	Residence	Age	Marital status	Academic level
I (n=5)	Female	Rural	75-87	3 widows 1 single	2 = never attended school 3 = 3 years of school
II (n=5)	Female	Urban	80-94	5 widows	3 = 4 years of school 2 = 12 years of school
III (n=5)	Male	Rural	76-94	4 widows 1 single	2 = never attended school 2 = 4 years of school 1 = 9 years of school
IV (n=5)	Male	Urban	76-85	2 married 2 widows 1 divorced	2 = 4 years of school 3 = 12 years of school

All the groups were given a brief introduction to the theme and objectives of the study and a guarantee of confidentiality. The questions were asked around the group by the first author, who *threw* them as discussion topics and asked participants to refer to concrete situations and examples (from personal experience or personal knowledge). The focus groups were held in a private room in the day centres which the subjects attended and lasted, on average 90 minutes.

Data Analysis

The interviews were recorded on video, transcribed and submitted for content analysis, taking family integrity as the conceptual framework (Table 1) (King & Wynne, 2004). The analysis aimed to describe and interpret family dynamics and processes associated with the management of material property and material inheritances from the elderly donors' point of view and also to establish links with the process of constructing family integrity. The procedure to analyse the data was as follow:

1. Definition of categories and sub-categories: the process of creating and testing the categorisation system was gradually refined by two independent judges (the authors). Each judge read the interviews and drew up a list of categories and subcategories.

They then met to compare and discuss their proposals until agreement was reached. Finally they produced a list of categories and sub-categories, which included definitions (Table 4).

2.   Classification of responses to the categories and subcategories that had previously been defined. The first author classified the interviews, which were then reviewed by the second author and both judges were in full agreement.

Table 4. Categories and subcategories

Sub/categories	Definition
1.Transformation of relationships	
1.1 Passing on the torch to heirs	Usually the illness, death or dependence of a donor initiates the process of passing on financial responsibility. Donors and heirs, typically parents and children, renegotiate their roles in managing family material resources (such as houses, property and money) and general financial responsibilities. Normally elders retain responsibility for money and pass on other resources.
1.2.Launching the inheritance	Generally this occurs in two phases: firstly, gift giving and verbal communication of wishes and intentions; secondly, initiating the legal procedures for succession and inheritance.
1.3.Exchanging material support with heirs	Parents continue to provide material support for their heirs, usually their children, in crisis situations or when they face unexpected expenses. Some elders receive material support from children or other significant persons or institutions to cover health expenses or compensate for poor living conditions.
2. Resolution or acceptance of losses/conflicts	
2.1.Managing (resolving/accepting) conflicts associated with material inheritance	Lingering resentment and/or family conflict over the distribution of property and the provision of care, in relation to siblings and in-laws in the past and in relation to heirs in the present.
2.2. Prevention of problems associated with inheritance	Communicating and explaining wishes and decisions concerning the distribution of property to heirs (who it is to be given to, and why).
2.3. Accepting material and social losses	Accepting economic losses and/or the loss of social status acquired in middle age.
3.Creation of meaning and legacy	
3.1. Attributing meaning to material possessions	Material possessions have symbolic and affective meanings: they mark key events in personal or family history, represent (social and material) achievements, successes or the specific talents of donors. In addition, material investment in children is re-evaluated (representing success in the parental/familial role).
3.2. Assembling the material inheritance	The material legacy is assembled throughout the lifetime, but in this phase becomes a more conscious and focussed process which aims to ensure the construction of a legacy that will be appreciated by heirs; sometimes donors play the role of keepers of valued older objects.
3.3. Striving to maintain family continuity	By conserving (not selling) material possessions such as houses or properties linked to family history or work.

Table 5. Distribution of responses by category/group

(Sub)categories	Rural women (n=5)	Urban women (n=5)	Rural men (n=5)	Urban men (n=5)	
1. Transformation of relationships					**Total**
1.1. Passing on the torch to heirs	2	2	4	4	12
1.2. Launching the inheritance	4	4	5	4	17
1.3. Exchange of material support with heirs	1	2	3	5	11
2. Resolution/acceptance of losses/conflicts					
2.1. Managing (resolving /accepting) conflicts associated with material inheritances	3	1	1	2	7
2.2. Prevention of problems associated with inheritance	2	3	0	1	6
2.3. Accepting material and social losses	1	0	0	2	3
3. Creation of meaning and legacy					
3.1. Attributing meaning to material possessions	1	1	4	4	10
3.2. Assembling the material inheritance	0	1	3	3	7
3.3. Striving to maintain family continuity	2	0	2	1	5

2.1. Material Inheritance: Challenges in Later Life Families

The results emphasise the emotional significance of the material inheritance for families in later life, which is revealed in exchanges between the elderly person (donor) and their multigenerational family (heirs) on three levels: changing relationships, resolution of conflicts and the creation of a legacy. The categories which emerge describe family processes associated with the management of property and material inheritances within the context of the construction of family integrity.

Transformation of Relationships

The transformation of family relationships which surrounds the material inheritance usually develops as a result of key events in family life: a real loss (death) or a symbolic loss (illness/dependency) affecting one member of the oldest couple in the family, and/or increased emotional and instrumental need on the part of elderly parents (donors). These marks in the family life cycle require a readjustment of financial relationships and support, linking two aspects associated with different areas of family life: money (instrumental) and care (emotional and symbolic). In either case, they testify to the challenges which the family has to face in ensuring that care is provided for the elderly and that material possessions are properly managed. The results show that three interconnected processes are activated: passing on the torch to heirs, launching the inheritance and exchanging material support with heirs.

Passing on the (financial) torch to heirs usually starts when one of the spouses passes away, and the elderly living parent negotiates the management of material resources and financial responsibilities with the adult children, typically maintaining power hierarchies in money management and financial independence (which is particularly important to males):

> "I've already put everything in my son's name but I'm still the first name on the bank account and if he wants anything he asks me first. I'm the one that controls the money!" [urban male, aged 76]

This is a difficult process for donors, since control over material possessions is a factor which affects security, particularly in old age. Maintaining the hierarchy (even if only in symbolic terms) is therefore a compromise solution. The women considered this less important, perhaps because their husbands had always been responsible for managing finances and they now expect someone else (their heirs) to take over.

This change in relationships implies establishing a balance between care for the elderly (donors) and the management of material possessions (ensuring that care can be paid for). Decisions on care and the management of material possessions tend to be combined, for example:

a) After the death of his wife, Donato decided that he would prefer to live in a home (so that he would not be a burden, above all, to his daughter-in-law). Before moving he knew that he would have to reorganise his assets and therefore sold some, kept some money for himself and divided the rest amongst his children.

b) Antónia thought of living with one of her daughters and the daughter agreed to this but in return wanted a greater share of the inheritance. Antónia did not like this idea and thought it was unfair. She therefore decided to sell her assets, divide the inheritance equally between her children and live in an old people's home.

When the elderly person in question is single and/or has no children or is not close to their family these decisions may imply that support is reorganised together with social institutions, which take on the role of the heirs in guaranteeing care:

> "Everything I have is for the home, because what I want now is to be well looked after and they take good care of me here!" [female, rural, aged 79]

Simultaneously the donors *launch the inheritance* (this was mentioned by almost all the participants), which involves: i) certain transfers (in the form of gift giving or legally formalised transactions); ii) compensation for support already provided or motivation for care to be provided in future by children or other heirs (these decisions usually lead to the initial conflicts associated with inheritance). The children or other heirs who are geographically closest or who provide the most instrumental and emotional care play a significant role in decisions associated with this process:

"My oldest son who lives nearby is the one who comes round the most and he knows all about my money!" [male, rural, aged 78]

The donors emphasised the strategic role of their material possessions, which constitute a security (and emotional) factor in facilitating contact and the availability (affective and instrumental) of heirs (children or others):

"Everyone knows this, it's like the old saying: those who've got a lot are worth a lot, those who haven't are worth nothing...if the parents haven't got any property, the children keep their distance" [male, urban, aged 76]

Whatever the situation, they regretted relationships that were based only on material exchange:

"The only help they want from me is financial...my son-in-law only comes round to see me to ask for money to buy a car for his son...and afterwards, when I was ill, he didn't even visit me!" [male, rural, aged 76]

In general, donors at this time in their lives are still concerned about saving money to cover their needs and to ensure the future inheritance. However, their children (heirs) do not always value this and would rather their parents ensured their own wellbeing (*"my son often says to me: dad, spend what you have to and don't worry about it ...we're not interested in an inheritance"*).

Relationships between donors and heirs also involve mutual exchanges of material support: parents (donors) provide material support to children (heirs) and/or parents receive material support from children. Parents (elderly donors) continue to provide material support for their children when they can, mainly to help them deal with family crises or unexpected expenses:

"My son came to see me the other day and he was really upset. He asked me to lend him 3000 euros and I did. It's for him, I don't want him to pay me back!" [male, rural, aged 76]

The women mentioned this aspect less, probably because they tended to be poorer and therefore had less opportunity to offer financial support and/or because they were not used to managing money (a traditionally male task). In Portuguese families, the support provided by women tends to be restricted to *small-scale*, everyday help or *gift giving*; whilst *large-scale support*, including inheritances or the passing on of businesses is reserved for men (Wall, 2005).

Only two male participants (one from a rural and one from an urban environment) said they received financial support from their children, which they described ambivalently. On the one hand, it was seen as reciprocal (the child gives in acknowledgment of the fact that they have received) but it also gave rise to feelings of being less worthy and being dependent on their children, which the elderly people preferred to avoid. It seems to be easier for elderly people to accept (or sometimes even demand) their children's (or other heirs') responses to their emotional and instrumental needs. It appears that men find it more difficult to accept material support provided by their children, since they are traditionally the breadwinners and the ones responsible for managing the family's finances. Acceptance of this kind of support may therefore entail a process of grieving and significant emotional readjustment.

Resolution of Losses/conflicts

In old age the elderly person faces the process of reviewing and integrating their life, which includes resolving or accepting past and present conflicts and resentments. Material inheritance is one of the most sensitive subjects in family life, leading to some of the most prolonged conflicts. The results show that in this phase of their lives, the elderly people sought to manage (resolve/accept) past and present conflicts centred on material inheritance, to prevent (present and future) problems concerning inheritances and also to accept material and social losses that affected the inheritance. Managing conflicts centred on material inheritances was a subject which many of the participants stressed. They mentioned that these conflicts were based on feelings of being treated unfairly and could occur:

a) Amongst heirs, usually because some heirs feel that others have maliciously influenced donors into leaving them a larger share, whilst those who are accused feel that this is unjust, thus leading to conflict.

b) Amongst donors, usually when the donor couple do not agree on how to organise and manage the inheritance (for example, one of the donors may prefer to divide it into equal parts whilst the other favours one particular heir, or one donor may prefer to spend and the other to save the inheritance in order to bequeath it).

c) Amongst donors and heirs, when there is disagreement on how the inheritances are managed and on the amounts involved in gift giving (for example, some heirs feel that they are being treated unfairly in comparison with others, whilst in other cases they feel that the donors could have given more than they did).

The participants mentioned their desire to resolve interpersonal conflicts associated with inheritances which they described as referring to two phases in their lives: i) old conflicts which had begun years ago when they received inheritances from their parents or in-laws, which involved siblings and in-laws and are still ongoing; ii) recent conflicts concerning the planning of the inheritance and the present-day division of property, involving children (or other heirs). In other words, the participants were referring to conflicts that emerged when they took on the role of heirs and again when they became donors.

Strategies used to attempt to manage (older and more recent) conflicts were aimed at preserving good family relations and assumed two different forms: i) avoiding conflict by blaming non-blood relations (daughters-in-law, sons-in-law, brothers and sisters-in-law ...); ii) minimising or downplaying the conflict, stressing shared values (*they don't mean it badly; they've got their own problems too*).

In fact, one of the major worries of the elderly (donors) at this stage in their lives concerned good family relations and the participants therefore referred to the need to prevent problems associated with inheritances, both now and in the future. They stressed the need to be fair and to explain their decisions to their heirs in order to preserve good family relations during their lifetime and after their death. They emphasised that it was important to justify decisions that involved: i) the unequal distribution of property, for example in order to repay a child for the support they had give them during their life (*"I've already thought that I will have to talk to them about this. The earrings and necklace have to go to my youngest because she's helped me the most"*); ii) the distribution of property to non-blood relations *("I've got to talk to them about this because I've already promised the home firewood from my property"*). The donor anticipates that these decisions (made out of a desire to be fair and to reward the care they have received) may generate conflict, probably because they contradict the myth of equality within the family (a deeply-rooted cultural norm) and centralisation of the inheritance within the family (which is also established in law).

The participants also pointed out the importance of accepting social and material losses (status) which affect the inheritance, reporting bad feelings concerning: i) significant material and/or social losses in the past which affect the possibility of building up and leaving a (good) inheritance; ii) failure to fulfil filial obligations towards elderly parents, justified by financial difficulties. The acceptance or resolution of these situations involves, in the case of the former, valuing what they had done when they had a higher income (*"when I had it, I gave everything I could"*). In the latter case, the elderly donors aimed to give their heirs what they were unable to give to their parents in order to deal with feelings of guilt. Therefore a process of continual reciprocity appears to emerge, translating into an extended exchange prolonged over time.

Creation of Meaning and Legacy

The creation of meaning and legacy is described in terms of sharing histories, values and material property and contributes towards creating family bonds and continuity in terms of the symbolic presence of deceased family members. The participants in this study revealed that the material and non-material (relational and symbolic) contents of the legacy are indissolubly linked. The transfer of the material inheritance is experienced as a reflection of personal worth by the participants when they assume the role of donors, even if the financial value is low. Some of the women, for example, had few economic resources, but stressed the importance of passing on material goods:

"I haven't got much to leave them...but if I had, it I would give me great pleasure to do so!" [female, rural, aged 82]

The participants, in particular the men, associated the creation of meaning and legacy with three aspects: attributing meaning to material property, assembling a material legacy and striving to preserve the family memory.

One of the challenges facing the donor when creating a meaning and legacy based on a material inheritance involves attributing affective and symbolic meanings to material possessions, namely:

i)   Recognition of life achievements – "I didn't inherit one penny from my parents but I've been able to show my children what I've made of myself because I've left them a whole building".

ii) Positive and significant events in personal or family history – "All the furniture in my house was made by me. My deceased wife was very fond of it".

iii) The specific skills and talents of the donors – "I'm leaving them a lot of needlework, because that's what I do best".

New meanings are ascribed to investments, especially financial investments in education and training for children and grandchildren made throughout their lifetime by male urban residents in particular. Before they had been seen as part of the parental role; now they are also transformed into an inheritance (the preparation of the next generation).

The material inheritance is assembled throughout life and at the end of the lifetime becomes more purposeful and focussed, with donors assuming an active leading role. For participants (especially males) it is an important concern, leading them to seek to actively construct a legacy that has real financial value and that will be appreciated and used by future heirs:

> "God gave me the inspiration…to put up this building … if not, I would have just had plots of land to leave them, which are no use to anyone!" [male, rural, aged 76]

The women (who were slightly older than the men) seemed to value this task less at this moment in time and were more concerned with the spiritual aspects of life. It was also important for them to assemble material possessions during the course of their lives, but they passed on these material possessions, usually at the time when decisions were being made about reorganizing care (for example, living in an institution or with one of their children). The present was dedicated to transmissions which were symbolic and/or involved spiritual values and they had already distanced themselves from the other task, leaving their heirs to assume responsibility.

Material possessions become the means by which the donor tries to safeguard family continuity (which was more important in a rural context), by preserving their memory within the family (so that it remained after their death) and keeping the identity of the family linked to the past and to its central values. Thus, certain material possessions (due to the meaning ascribed to them) assumed greater importance, for example possessions associated with family history (*"my son won't sell the land where I grew my vegetables and I'm pleased about that"*) or working life (*"my tools are going to my son"*). However, this continuity depends mainly on the value that heirs ascribe to the possessions. Various situations were mentioned by the participants: i) some elderly donors had negative expectations which made it difficult to create meaning (*"my daughters don't want to know about anything"*); ii) others had positive expectations which consolidated the creation of the legacy (*"I've left a lot of furniture in their house that I made myself: one day they'll look at it and remember that it was me who made it"*).

3. DISCUSSION AND IMPLICATIONS

3.1. Material Inheritance and the Construction of Family Integrity

The results of this study suggest that material inheritance implies a reorganisation of functions and transactional patterns in later life families, in the following areas (Figure 1): instrumental (reorganisation of material transmissions and support), relational (redefinition of the relationship between donor(s) and heir(s) and the safeguarding of family bonds) and emotional/symbolic (emotional and relational reassessment of the material legacy and reintegration of individual and family history).

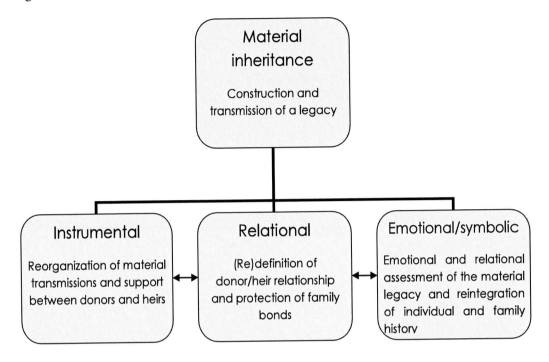

Figure 1. Dimensions of the material inheritance

Instrumental

Economic and instrumental needs tend to increase in families in later life and become a source of stress for the elderly and intermediate generations. Olson (1988) states that 30% of the stressors for the couple in the oldest generation are rooted in economic constraints. In addition, financial resources affect the options and resources available to families to help them deal with certain normative challenges, such as providing care.

The instrumental aspect of the material inheritance includes the reorganisation of material transmissions and support between heirs and donors. Families in later life make use of the material inheritance to carry out tasks which are central to their development and to respond to practical everyday needs, namely reorganising the management of material goods and guaranteeing care for elderly parents (donors). In this sense, the material inheritance may be understood as a practical provision for elderly parents (donors) and their children (heirs), testifying to the function of family relationships: responsibility for other members of the family (i.e., protection). Family theorists (Sussman et al., 1970) have argued that inheritance dispositions reveal the processes underlying relationships between the generations: children care for elderly parents and are in turn recompensed with an inheritance.

This instrumental dimension of the material inheritance reveals how the family system activates its protection and survival functions and its capacity for self organisation (the system autonomously and spontaneously modifies its structure to create the conditions for its survival). Literature on the subject documents how families, in particular donors, adapt the rules of succession to (economic and emotional) family needs. For example, socio-historical studies (Hareven, 1996) on systems of succession and strategies for the transfer of family possessions reveal that in pre-twentieth century samples of wills the exchange of care-giving for inheritance was often explicitly described. Also, cotemporary studies on family transmission processes (MacGarry, 1999) show that families are involved in transmission at two stages in their lives: part of the property is transferred during the life course to help children (heirs) and the rest is reserved for transmission after death and to cover any future needs. Donors use this transmission strategy above all when they fear for their security and financial stability.

The instrumental dimension of material inheritance is combined with one of the most important emotional processes in this stage of life: passing on the torch to the next generation (Carter & McGoldrick, 2005). The results show that the passing on of property and financial responsibilities from donors to heirs (together with launching the inheritance) occur in such a way as to safeguard the power and (real or symbolic) hierarchical position of the parents (donors). One of the chief impediments to personal integrity is the fear (or reality) of financial, physical or emotional dependency (Schaie & Willis, 2002). The major contribution made by the instrumental dimension of the material inheritance towards constructing integrity is based on the possibility that the family can use it to achieve a balance between: i) management of property and provision of care (choice of main carer, living arrangements, health care plans); and ii) the autonomy and (financial, physical and emotional) dependence of donors in relation to their heirs. This balance enables the family to carry out instrumental and practical duties which the donor may no longer be able to manage (due to physical and/or cognitive decline), whilst the donor preserves his autonomy, the respect of the family and the continuity of their role within the family.

Relational

The transmission of the material inheritance (and the preparation this involves) provides an opportunity (or, alternatively, a risk) for redefining the relationship between the donor and their heirs and for ensuring good family relations.

Within the family, material possessions hold secret meanings, normally associated with certain aspects of the history of relationships, such as family myths, family secrets or transactional patterns of power. Literature on the subject reveals that the material inheritance may be understood as a gift passed down from donors to heirs (Kemp & Hunt, 2001), which is submitted to the relational and symbolic processes that govern this kind of informal material transmission. For example, Ruth *et al* (1999) found six meanings for the act of giving/receiving which have an impact on the quality of relationships between donor and receptor: strengthening, affirmation, negligible effect, negative confirmation, weakening and severing. The material inheritance therefore has a relational aspect that is as important, or more important, than the economic aspect.

In addition to the financial and economic aspects (the more instrumental aspects), strategies employed by donors for the transmission of material property are aimed at: i) creating social bonds; ii) protecting heirs if, for example, they are less well-off or have mental health or health problems; iii) safeguarding family ties and harmonious relations. The results suggest that the donor recognises the relational power of the material inheritance and aims to control the process and the negative implications of transmission (for example, conflicts). It seems that the parental role in later life may encompass the responsibility of ensuring the welfare of future generations, including maintaining harmony between children and their descendents (Drake & Lawrence, 2004). Factors such as a desire to avoid conflict amongst potential heirs may guide the donor's decisions regarding allocation. For example, parents may be motivated by a wish to avoid envy in generally treating children on strictly equal terms, sometimes at the expense of responding to different needs.

However, the real guiding principles of the donor may not be explicit. For instance, explicit acknowledgement of the exchange of inheritance for assistance may be less common in contemporary arrangements than in pre-twentieth century wills. Rendering such exchanges explicit may, in fact, undermine the basis for relationships in families, rather then creating closer bonds between family members (Clark & Chrisman, 1994). In fact, close relationships may be characterised by the avoidance of exchange behaviours, especially when people see themselves as joined by ties of affection rather than obligation. Thus, unlike equality, principles such as reciprocity are likely to operate implicitly in the donor's decisions, rather than being acknowledged explicitly. In addition, other implicit relational processes exist which influence the donor's decisions, such as family secrets (the family may be guarding the secret of an illegitimate child who is not included in the transmissions as he/she is not a blood relation), invisible loyalties (the donor/heir relationship may be dominated by debts and obligations associated with family alliances which heirs know nothing about) or family myths (belief systems passed down over generations which unconsciously guide transmission, such as the myth of family equality which obliges all children to be treated equally).

The relational dimension of the material inheritance translates into the construction of integrity through the donor achieving feelings of peace/satisfaction in relation to their material legacy, the assurance that the process responds to their wishes and objectives (for example, rewarding the care provided by a child) and the knowledge that they have done everything to avoid conflict in family life. The donor may want to be assured that any problems associated with the material inheritance they received from their parents are not repeated, and they attempt to remedy this (to prevent any repetitions leading to conflict) when preparing the material inheritance (Patrão & Sousa, sd).

Emotional/Symbolic

The symbolic dimension of the material inheritance is the dimension which most reveals the individual skills and self of the donor. Material possessions plays a specific role in each phase of the life cycle; in the final phase of life it serves as an anchor for meaning and time-space references, representing significant people and events in the life story (Csikszentmihalyi & Rochenberg-Halton, 1980). MacAdams (1993) argues that identity development via life story creation is the major psychosocial task permeating adult life and that generativity (taking care of the next generation) is incorporated into it as one of its most important aspects. In constructing the material inheritance (choosing and assembling the property to be transmitted and deciding *what, when and to whom* it should be given), the donor is also ascribing values and relational and emotional meanings to it which boost the process of the life review and the creation of the life story (e.g. Butler, 1963). In this way, the narrative of the donor relating to their material legacy (what it tells them about their possessions and what it tells others, particularly their heirs) enables them to integrate their life story and provide it with coherence and consistency. The public nature of inheritance confers on it the nature of a social test in which donors use material legacy as a sign of status or accomplishment. In addition, it enables them to express their generativity by ensuring continuity for the parental role of taking care of the next generation (care in old age and beyond death).

Through reassessment of the property that is transmitted, this emotional/relational dimension enables the material inheritance to serve as an opportunity (ritual) for reviewing and integrating personal and family history, thus contributing towards recreating (individual and family) identity.

Material Inheritance and Family Integrity

Table 6 summarises the three dimensions of the material inheritance and shows the role it plays in the construction of family integrity and the family skills which are put to the test during this process.

The elderly person's satisfaction with their material legacy appears to translate into:

- Satisfaction with decisions taken concerning reorganisation of the management of material possessions and care, living arrangements and launching the inheritance.
- Acceptance of their social and economic condition and status (accepting what they have, putting what they do not have or have not achieved into perspective).
- The connection with the multigenerational family through a valued and recognised exchange of material possessions (with symbolic and/or real financial value).

In these circumstances, donors may distance themselves emotionally from the material inheritance and considered it "settled", (satisfactory resolution and integration of task).
Dissatisfaction with the material inheritance may take the form of:

- Discontent with decisions taken concerning the management of property, the launching of the inheritance, living arrangements and care.
- Resentment of their social and economic condition and status.
- The feeling that the connection with the family is restricted to material transmissions and/or that the legacy is not appreciated and acknowledged by heirs.

Dissatisfaction and resentment prevent the elderly person from emotionally integrating the task, meaning that they return endlessly to the subject. Conflicts and emotional distancing may occur and family relations may remain *frozen*, threatening basic family functions (such as the reorganization of care for the elderly donor).

In short, transmission of the material inheritance emerges as a fulcral point in the family system in terms of the construction and consolidation of family integrity: it represents the objective confrontation with mortality and an (emotional and relational) context for the life review, facilitating the emotional process of transition at this stage in the life cycle. It also represents an opportunity for increased closeness within the family, trust and respect for (individual and family) needs, and gives donors a sense of meaning and continuity in their lives.

Table 6. Material inheritance and family integrity

Dimensions of material inheritance	Contribution towards achieving integrity	Individual and family skills
Instrumental Reorganisation of material transmission and support between donors and heirs.	Balance between material possessions and care (security); symbolic continuation of family roles (the parental role); equilibrium between autonomy/dependence.	Parental maturity and filial maturity; mutuality; resilience to financial strains; adaptability and joint problem solving; care giving and attachment.
Relational Redefinition of relations between donor and heir; resolution of (past and present) conflicts concerning inheritance; prevention of future conflicts.	Preserving and improving family relations through material transmissions (ensuring the welfare of future generations, including maintaining harmony between children and their descendents).	Open communication style; joint problem solving; family cohesion, forgiveness.
Emotional/symbolic Construction of legacy; ascribing meaning to material possessions; safeguarding (individual and family) memory.	Maintaining generativity (taking care of the financial wellbeing of heirs), recreating identity (creation of meaning in relation to material conquests and the use of material possessions in relations) and ensuring continuity (preserving individual and family memory).	Valuing self and others; stimulating and maintaining mutual interests; creating opportunities for interaction; sharing values.

3.2. Material Inheritance: A Lifelong Process

One of the most significant aspects of this study is the extension through time of the process of transmitting the material inheritance. Just as (individual and family) integrity is constructed throughout life, the material inheritance (the construction and transmission of the material legacy) is not restricted to a set period of time.

It is a process which is intrinsic to the family life cycle (we all begin as potential heirs and become donors one day) and is governed by the principal of the circulating legacy (Prieur, 1999) in which the roles of donor and heir succeed each other over time. Parents, for example, repay grandparents (their parents) for the legacy they have received by passing on a legacy to their own children.

Donors seem to consider the construction of their material inheritance a life task. They see it as an obligation and a necessity that is intrinsic to their role and parental function. In older families, the *"material inheritance"* becomes more pressing, gaining in emotional importance with the real or symbolic loss of one of the members of the older generation (generally one of the parents).

The transmission of the material inheritance involves specific (emotional, relational and legal) protagonists and processes both before and after the death of the donor. In the period before death, the material inheritance is a task for both donors and heirs, although donors assume the more important role. After the donor's death, the process acquires a greater legal importance (property is distributed in accordance with the current law on succession, using formal legal procedures).

Schaie & Willis (2002) recently expanded their stage theory model of adult cognitive development to differentiate between the various groups contained within the broad concept of "old age". Originally the authors viewed old age as a stage of re-integrative cognitive work. This paralleled Erikson's idea of ego integrity. Schaie and Willis have now labelled old-old as a stage of reintegrative cognition and have added reorganizational cognition to characterize the young-old who are dealing with reorganizing priorities and finances in the post-work stage of life. They have also added a final stage for the creation of a legacy by the oldest-old. This stage often includes writing or revising autobiographies, putting one's effects in order, distributing prized possessions, providing an oral and material history for the next generation through family pictures and heirlooms, making funeral arrangements and perhaps undertaking a final revision of their will.

Bearing in mind the concept developed by Schaie & Willis (2002) and the results of this study, a more precise understanding of the dynamics of material inheritance can be obtained, involving two phases:

- An initial instrumental or reorganizational phase which implies instrumental decisions taken more or less strategically in order to reorganise the material resources required to provide care for the oldest generation and preparation for transmission after death. At this point heirs may still need material support from elderly parents.
- A second emotional or reintegrative phase which is more emotional in character and implies revising the previous options (such as reassessing the will), clarifying decisions and balancing the desire to redefine or amend with establishing fairness in relationships with heirs.

In some cases a third phase may also emerge when, for example, the donors are extremely elderly (a common situation now that life expectancy has increased) and if they have begun to consolidate transcendence (Tornstam, 1997). Whilst they are still living, donors may emotionally (and objectively) detach themselves from the role of donor on the expectation that their heirs will take on this role.

In each of these phases the instrumental, relational and emotional/symbolic dimensions of the inheritance acquire a different weight. For example, in the instrumental phase the instrumental and relational dimensions are more salient, indicating the donor's very active involvement in the process, whereas in the reintegrative phase the emotional/symbolic dimension is more significant and processes that are more closely connected with the self (and with individual development) become more important.

After the death of the donor, the task remains (i.e., survives them), but the current protagonists are now the heirs, who ensure its (legal and emotional) completion. At this point, the relational and emotional dimensions of the inheritance become extremely important. Resentment and rivalry between heirs (often in relation to the donor) tend to become accentuated, based on feelings of unfairness and injustice in the distribution of the inheritance. In addition, the absence of the donor implies that the transmission assumes the status of the *last word* on the relationship between donor and heir(s). The relational and emotional character of the material legacy remains: the way in which the heirs receive (or reject) the legacy and use it (for example by saving it, spending it, using it in accordance with the wishes expressed by the donor when they were alive, or passing it on to others) reveals the nature of their relationship with the donor and the meaning they attribute to it. At this point, the heirs move up one generation and assume the role of future donors and the process advances cyclically to the rhythms of family time.

3.3. Implications for Intervention

Material inheritance, like any other family challenge, (changing roles and functions in order to respond to the needs of the family) activates the usual skills and patterns within family functioning.

The results show that the material inheritance challenges individual and family skills in terms of three central themes:

i)   The transformation of relationships in order to provide care for elderly donors whilst maintaining the family hierarchy and power structure.
ii)   The resolution or prevention of conflicts associated with the inheritance in order to preserve family harmony.
iii) The combined construction of meaning and continuity on the basis of the material legacy.

All these aspects are related to the basic dimensions of family functioning (Olson *et al.;* 1988; Wynne, 1988).

Changes in relationships emphasise the adaptability of the system (reorganisation of the rules for participation and the boundaries between generations), the capacity for joint problem solving (for example finding creative solutions which preserve the elderly person's autonomy and meet their basic protection needs, such as provision of care or living arrangements).

The resolution or acceptance of conflict requires opening up communications on the subject of the transmission process. Conflicts surrounding the material inheritance tend to centre on mutual ignorance of intentions and desires on the part of donors and heirs (Stum, 2000). The way in which the donor transmits (or intends to transmit) implies a (more or less deliberate) relational proposal which is not made explicit or is not able to be understood by heirs and whose effects may be felt in terms of relations, leading, for example to conflict if certain perspectives and values (such as equality vs. reciprocity in transmission) are not compatible. Therefore clarifying the objectives of transmission to one's heirs and unveiling the meanings which donors and heirs attribute to them may prevent or facilitate resolution of the usual conflicts associated with fairness and justice.

The construction of meaning and continuity on the basis of the material legacy is associated with another skill: the capacity to value the legacy bequeathed by the donor. This depends on how close the various relationships are, but also on shared values and the ability of the family to get to know and take an interest in family history and therefore in what the donor is to transmit, even if differences in values makes this difficult. Opportunities for family interaction, ritualised moments for transmission and the openness of the family to transmission are essential aspects of this process.

In addition to activating these family skills, it may also be necessary to deal with more dysfunctional patterns of exchange. The emergence of the inheritance is associated with a crisis (the real or symbolic threat of the loss of a member of the oldest generation – the donor) in which relational patterns may be exacerbated and the family may not have enough emotional resources to deal with the challenge. In fact, the biggest difficulties within the relational system arise when the quality of relating is inappropriate or when it provides poor benefits to individuals during this time of structural change (Wynne, 1988). In this context and given the potential for conflict surrounding the material inheritance, the importance of psycho-educational programmes (based on a multidisciplinary approach) should be stressed. These are aimed at donors, heirs and the professionals to support them in dealing with instrumental matters (e.g. finance, living arrangements, care), relational matters (e.g.. family histories of conflicts between parents, children, siblings, the involvement of in-laws, family secrets) and emotional matters (e.g.. coping with illness/death, guilt, emotional burden) and help them to make informed decisions. Their usefulness in preventing family conflicts and financial abuse of elders (mismanaging money or stealing property or savings, forcing an elder to sign documents such as a will or to transfer ownership savings) should be stressed. In fact, guidelines for the prevention of elder abuse (Douglass, 1987) refer to measures that imply providing assistance to elderly people, as well as advance planning of the inheritance and the provision of care.

As with other family interactions which imply power relationships, the perspective of entitlement (Winslade & Monk, 2001) provides an interesting approach to mediating in conflicts based on inheritance, especially those which involve providing care for elderly donors. People often find themselves believing that others should treat them well and take care of their needs. They are particularly sensitive to being treated unfairly when they have contributed to another's person well-being and their actions are not reciprocated. When one party experiences a discrepancy between what he/she believes is deserved and the favours he/she has actually received, this may produce a strong negative response. Therefore, donors who do not feel reciprocated because they have not received the care, nurturing and love which they consider they deserve from their heirs and heirs who do not feel recompensed for the care they have provided for their elderly parents through recognition, love or material reward by donors and/or other heirs, often will seek to replace these emotions, in a destructive manner, using threats, manipulation or even more dysfunctional behaviour.

In family and community interventions involving later life families, material inheritance represents a *window* on family dynamics during a moment of crisis. Material inheritance provides the therapist with a context in which to explore affections, transactional patterns, alliances, triangles, and also family myths and the norms of filial responsibility and obligation. At the same time, it may serve as an intervention point for the therapist to work on old relationship patterns (such as keeping secrets, over or under-functioning or repeating inappropriate past family behaviours) and/or rediscovering new ones.

FINAL REMARKS

Material inheritance emerges as a central element in the construction of family integrity and an opportunity to consolidate or reconstruct security/protection, connection, meaning and continuity in the multigenerational family.

We hope to have contributed towards extending knowledge of the inheritance and its role within the framework of normative processes involving later life families. However, what we have been able to show is derived from a very specific context: the sample is restricted to the perspective of donors who belong to a particular *cohort* of Portuguese society in which traditional family values such as honour, kindness and generosity prevail and there are many links to beliefs and expectations associated with family obligations and responsibilities. It would therefore be interesting if future research: i) approached material inheritance from a multigenerational perspective, emphasising the links between the perspectives of donors and of heirs; ii) studied the process in different socio-cultural and economic contexts and in other family contexts such as reconstituted families, single people or childless couples, since, in addition to challenging the traditional (and legal) framework (based on the biological family), this may reveal other values and meanings and other family skills and strategies.

Professionals and families are not used to talking openly about material inheritance, probably because it metaphorically combines two *taboo* subjects: death and money. However, increased life expectancy poses a challenge to the management of (instrumental, financial and emotional) family resources, traditional family functions and values and the theoretical models used to understand them. Studying the three dimensions of material inheritance (instrumental, relational and emotional) may therefore contribute towards reaching an understanding of the dynamics of later life families.

REFERENCES

Becker, G. (1974). A theory of social interactions. *Journal of political Economy*, 82(6), 1063-1093.

Bernheim, Shleifer & Summers (1985). The strategic bequest motive. *Journal of Political economy*, 93(6): 1045-1076.

Butler, R. (1963). The life review: an interpretation of reminiscence in the aged. *Psychiatry*, 26(1): 65-76.

Caputo, R. (2005). Inheritance and intergenerational transmission of parental care. *Marriage and the Family Review*, 37 (1/2): 107-127.

Carter, B. & McGoldrick, M. (Eds.) (1999). *The expanded family life cycle.* (3 ed). Needham Heights: Allyn & Bacon, 362-372.

Clark, M & Crisman, K. (1994). Resources allocation in intimate relationships: trying to make sense of a confusing literature. In M. Lerner & G. Mikula (eds). *Entitlement and the affectional bond.* New York: Plenum Press: 65-88.

Coleman, M. & Ganong, L. (1998). Attitudes toward inheritance following divorce and remarriage. *Journal of Family and Economic Issues*, 19(4): 289-314.

Cox, D. (1987). Motives for private income transfers. *Journal of Political Economy*, 95(3), 508-546.

Csikzentmihalyi, M. & Rochenberg-Halton, E. (1981). *The meaning of things: domestic symbols and the self*. Cambridge: Cambridge University Press.

Douglass, R. (1987). *Domestic mistreatment of the elderly – towards prevention*. Washington: American Association of Retired Persons.

Drake, D. & Lawrence, J. (2000). Equality and distributions of inheritance in families. *Social Justice Research*, 13 (3): 271-290.

Haraven, T. (Ed.) (1996). *Aging and generational relations*. New York: Aldine de Gruyter.

Hunter, E. & Rowles, G. (2001). Leaving a legacy. *Journal of Aging Studies*, 19: 327-347.

Kane, R. (1996). From generation to generation. *Generations*, 20(3).

Kemp, S. & Hunt, F. (2001). Exploring the Psychology of inheritances. *Zeitschrift für Sozialpsychologie*, 32 (3): 171-179.

King, D. & Wynne, L. (2004). The emergence of "family integrity" in later life. *Family Process*, 43(1): 7-21.

Kohli, M. & Künemund, H. (2003). Intergenerational transfers in the family. In. Vern Bengston & Ariela Lowenstein (Eds.). *Global aging and challenges to families*. New York: Aldine de Gruyter, 123-142.

Lustbader, W. (1996). Conflict, emotion and power surrounding legacy. *Generations*, 20(3): 54-59.

MacAdams, D. (1993). *The stories we live by: personal myths and the making of the self*. New York: Morrow.

Marcoux, J. (2001). The "casser maison" ritual": constructing the self by empting the house. *Journal of Material Culture*, 6(2): 213-235.

McGarry, K. (1999). Inter-vivos transfers and intended bequests. *Journal of Public Economics*, 73: 321-351.

Olson, D. H. (1988). Family types, family stress, and family satisfaction. In. C. Falicov (Ed.). *Family transitions*. New York: The Guilford press, 55-80.

Piercy, F. & Hertlein, K. (2005). Focus group in family therapy research. In D. Sprenkle & F. Piercy (Eds.). *Research methods in family therapy*. New York: The Guilford Press.

Price, L., Arnould, E. & Curasi, C. (2000). Older consumer's disposition of special possessions. *Journal of Consumer Research*, 27(2): 179-201.

Prieur, B. (Coord). (1999). *As heranças familiares*. Lisboa: Climepsi.

Rubinstein, R. L. (1996). Childlessness, legacy and generativity. *Generations*, 20(3).

Ruth, J. *et al* (1999). Gift receipt and reformulation of interpersonal relationships. *Journal of Consumer Research*, 25: 385-402.

Schaie, W. & Willis, S. (2002). *Adult Development and Aging* (5th ed.). New Jersey: Prentice Hall.

Sussman, M., *et al.* (1970). *The family and inheritance*. New York: Russel Sage foundation.

Stum, M. (2000). Families and inheritance decisions. *Journal of Family and Economic Issues*, 21 (2): 177-202.

Tornstam, L. (1997). Gerotranscendence: the contemplative dimension of aging. *Journal of Aging Studies*, 11(2): 143-154.

Wall, K. (Ed.) (2005). *Famílias em Portugal*. Lisboa: ICS.

Webster, G. (2003). Prosocial behavior in families: moderators of resource sharing. *Journal of Experimental Social Psychology*, 39: 644-652.

Winslade, J. & Monk, G. (2001). *Narrative Mediation*. San Francisco: Jossey Bass.

Wynne, L. C. (1988). An epigenetic model of family processes. In C. Falicov (Ed.). *Family transitions*. New York: The Guilford Press, 55-80.

In: Families in Later Life: Emerging Themes and Challenges   ISBN 978-1-60692-328-3
Editor: Liliana Sousa   © 2009 Nova Science Publishers, Inc.

Chapter 3

COUNSELING OLDER ADULTS WITH FAMILY ISSUES: FORGIVING AND EMPOWERING

Margarida P. Lima

ABSTRACT

Counseling older adults with family issues addresses problems of older adults within their primary interpersonal context, the family. Although it is still a rare topic and practice, it is, however, an important response to challenges faced by older adults in later life.

With the purpose of making a review of the current state of knowledge in this field and in order to reflect on some aspects that have not yet been the object of many studies, this chapter combines theory and research with case examples, emphasizing the practical clinical decisions faced when working with older people in either individual or institutional settings. It addresses issues relevant to counseling with older people and aims to be useful not only to those readers who are involved in the provision of psychological services but also to those who are interested in the challenges and concerns faced by older people.

It closes with the importance of using empowerment and forgiveness when the older patient is confronted with the need to deal with complex family situations. It also stresses the need to do more research in the field.

1. THERAPEUTIC INTERVENTIONS

1.1. Community Resources for Older Adults

«When a door is closed somewhere a window is opened». (Cited by F, 76 years)

A popular quotation says: «what kind of monster are we, if we don't accept confusion», meaning that it is important to accept (and face) reality in all its complexity and paradox. This quotation is even truer when we confront the challenge of responding to the more or less explicit appeals of older adults.

Many of these appeals, as we shall see, are related to family, issues to which we must provide a solution. The aim, of course, is to improve the quality of life and the happiness of the elderly and of their family.

As far as happiness is concerned, Csikszentmihalyi's work (2002) sums up two decades of research on the positive aspects of human experience, such as joy, creativity and the process of full immersion in life, which the author refers to as flow, and aims to present the general principles that will allow a transformation of lives dominated by boredom and by the absence of meaning into fulfilling ones. The thesis defended by the author can thus be summed up as: happiness is not something that «happens», connected to luck or chance; it does not depend on external events but on the way an individual interprets these events; thus, happiness is a condition that should be prepared, cultivated and defended by each person. The perceptions we have of our lives result from multiple forces that shape experience, many which are beyond our control: physical appearance, personality traits, genetics, family background, the cohort into which we are born, and nationality. These are just some of the countless conditions that determine what we do, see and feel. Therefore, it is understandable to think that external forces, first and foremost, impose on one's destiny. Nevertheless, Csikszentmihalyi identifies moments in which every individual has felt in total control of his/her actions and absolute master of his/her own life. These moments, usually rare, and characterized by a deep feeling of euphoria and absolute satisfaction, remain in one's own memory as ideal situations or optimal experiences, to use the author's terminology.

Optimal experience is something the individual causes to happen, which gives him/her a sense of control and integration and adds meaning to life by making him/her feel that he/she participates in his/her own destiny. In psychology, the concept is applied to countless areas, but the one that concerns us is the organization of activities with the objective of promoting the wellbeing of older adults in the community and in institutions for the elderly.

As a matter of fact, cognitive and physical experiences that challenge the individual to overcome his/her limits, which are guided by realistic aims, that develop attention, imagination, memory and the ability to concentrate are indispensable factors in order to be able to experience the flow. These are experiences in which the individual finds himself/herself intrinsically motivated by activity and in which he/she would get involved even if he/she had nothing to gain, except from the satisfaction taken from it. Subjective experience is not just one dimension of life, but life itself; material conditions only affect us indirectly, by way of experience.

Having as a starting point the empirical evidence that quality of life is associated to meaningful activities and interpersonal relationships, it is important to emphasize learning that is centered on the «here and now» and on the availability to enjoy the immediate experience in which the family /(and institutions) have a fundamental role in their functions of encouraging individuality and integrating the experiences lived by its elements, so as to transform potentially entropic experiences into optimal experiences.

A unified purpose (meaning) is what gives meaning to life, wherever it may come from and whatever it is. This unified purpose can be broken for many reasons. For example, by the life events that are inevitably responsible for the unfolding of our lives. Counseling appears as one of the possible solutions to help re-establish the experience of flow that unites and gives meaning to individual life starting from purposes, determination and inner harmony.

Many therapeutic and counseling interventions, whether carried out in an institutional setting or not, either individually or in group, have been suggested, which can actually relieve negative states and have been found effective (Knight, 1999; Gatz, 1998; Gallagher-Thompson et al., 2000; Barrowclough et al., 2001). This effectiveness occurs in many settings and for many conditions and problems like depression (Gallagher-Thompson & Steffen, 1994; Scogin & McElreath, 1994; Scogin, 2000; Cappeliez, 2001), stroke (Evans et al., 1994) and aging families (Qualls, 1996; O'Rourke, & Cappeliez, 2005). Behavioral and environmental interventions for older adults with dementia are considered well-established, empirically-supported therapies (Gatz & Knight, 1998). Probable effective therapies for the older adult include cognitive behavioral treatment for sleep disorders and psychodynamic, cognitive, and behavioral treatments for clinical depression. For nonsyndromal problems of aging, memory retraining and cognitive training are probably effective in slowing cognitive decline. Life review and reminiscence are probably productive in improving depressive symptoms or in producing higher life satisfaction. Scogin & McElreath (1994) reported a meta-analysis of psychological interventions for the treatment of depression in later life which showed an aggregate effect size (d = .78) roughly equal to that found in another meta-analysis for anti-depressant medications (d = .57, Schneider, 1994) and roughly equal to that found for younger adults in meta-analyses using cognitive-behavioral approaches (d = .73; Robinson, Berman, & Neimeyer, 1990). Thus, in general, available evidence supports the effectiveness of psychological interventions with older adults.

Nevertheless, it should be noted that psychological assessment with older adults is more specialized than interventions are because of the higher prevalence of dementia in later life, which makes some level of neuropsychological screening essential. On the other hand, the higher prevalence of medical disorders in the older population makes paying attention to physical causes of symptoms and to the effects of medications as causes of symptoms highly important as well (Bortz & O'Brien, 1997).

Older adults are particularly open to the short-term, focused psychotherapies developed in recent years, which emphasize clinical problems and treatment goals. Concerning family issues, counseling has been considered an essential tool and as for community resources for older adults there are a number of ways in which an older person can contact a counselor besides counseling and psychotherapy associations or private consultation: many surgeries provide a counseling service, although there is often a waiting list[1]. Health and social institutions offer a free counseling service to older people. This facility may be particularly beneficial to those who are housebound, as often counselors will visit the older person in their own house.

The richness of experience and individuality of older people means that counseling them is perhaps one of the most rewarding and fulfilling experiences for counselors and, consequently, for clients. If counselors can cope with complexity then both client and counselor can learn a lot that can help the older client achieve one of life's greatest purposes – a happy old age.

On the following pages we will try to present a general vision about counseling older adults with family issues and the importance of forgiving and empowerment as counseling tools.

---

[1] This information refers to the Portuguese reality.

2. COUNSELING

2.1. General Issues

«Whatever it is that you decide to do, it's what you decided to do. Whatever you are thinking right now, that is what's on your mind. Whatever happened to you, it has already happened. The important question is: how are you going to deal with it? In other words, «what now?»» (Jon Kabat-Zinn, 2000).

The term counseling is a nebulous one (Rainsford, 2002). Many issues can and should be addressed, namely the definition and delimitation of the concept of counseling, theories and models of counseling, fields of socio-professional using, ethical, personal and developmental/supervisional dimensions in counseling, relationships with the processes of psychological assessment, psychotherapy and counsultory (Yalom, 1985; Corey, 1999; Culverwell & Martin, 2000).

However, for the purposes of this chapter, counseling refers to a therapeutic approach that places value on the person's subjective experience and challenges the person to accept responsibility for his or her own life. The relationship that develops between counselor and client can foster personal growth. The overall aim is to provide an opportunity for the client to work towards living in a way he or she experiences as more satisfying and resourceful. Counseling may be concerned with addressing and resolving specific problems, coping with crises, making decisions, working through conflict or improving relationships with others and empowering older clients. As Smith (2006) stated, "the strength perspective provides a corrective paradigm that allows [therapists] to see the glass as half full rather than half empty" (p. 16). This view of clients clearly facilitates the therapeutic alliance, in that clients appreciate being seen as a repository of assets rather than as a confluence of problems; this view "validates them in positive ways as worthwhile human beings" (Smith, 2006, p. 39). Moreover, this perspective also creates a more egalitarian client-therapist relationship in that clients are viewed as active, equal agents of change in their own lives (Smith, 2006; Christopher et al., 2006). Strengths-based practice is founded on a collaborative endeavor between therapist and client, with their respective expertise (Clients as expert in their own lives and therapist as expert in therapeutic process). Thus, with a foundation in strengths-based practice, the counselor encourages a partnership relationship with the client, in which the counselor encourages hope and inspires change, validates clients' experiences and supports clients to mobilize their potentialities and capacities towards the desired end (Smith, 2006).

General benefits of Counseling with older people are to assist in reducing stress, in coming to terms with their losses, to give the opportunity to share past and present problems in a confidential and supportive environment, to help adjust to a new situation and to think afresh and explore ways of coping more effectively, and to give a greater sense of acceptance so they can have a better quality of life. In this endeavor, little relevance has been given to older adults facing family problems and conflicts.

2.2. Adaptations to Older Adults

"Age is an empty variable" (Simões et al., 1999)

The contextual, cohort-based, maturity, specific challenge model (CCMSC) proposed by Knight (1996; Knight & McCallum, 1998) integrates concepts from life span developmental psychology, social gerontology, and clinical experience into psychotherapy with older adults. The model suggests that older adults display greater maturity than younger adults but may also be facing some of the most difficult challenges of adulthood. The model further asserts that the social context of older adults and the fact that they are members of earlier-born cohorts should be recognized and incorporated into the psychotherapeutic process. Although the model outlines important differences between older and younger adults in therapy, similarities often outweigh differences between the groups as the process of psychotherapy unfolds (Knight, 2004).

Psychotherapy and counseling need to be adapted, but mostly not due to developmental differences but to context effects, cohort effects, and specific challenges common in later life. Context effects require changes and adaptations on the psychotherapy and counseling dynamics for older clients living in age specific contexts, such as retirement communities, long term care settings, hospitals and outpatient medical contexts. The differences are due to the specialized environmental context rather than to the age of the clients. It is likely to be somewhat similar to working with younger adults in medical care settings and rehabilitation settings. While somewhat less different and therefore less specialized than the institutional settings, as the counselor must be aware of the need to attend to these differences, because seeing clients who are living a post-retirement lifestyle, especially if some of their lives are spent in age-segregated environments, requires knowledge about the social rules of those environments which can be learned from older clients. Otherwise, judgments will be made based on the norms and folkways of young and middle-aged adults whose lives are shaped by school, work, and young families rather than by leisure time, senior community centers or meal sites, and the dispersed networks of older families (Knight, 2004).

Cohort effects require modifications because earlier born cohorts have different skills, different values, and different life experiences than later born ones. The specific challenges of later life require specific knowledge and therapeutic skills because of the problems they pose for clients, not because of the client's age (Knight, 2004). Adapting to working with members of other cohorts is similar in difficulty and in the flexibility required to work with clients of a different gender, ethnicity, class background, or occupation-based lifestyle. It does require sensitivity to the possibility of difference. It also requires some knowledge of history before the time one was born or at least the willingness to learn about that generation.

However, elderly people are categorized, and typical topics are referred as characterizing this life period, but we should not forget that aging is a highly individual experience. What makes individuals, as they age, different from one another is a combination of many socio-historical and biological factors (for example, place of birth, place of residence, birth cohort, the food eaten and not eaten, education, heredity, physical and mental health, family size and composition...). There is also a time period effect on an individual; in other words, a person's age when he or she experiences a particular time period also influences how they age. Therefore, the factors that influence the manner in which people age are numerous. It is, actually, a series of processes that begin with life and continue throughout the life cycle. As individuals move through the processes, they become increasingly different from everyone else, which explains the heterogeneity of the aging population.

Older people's reactions to events and situations are no different from those of the rest of the population and their capacity to cope will vary from person to person. Chronological age may differ considerably from a person's functional age, and age-related changes occur at different rates for different people. Age-related changes do not begin at the same time nor do they all occur simultaneously and the effect of this aging losses differs between individuals. Whatever changes come with aging, most older adults are in relatively good health. Physiological, sensory, emotional, and physical changes do occur, but the human body and a person's ingenious methods of compensation often allow the older person to successfully function in today's complex world.

Because of the growing number and heterogeneous nature of our aging population, there is a rapidly increasing need to understand both the normal aging processes and the consequences of aging on the population.

In terms of specific challenges, if the older clients are physically ill, this will raise new issues in both assessment and also in interventions with them. Sorting out physical and psychological influences on symptoms and problems is an ongoing assessment issue. Specific knowledge about the effects of different chronic illnesses as well as both the skill and emotional readiness to work with physically disabled clients become essential. Consultation and supervised experience with psychologists who have such experience is likely to be needed, in addition to didactic instruction.

The more of these factors that are present, the more specialized working with older adults becomes. For instance, the counselor should be more flexible in setting the duration and the frequency of the session, as compared to therapeutic work with younger adults (Northus & Nielsen, 1998). Other things being equal, the larger the proportion of older adults in one's caseload, the more likely it is that these factors will be present, whether the therapist is immediately aware of them or not (Knight, 1999). Many of these factors are related to family issues or will have an impact on the family of the aging adult.

Working with frail, older adults requires some basic understanding of the stress and coping processes that affect caregivers. Sometimes intervention with caregivers will be necessary and will usually include some need to explore relationship issues and family issues as well. This work often includes a dual focus on emotional issues for the caregiver and problem solving in order to reduce the real stress and strain of long term caregiving for a seriously disabled family member (Knight, 1999).

Although there is a diversity of ways to live old age, for some people the problems in everyday life can become too much to deal with on their own. And there are a number of issues that although not unique to older people many older people may encounter them and therefore bring them to be dealt with in therapy: loss, depression, anxiety, fears about the future, loneliness, and awareness of their own mortality. Many of them feel awkward discussing these problems and concerns with friends or members of their family and would benefit from talking to a trained and experienced counselor.

There are many losses that older people can experience. These include: loss of independence, of health, of mobility, of family home and of loved ones. Many older people have been with their spouse or partner for a considerable amount of time and it is likely that each partner will have a strong attachment to the other. When a spouse dies, it is often difficult for the widow/widower to adjust. Also, as we get older the number of deaths of close friends and family members increases and so older people can often experience an overload of grief.

Older people often have concerns regarding their own health and wellbeing. They may also become anxious about practical and financial issues or worry about how they will cope on a day-to-day basis and remain living independently in their own homes.

Some older people can experience intense feelings of loneliness. This can happen particularly when an older person remains living in their own home after the death of the spouse. Many older people can experience feelings of isolation and of being "cut off" from society.

Often, when older people have experienced the loss of a spouse, and/or friends and family, they have a greater sense of their own mortality. When working with clients on death and dying issues, the therapist needs to have basic skills in death counseling and in grief work (Knight, 1999). The nearness of death gives a special urgency and motivation to the work and a time-limited therapeutic contract mirrors the reality of having only a short time left. Making counseling available to older people also represents an important valuing and validation of their experience.

In short, in Knight's (1999) perspective, seeing some older adults that are much like the other adults in one's practice does not require much further specialization. Seeing a lot of older adults, seeing older adults who have different problems, or seeing them in different settings requires specialized knowledge and supervised experience. This challenge must be met so that the confidence given by the elderly will not be defrauded.

2.3. Building Counselor Client Relation in Counseling Older Adults

"It is through feelings that we experience our way of being in the world. In other words, we always are as we feel." (Guidano, 1995, p.95)

We have seen that a growing literature has documented the effectiveness of psychotherapy with older adults (Haley, 1999; Zarit & Knight, 1996). However, a recurring concern in the literature has been that older adults rarely present their problems to traditional mental health settings. Rather, older adults present them predominantly in medical settings. This is of great concern because most physicians have not been adequately trained to assess or treat clients' psychological problems effectively (Haley, 1999). Successful psychotherapy and counseling with older clients in medical settings requires primarily the same clinical skills that are necessary in all psychotherapy. The ability to establish a successful therapeutic relationship, and to provide emotional support as well as technical expertise, is essential. But, it requires that the psychotherapist is able to work in unconventional ways, being more flexible in setting the place, duration and the frequency of the session; and having the capacity to assume multiple roles in order to respond to older adults in need of psychological services (Haley, 1999), who sometimes have multiple medical and psychological problems, or comorbidity. Complexity is further introduced with the presence of multiple psychosocial issues. This comorbidity forces counselors to focus on the most relevant problems, that have a reasonable likelihood of change and that are vital to the client's quality of life.

The helping relationship is a transactional encounter between two people where the quality of the relation is of vital importance. The one who helps must possess the characteristics of focusing on the person mentioned by Rogers. These are, empathy, unconditional acceptance and consistency as well as training in techniques of counseling in primary prevention programmes and in promoting personal and social development of older adults. Knowledge of gerontology, counseling techniques, and communication skills are necessary to work with older adults in a therapeutic relationship, always stressing the human element when working with older adults as is possible to see in the case that follows.

> Louisa (76 years) was recently assessed and is in full possession of her cognitive faculties. Her children put some pressure on her to go to an institution and she, who had always been an active and independent woman, gave in to please them and give them no trouble. Shortly after, she was committed to the hospital as a result of not taking the medicine the institution's doctor had prescribed for her. A conflict broke out between the children, who defended that their mother should have been forced into taking her pills, and the institution that felt divided between the duty to protect their patients and the duty to accept personal responsibility and options. A solution was found through a conversation with this patient's counselor who asked her the not-yet-asked question «why did you decide not to take your pills?"

Independently of the institutional frame where the counseling will take place, the basic communication skills developed by the counselors in their personal training are very important for the success of the intervention. The relationship with the patient is the first tool of the counselor. Being present and available in the interaction gives the possibility that the words spoken are self-transformative. Listening and answering requests with interest and openness is important, especially when there is sensory impairment. Talking clearly, without using technical jargon or harsh words is essential. Finally, being creative and willing to question our habits of thinking and doing will help clients tell their story and eventually recreate their lives.

However, the transference and countertransference sometimes encountered with older adult patients can lead to a therapeutic impasse and resistance to treatment (Knight, 2004). Societal taboos and counseling, within the context of institutional settings (e.g., nursing homes), can make the management of these dynamics particularly challenging. Although difficult to broach, an analysis of the relational dynamics can provide valuable information regarding an elderly patient's sense of intrinsic value, beliefs about power and agency, and difficulties with family members. The most frequently encountered are transferences relating to a counselor as son, as grandson, as father/mother, as magical expert and the erotic transference. Transference and countertransference depend mostly on the types of previous relationships of both the client and the therapist. Namely, it is important to be aware of family relations and beliefs about aging and death.

A practitioner has a responsibility to examine personal ageism, sexism, and countertransference limitations unconsciously conveyed: including projections of conflicts with grandparents or parents on the older patient. Otherwise, the counselor's ability to be receptive to clients who want to explore themselves is hindered. Altschuler & Katz (1999) describe a method that has been effective in helping students, paraprofessional counselors as well as mental health professionals identify countertransference reactions in themselves which consisted of a sentence completion exercise that can be used to elicit and uncover countertransference responses toward elderly people.

Generally speaking, the counselor will get stuck where he gets stuck as a person. The analysis of the counselor's countertransference "how do I feel with what the client said? What does it mean to me?" becomes crucial in a relationship that is often regulated by unusual changes in the therapeutical setting and by little control of some variables on the part of the therapist. These changes can make the therapist have feelings of inefficiency and difficulty in establishing limits with the client, who may often see him/her as a friend or as a «visitor». Boundary management refers to the challenges of the clinician's ability to maintain the boundaries of treatment.

Taking into consideration the keys to success for psychologists in primary care settings, as proposed by Haley (1999), can help create a positive rapport with older clients: Namely, do not wait for clients to come to you; many of your clients are really sick; work in interdisciplinary teams; psychotherapy is not enough, it is necessary to assess, educate, develop programs and do research; be prepared for anything and everything; refer out when necessary; stand up for what you know and ask what you do not know.

2.4. Helping Clients Tell their Stories

"Anyone who went through life and did not suffer
Was a ghost and not a human being
Who just passed life by and did not live...»[2]

(M, 68 years)

Telling the stories of one's life and retelling them from a new perspective can be a transformative experience (McAdams & Ochberg, 1988; Csikszentmihalyi, 2002). On the contrary, psychopathology can be described meaningfully in terms of vicious circles or repetitive maladaptive interpersonal functioning in the client's interaction with others. Gonçalves (2000, p.134) refers to this saying that what brings "most clients to psychotherapy is the lack of creativity and a centering on the same polarities and subjects. Thus, mental health presents itself as the possibility to paint in color and not in black and white. It implies the capacity to have alternatives, to experience roles, to be able to be the author of one's life." Moreno, the father of psychodrama, spoke about spontaneity as a fundamental tool for

---

[2] Sentence inspired in the Brazilian poet Vinícius de Moraes:
   Quem já passou por essa vida e não viveu
   Pode ser mais, mas sabe menos do que eu
   Porque a vida só se dá pra quem se deu
   Pra quem amou, pra quem chorou, pra quem sofreu
   Ah, quem nunca curtiu uma paixão nunca vai ter nada, não
   Não há mal pior do que a descrença
   Mesmo o amor que não compensa é melhor que a solidão
   Abre os teus braços, meu irmão, deixa cair
   Pra que somar se a gente pode dividir
   Eu francamente já não quero nem saber
   De quem não vai porque tem medo de sofrer
   Ai de quem não rasga o coração, esse não vai ter perdão
   Quem nunca curtiu uma paixão, nunca vai ter nada, não

wellbeing and self development and defined it as a new response to an old situation or an adequate response to a new situation.

A strategy to promote wellbeing is instilling hope (Seligman & Csikszentmihalyi, 2002 Snyder et al. 2002). Another, is the building of buffering strengths, such as courage, interpersonal skill, insight, optimism, authenticity, perseverance, realism, pleasure capacity, future-mindedness, personal responsibility, and purpose (Seligman, 2002). A final illustrative strategy is narration (McAdams et al. , 1997).

It has been considered that narratives and, in particular, autobiographical narratives, constitute a privileged form of human beings attributing meaning to their personal story (Bruner, 1990).

Our stories are also, simultaneously, a process of construction or (re)invention of our personal pathway, becoming in this way our personal identity (Faust, 2003). In this sense, we can say that "to be a person is to have a story, is to be a story" (Kenyon and Randall, 1997, 1). If we consider that our self develops through narratives, to construct a coherent self through narratives is a psychosocial and educational challenge.

Focusing on biographical episodes within the counseling process constitutes an important transformative element. When we construct stories about our past, we do it in accordance with our personality characteristics and motives. The narratives lie in facts, but they are also an imaginative form to redeem the past and to give meaning to the future. They lie "somewhere between pure fantasy and slavish chronicle", and the apparent memory failures must not be considered as errors but as an attribution process that provides life with a sense of unity and purpose. "Life histories are psychosocial constructions that try to state the personal truths about ourselves" (McAdams et al. 1997, 3).

Wellbeing has been defined by a number of scholars as being action-oriented as well as feeling-oriented. Thus, wellbeing is concerned with pleasant feelings and experiences as well as the way in which people make choices and live their lives (Lent, 2004; Ryan & Deci, 2001). Davidson and colleagues (2006) indicated that life events, both positive and negative, do not just happen to people, "but are, in part, actively generated by them" (p. 153). This action orientation facilitates the clients' engagement in their own change process. This perspective creates numerous possibilities for interventions designed to change behavior, to update goals and aspirations, and to engage clients in their own process of building a meaningful life. In this perspective, counseling provides a space and time that allows the older client to tell their story. And, therefore, to gain new possibilities regarding lost dialogue with family members or a new script for his/her life.

3. COUNSELING OLDER ADULTS WITH FAMILY ISSUES

3.1. Main Topics and Challenges

«Mothers are the highest things their children create.» Herberto Helder[3]

Not so long ago, older generations remained within the family, integrated in the social and productive economic systems practically till they died. Natural sympathy between

---

[3] Considered one of the most important living Portuguese poets.

generations was still deeply rooted and the older individuals were welcomed and taken care of in their families; the problems of old age were individual problems and the private space of home and family closed in on them. Families have always been recognized as the main context for the promotion and support of the independence and health of its members, as the main providing entity in situations of dependency of their relatives and as the institution where people's lives unfold, where most of their rights, obligations and needs are expressed and fulfilled, from the cradle to the grave. In Europe, the majority of the support the old receive comes from their family.

Although nowadays the family still plays a significant role as far as its elderly are concerned, there is an increasing difficulty in accomplishing this function. Home, residence, intimacy and family roles are now confronted with the impact of new cultural models, new lifestyles, and new demands. Actually, the family has been marked by processes of transformation over time, and from the traditional enlarged family, in which different generations lived in the same house, we now have the nuclear family, where the physical, affective and relational space changed .

Thus, the presence of woman in the work place (who were previously seen as the main caretakers of parents and in-laws); the decrease in the birth rate, which reduces families and reduces the availability of family caretakers; the new types of family – single men/women, single mothers, divorced or childless couples, and children who leave their homes early – make the chances of experiencing growing old in a safe family environment difficult. Consequently, the increase in the institutionalization rates reflect not only the growing aging of the population, but also the increasing difficulty of families in providing support for their elderly.

The aging of the population is one of the most important challenges of the 21st century and it compels us to consider increasingly important issues, such as retiring age, the means to live, the situation of the elderly within society, intergeneration sympathy, the sustainability of health and social security systems, and old people's quality of life (Diener & Suh, 1998). It is urgent to develop the means that will best attend to the difficulties/problems of the increasing number of elderly people. Counseling appears in this scenario as one of the institutional and communitarian answers that should be promoted.

The family's evolving cycle has been described as cyclical, or better, as a spiral in which in some periods of a family's life its members evolve, counting on intrafamily centripetal forces. In other periods, the family members show a tendency to individuate, to distinguish themselves from the others, heading towards extrafamily interests, dominating then the centrifugal forces where there is the opportunity to appreciate the difference and the independence. It is an opportunity for each member to expand to what is least known of oneself, instead of wanting the other members to be like him/her.

This means that one person moves from one generation to another when the family is at its closest and consolidates his/her individual integrity when the family is furthest apart.

When a family asks for help that is because its members are limited in their capacity to face new circumstances. When one is unable to respond to change, a family crisis will take place so that change will happen.

Counseling and therapeutic interventions will then have as one of their goals to make the family change and provide answers to the continuing demands, both inside and outside the family system.

3.2. Client's Counseling Goals

"Good fences make good neighbors."[4]

We know that family and social support are a guarantee to better mental and physical health and to subjective wellbeing. Still, conflicts are frequent or recurring family topics that interfere with the happiness of the elderly and their families: feelings of abandonment and sadness on account of their children not visiting them or not paying them the attention they want; parental role reversal, in which the situation of power is reversed and the children think they can decide about «their parents' welfare» for them and for their own good; lack of dialogue concerning questions that implicate the elderly or the opposite; feelings of guilt, of injustice, of ungratefulness, of anger and revenge on the children's as well as on the parents' part; family problems that last from childhood till the present moment; transgenerational problems, brotherly rivalry; autonomy and dependency problems; and sadness, love and longing. Many of these topics could be worked in a counseling frame with multiple gains. Many of them imply problem resolution and decision making and, therefore, the empowerment of older clients. Age-relevant adaptations with special attention to medical comorbidity, cognitive capacity, and the role of family members and caregivers are often necessary to make the endeavor effective. In addition, modifications of the therapeutic goals to include increased self-reliance, reduction in primary-care-service needs, improved social or family functioning, and long-term health care planning can further optimize treatment outcomes.

Other topics do not imply so many external changes (or it is not possible to make the desired changes) but rather mainly internal reorganization, acceptance and forgiveness. The aim of counseling may be then to help make sense of conflicting emotions of love, anger, anguish, guilt and exhaustion.

One general guidepost is that the more severe the personality pathology and the more poorly the individual is functioning, the more appropriate it is that the intervention be directed to the environment. The more functional the individual is, the more appropriate are therapies directed at the deeper level of the individual. When planning treatment, the question that should be addressed is where in the individual or in the system can I anticipate the least resistance and the greatest openness to positive change? Recent empirical findings (Northus & Nielsen, 1999) indicate the most frequent complaints of older adults' close relationships, are with children, followed by spouses and then by the clients' siblings. These issues are generally described in terms of common problems that bring older adults to counseling (Knight, 1996).

Older people in special conditions are more likely to be coping with more than one problem at once, so they will need more than one sort of help at once. So, working in multidisciplinary teams that are flexible and communicate well is crucial.

As with other aspects concerning health and social care, the goals of counseling should be agreed in a discussion with the client about his needs. Many times, that help should be

---

[4] Robert Frost (1874–1963) published the metaphorical poem "Mending Wall" in 1914. The poem is set in the countryside and is about one man questioning why he and his neighbor must rebuild the stone wall dividing their farms each spring. The line has passed into popular culture as a positive aphorism.

extended to other members of the family, namely eventual caregivers. As in Susana's case that follows:

> 40-year-old Susana started taking care of her dependent mother four months ago. She notes how the situation has changed and from a person who was looked after by her mother, she has now become the caregiver (reversal of roles), which has called for a need of emotional changes (restructuring the affective relationship).
> Quite often the feeling of overload leads her to send affective messages she did not wish to, such as: «we were so happy before you got sick... I love you very much but this situation is tearing my life apart.»

Most caregivers are women and although most of these women have taken on this role willingly, the unrelenting demands exact a high toll. Some are serial caregivers. Many experience depression (Figueiredo, 2007) and stress-related illnesses. The price of burnout is high both for the caregivers and their ageing parents. Ironically, burnout is the leading reason caregivers give for why they eventually put their loved ones into a nursing home. Adequately supported families do not usually neglect their elderly.

But there are also positive outcomes of being a family caregiver, especially if they recognize the warning signs of burnout and seek support in time, if needed. Care of the care provider cannot be overemphasized. Counseling and support groups for caregivers are also available and are an effective solution. When the family has quite different goals from the older client then family therapy can be more appropriate

4. THE ROLE OF FORGIVENESS AND EMPOWERMENT

«How can I use what's happening to me to grow up?» (P, 65 years old)

All family interventions or about family topics should be performed according to a series of fundamental premises: forgiving, so as to establish a bond that will facilitate the path to reach the established purposes with self, family and community. Formation and information on what is happening, what is going to happen, why, how to face it and with what strategies. Empowerment, that is, giving both the older person and his/her family the resources to fulfill their needs for themselves, as much as possible, or to ask for help. And finally, the motivation to perform the task together with different family members.

With the purpose of identifying the family's characteristics, its needs and problems, one must make a preliminary evaluation which should include: the type of communication and interaction between family members, who makes the decisions, if the family is facing an unstable moment or is at a crisis point, ideas, beliefs, attributions, and expectations towards relevant issues (growing old, sickness, and care). Endowing the family with communicative skills is also fundamental, as problems at this level often make relationships difficult.

All intervention should start by working on beliefs and conduct. In particular, the staff of institutions and therapists should be non-prejudiced role models in their attitudes towards the elderly and their families. These attitudes are reflected in language and behavior, namely by not blaming the family if the old person is committed to an institution or lives alone and by not seeing old age as a synonym for dependency and disability. An environment free of anxiety and of excessive demands is the grounds for learning and evolvement in these processes on the part of elderly and on the part of their families. Demand implies the need to do things correctly, to be perfect, and thus, the non acceptance of failure, in other words, the non acceptance of ourselves.

4.1. Conceptual Definitions

Within the past decade, social scientists and practitioners have become increasingly interested in forgiveness and its potential for improving personal wellbeing and interpersonal relationships (McCullough et al., 1998), as a fundamental strength that a person can employ to deal effectively with life's challenges (Snyder & Lopez, 2002) and it is associated with emotion-focused coping (Konstam et al., 2003) and related to personality traits (McCullough et al., 1998; Walker & Gorsuch, 2002), particularly emotional stability. Forgiveness can be a helpful counseling tool for a wide range of populations, including incest survivors, substance abusers, cancer patients (Enright et al., 1992; Pingleton, 1998), and for couples with guilt issues and marital insatisfaction (DiBlasio, 2002).

To date, however, the social literature and the clinical psychological literature that are related to forgiveness have not been integrated, leaving many questions unanswered.

Currently, ambiguity exists with respect to a myriad of issues related to forgiveness, including definitional issues, measurement issues, how the process of forgiveness unfolds, and optimal intervention models for differing populations, including older adults.

Although cautionary views of forgiveness in psychotherapy are still needed (Cosgrove & Konstam, 2008), there are areas of convergence, including the idea that forgiveness helps the therapist elaborate upon the challenge of self-acceptance that poor self-esteem poses for older adults engaged in life review or dealing with family problems, as we can see in the case of Alvaro.

> Alvaro is 80 years old and has been in a home for a short while. While talking to the institution's counselor he told her he had had a dream that night that had changed his mood and left him very sad and anxious. In his dream he was 15 or 16 and he was trying to reach his parents but they had disappeared, they weren't there. He began to wonder whether he had led the kind of life that had not stained and embarrassed his family's name. He knew he was going to die soon but he wanted to make sure he wouldn't leave anything unresolved. At a certain time in his life he had divorced his wife and married another woman. Although he had kept supporting his first wife, he felt guilty for the pain he had caused her.

Forgiveness and a holistic understanding of his past and evoking insights about the meaning of their personal history helped Alvaro to deal with these unresolved issues.

Focusing on the multi-dimensional nature of compassion, which is linked to various capacities such as sympathy, empathy, warmth and forgiveness, international contributors focus on how therapists bring compassion into their therapeutic relationship and examine how it can help alleviate psychological problems.

For Gilbert (2000), forgiveness allows us to learn how to change - through forgiveness we are open to our mistakes and learn from them. Learning forgiveness, however, is not easy because our self-critical part is often very unforgiving, and will usually see any opportunity to attack or condemn as an opportunity not to be missed.

The word "forgive" is derived from the root "to give" indicating that forgiveness is an action that is originated by the person. Thus, it is an action that is «our responsibility» and is under our control.

We forgive more easily when we feel better with ourselves and when we have control over our life. Beliefs of environmental control is known as another factor that positively influences our satisfaction towards life (Argyle, 2001).This way, those who are happier and more pleased with life tend to believe they can influence their everyday events (Bandura, 1986), understand, positively, the circumstances of life (DeNeve e Cooper, 1998) and trust their abilities and skills (Lyubomirsky et al., 2005). In the same manner, a causal relation between the subjective welfare and the positive changing of environmental control beliefs, on behalf of groups of elderly individuals, was found (Veenhoven, 1997).

To empower the elderly is, therefore, one of the most efficient tools in the promotion of the welfare of older people and an answer to the abuse against the elderly. By offering self-acceptance and self-responsibility through empowerment and forgiveness, counseling helps the creation of more solid family relationships or the acceptance of a non-ideal reality.

4.2. Process

«How can I use what's happening to me to enhance my self development?» (M, 76 years old)

Many older people have "issues", and family issues, in particular, that diminish their social relationships and their ability to exchange and to dialogue. These issues can be handled, as in the case presented below, in counseling with forgiveness and with empowerment at an individual, group and institutional level.

> During the first weeks she attended the group, Lurdes (79) spoke incessantly of how sad she felt that her son did not call her or come to visit her. Some of the other elements in the group told her that the same thing happened to them or that it was normal as children had their own lives and that was it. Only one member mentioned she was very happy and that her daughter visited her everyday and was very affectionate.
> Lurdes remained downright sad. One day I asked her to tell her story, the story of her relationship with this son. She then told how she had had a hard working life, she was very poor and she had been a single mother. In those days it was very difficult and because she had been unable to raise her son alone, she had to place him in an institution. There, he studied and she worked to pay for his studies through university. When she had the means for it, she picked her son up. Now he is a highly-thought of doctor. After telling her story, Lurdes looked at us and said:«He is doing the same to me, isn't he?» Slowly, she was capable of expressing her feelings of sadness, grief and misunderstanding. «Doesn't he understand that I didn't have any other option? That he wouldn't have studied, he wouldn't have been a doctor if I hadn't done what I did?»

We cannot make other people forgive us but we can forgive ourselves. Understanding that we did our best at that time, that was what we were able to do and that is what we really did. This personal task is a process that often may not change reality. But many times, it does.

Lurdes gradually came to understand her son's perspective and stopped discriminating and depreciating herself, and with the day center counselor support she started developing some hobbies. Today, they see each other more and she is really thankful that he has given her the opportunity to help raise her granddaughter, whom she loves very much.

But Lurdes's story is a case that has been followed through and with success. Our institutions are filled with cases like the one that follows. People that feel anxiety, anger, frustration and impotence, who ask themselves "why don't they come see me and talk to me, I want to know. Why did diseases undermine my family?"

> Guidana has been waiting for a visit from her son for a year. She's sitting on her bed looking patiently. She doesn't leave the bed as he may arrive any moment. She doesn't get involved in many activities because «he may come when I'm away... you know miss, he already has two children. He works a lot and lives far from here... he can't waste much time. He'll come then, I'm sure...»

When an (older) person feels he/she is the victim, he/she shuts down his/her ability to communicate, because now he/she has "issues" with the person or persons who "victimized" him/her. DiBlasio (2002) presents a study with a forgiveness intervention with 13 steps to be able to forgive. For the majority of authors, the first step in forgiving is to get into contact with our emotions about the incident. "Working through" each incident and "running out" the emotions connected. After the emotions revolving around that incident are vented, it makes it easier to forgive. After the description and ventilation, the counselor can try to determine where the client is holding the pain, in what part of the body. Techniques like writing down the feelings, and mindfulness that makes the patient stay in the present time, and admire what he/she has will also help.

Concerning forgiving 'what you have done to others', it is first necessary to communicate what your blames are before working to receive forgiveness, mostly from yourself. Afterwards, it is important to be aware at the time of the event, what feelings the client was not able to experience, what problem he/she was trying to solve and what were the implications for his/her family.

Genuine forgiveness is a process, not an event. It takes time and hard work. It is a voluntary act that gives meaning to the injury, disengages the offended from the offender, and frees the injured person from the ills of bitterness and resentment and gives peace, freedom, self-acceptance, and release from self-pity. Forgiveness needs not be connected to the offender's repentance. When we say, "I forgive you," we are saying "I let it go." It implies a change of heart. It also conveys a change in expectations concerning the forgiver's future thoughts and behavior. It is my responsibility to stop spending time in thought, action, or reaction concerning the issue.

Sorrow is a natural response to loss and will come naturally as the person is able to name the offenses and explore and reveal the injuries in detail to the counselor. The expression of sorrow may lead to a sense of restored wholeness and new perspective.

It is important to insure protective measures against future injuries or feelings of injury, empowering the older person and therefore strengthening family resilience. Helping others in support groups can be a way of restoring the sense of belonging and giving meaning.

Many hurt people spend so much energy on revenge or validation, continually seeking assurance that the offense was real and that they have the right to feel injustice, that their lives are put on hold while they keep on waiting for justice. When one has spent so much energy seeking justice, it is hard to imagine a different life. The injured often struggle with the vision of repentance and forgiveness because their "victim lifestyle" is accomplishing something for them, and change is frightening. Once they turn the table, they see themselves as whole, free, and in control, in other words as being responsible. That it is why it is essential not to excuse. Excusing means you believe there is some logical reason a person behaves the way he behaves.

When one has been deeply wounded, there is no way to forgive genuinely without experiencing a great deal of personal growth.

Perhaps the value of forgiveness is often misunderstood because we underestimate how difficult it is to forgive genuinely, in a way that strengthens and brings enriched meaning to life. Injured people who embark on the journey of forgiveness must be willing to be patient and take the time necessary to complete the process in a meaningful way, accepting pain as a part of life and developing a new philosophy about people. This is truer when we work with people at the end of their lives where sometimes there is a profound need to express unresolved feelings of deep personal hurt caused by past injustices. Forgiveness at the end of life may provide a sense of inner peace with oneself and with others, provide an opportunity for personal growth, and assist the dying with a sense of completion and completeness.

In sum, the study of forgiveness in the family is important for both advancing understanding of forgiveness more generally, as well as for understanding family functioning. In particular, the findings point to the centrality of forgiveness for many aspects of healthy, family functioning.

5. CONCLUSIONS: FUTURE TRENDS

"(With age) Our sight diminishes so we can see better." (A, 80 years old)

Old age is still young in many aspects, namely concerning intervention research. Nevertheless, we have gone far enough to understand the capacity of the human mind to reorganize even when the prospects seem most wretched.

The purpose of this chapter was to review what is currently understood about using forgiveness and empowerment as counseling tools in intervention with older adults with family issues. Aging is a privilege and a challenge and many people experience full lives and can live well beyond 60 years of age. Understanding adaptive capacities that enable many older people to change, cope with loss, and pursue productive and fulfilling lives is a social gain. For others, living longer is a problem and living longer in families that may have four living generations is very difficult. Therefore, reflecting on how to apply counseling approaches to later-life family problems should be an aim of counselors doing therapeutic work with older people.

Adjustments should be made in mental health services and counseling support, so that older people can receive help that extends beyond traditional, formal treatment settings. The challenges are to make interventions that also explore the role of families, institutions and services. With the aim of promoting wellbeing, we already know what changes to operate in institutions. These should be little changes that include relaxing music, using agreeable odors, providing interesting routines, creating learning situations, caring for self-esteem, health and inter-personal relationships, providing activities that match peoples' tastes and interests and that allow for personal and context control, and finally carrying out projects and learning how to thank and forgive.

What to do to promote wellbeing in families in the last stage of life is one of the most recent challenges. Of course, satisfactory relationships at this phase have been built through flexible and strong relationships in other stages of the family's life cycle. Still, transitional moments, conflicts, and mourning are to be expected in any family. So, empowering the different family members and promoting the capacity of letting go of conflicts and misunderstandings, that is, to forgive and to let go, is essential in a society in which the future will necessarily be one of «aging together».

REFERENCES

Altschuler, J. & Katz, A.D. (1999). *Journal of Gerontological Social Work*, 32(2), 81-93.

Argyle, M., (1999). Causes and correlates of happiness. In Kahneman, D. Diener, E. & Schwarz, N. (Eds.), *Well-being: The foundations of hedonic psychology*, 213 – 229. New York: Russell Sage Foundation.

Bandura, A. (1986). *Social foundations of thought and action: A social cognitive*. New York: Prentice Hall.

Barrowclough C., Haddock G., Lowens I., Connor A., Pidliswyi J. & Tracey N. (2001). Staff expressed emotion and causal attributions for client problems on a low security unit: An exploratory study. *Schizophrenia Bulletin.* 27(3), 517-526.

Bortz, J.J., & O'Brien, K.P. (1997). Psychotherapy with older adults: Theoretical issues, empirical findings, and clinical applications In P.D. Nussbaum, (Ed.), *Handbook of neuropsychology and aging.* Critical issues in neuropsychology, 431-451. New York: Plenum Press.

Bruner, J. (1990). *Acts of Meaning*. Cambridge: Cambridge University Press.

Cappeliez, P. (2001). Presentation of depression and response to group cognitive therapy with older adults. *Journal of Clinical Geropsychology*, 6(3), 165-174.

Corey, G. (1999). *Theory and practice of counseling and psychotherapy*, 5th ed. Pacific Grove, C A: Brooks/Cole.

Cosgrove, L. & Konstam, V. (2008). Forgiveness and Forgetting: Clinical Implications for Mental Health Counselors. *Journal of Mental Health Counseling.* 30 (2008): 1-13.

Csikszentmihalyi. M. (2002). Fluir. A Psicologia da Experiência Óptima. Título Original: *Flow. The Psychology of Optimal Experience* (1990). New York: Harper Perennial. Tradução: Marta Amado. Lisboa: Relógio d'Água Editores, 309.

Culverwell, A., & Martin, Carol. (2000). Psychotherapy with older people In G. Corley, (Ed.), *Older people and their needs: A multi-disciplinary perspective.* 92-106. London, England: Whurr Publishers, Ltd.

Diener, E. & Suh, M. E. (1998). Subjective well-being and age: An international analysis. *Annual Review of Gerontology and Geriatrics*, 17, 304 – 324.

Davidson, L., Shahar, G, Lawless, M., Sells, D., & Tondora, J. (2006). Play, pleasure, and other positive life events: "Non-specific" factors in recovery from mental illness? Psychiatry, 69, 151-163.

DeNeve, K. M., & Cooper, H. (1998). The happy personality: A meta-analysis of 137 personality traits and subjective well-being. *Psychological Bulletin, 124*(2), 197-229.

DiBlasio, F. (1992). Forgiveness in psychotherapy: Comparison of older and younger therapists. *Journal of Psychology and Christianity*, 11(2), 181-187.

Enright, R., Eastin, D., Golden, S., Sarinopoulos, I., & Freedman, S. (1992). Interpersonal forgiveness within the helping professions: An attempt to resolve differences of opinion. *Counseling and Values*, 36, 84-103.

Faust, Drew Gilpin (2003). Personality, Psychobiography, and Psychology of the Life Story. *Harvard Magazine*, electronic version. Retrieved 01.07.2005 from http://web.lemoyne. edu/~hevern/nr-pbiog.html

Figueiredo, D. (2007). *Cuidados Familiares ao Idoso Dependente*. Cadernos de saúde. Climepsi. Lisboa.

Gallagher-Thompson D, Steffen A.M. (1994). "Comparative effects of cognitive-behavioral and brief psychodynamic psychotherapies for depressed family caregivers." *J Consult Clin Psychol.*; 62: 3: 543-9.

Gallagher-Thompson, D., McKibbin, C., Koonce-Volwiler, D., Menendez, A., Stewart, D., & Thompson, L.W. (2000). Psychotherapy with older adults In C.R. Snyder & R.E. Ingram, (Eds). *Handbook of psychological change: Psychotherapy processes & practices for the 21st century*. 614-637. New York: John Wiley & Sons, Inc.

Gatz, M. (1998). Towards a developmentally-informed theory of mental disorder in older adults. In J. Lomranz (Ed.), *Handbook of aging and mental health*. 101-120. New York: Plenum.

Gatz, M. & Knight, B.G. (1998). Psychotherapy with older adults. In G.P. Koocher, J.C. Norcross, & S.S. Hill (Eds.), *Psychologist's Desk Reference* .370-373. Oxford University Press.

Gilbert, P. (2000). Social mentalities: internal 'social' conflicts & the role of inner-warmth & compassion in cognitive therapy. In Gilbert, P.& Bailey, K.G. (Eds). *Genes on the Couch: explorations in evolutionary psychotherapy.* London: Brunner-Routledge.

Gonçalves, O. (2000). *Viver narrativamente*. Climepsi. Porto.

Guidano, V.F.: (1995). Constructivist Psychotherapy: A theoretical framework. In: Neimeyer, R.A., Mahoney, M.J. (Eds.) *Constructivism in Psychotherapy*, APA. Washington D.C.

Harley, B. (1999), "The myth of empowerment: Work organisation, hierarchy and employee outcomes in contemporary Australian workplaces", *Work, Employment and Society*, Vol. 13 No.1, 41-66.

Christopher, J. C.; Christopher, S. E.; Dunnagan, T. and Schure, M. (2006). Teaching Self-Care Through Mindfulness Practices: The Application of Yoga, Meditation, and Qigong to Counselor Training; 46; 494 *Journal of Humanistic Psychology.*

Konstam, Varda., et al. (2003). "Forgiving: What Mental Health Counselors Are Telling Us." *Journal of Mental Health Counseling*, 22.253-267.

Kabat-Zinn, J. (2000). *Aonde quer que eu vá*. Sinais de fogo. Gradiva. Cascais

Kenyo, G. e Randall, W. (1997). *Restorying our lives: personal growth through autobiographical reflection*. Weslport, Praeger, 1997.

Knight, B. G. (1996). *Psychotherapy with older adults* (2nd ed.). Thousand Oaks, CA: Sage Publications.

Knight, B.G. (2004). *Psychotherapy with older adults*, 3rd edition. Thousand Oaks (CA): Sage. Publications.

Knight, B.G. & McCallum, TJ (1998) Adapting psychotherapeutic practice for older clients: Implications of the contextual, cohort-based, maturity specific challenge model. *Professional Psychology*. 29, 15-22.

Knight, B.G., & Satre, D.D. (1999). Cognitive behavioral psychotherapy with older adults. *Clinical. Psychology: Science and Practice*. 6, 188-203.

Lent, R. W. (2004). Toward a unifying theoretical and practical perspective on well-being and psychological adjustment. *Journal of Counseling Psychology*, 51, 482 - 509.

Lyubomirsky, S. King, L. & Diener, E. (2005). The benefits of frequent positive affect: Does happiness lead to success? *Psychological Bulletin*, 131, 803 – 855.

McCullough, M. E., Rachal, K. C., Sandage, S. J., Worthington Jr., E. L., Brown, S. W., & Hight, T. L. (1998). Interpersonal forgiving in close relationships II: theoretical elaboration and measurement. *Journal of Personality and Social Psychology*, 75(6), 1586–1603.

McAdams, D.; Diamond, A.; St. Aubin, Ed; Mansfield, E. (1997). Stories of commitment: the psychosocial construction of generative lives. *Journal of Personality and Social Psychology*,72, 3, 678-694.

McAdams, D. & Ochberg., R. L.(1988). *Psychobiography and life narratives*. Durham: Duke University Press.

Nordhus, I.H. & VandenBos, G. (Eds.), (1998). *Clinical Geropsychology*. Washington, DC: American Psychological Association.

O'Rourke, N. & Cappeliez, P. (2005). Marital satisfaction and self-deception: Reconstruction of relationship histories by older adults. *Social Behavior and Personality*, 33, 273-282.

Pingleton, J.P. (1989). "The role and function of forgiveness in the psychotherapeutic process." *Journal of Psychology and Theology*. 17 27-35.

Qualls, S. H. (1996). Family therapy with aging families In Zarit, S.H. & Knight, B.G. (Eds.), *A guide to psychotherapy and aging: Effective clinical interventions in a life-stage context* (pp. 121-137). Washington: American Psychological Association.

Rainsford, C. (2002), Counselling older adults. *Reviews in Clinical Gerontology*. 12: 159-164 Cambridge University Press.

Ryan, R. M. & Deci, E. L. (2001). On happiness and on human potentials: A review of research on hedonic and eudaimonic well-being. *Annual Review of Psychology*, 52, 141 – 166.

Scogin, F. & McElreath L. (1994). Efficacy of psychosocial treatments for geriatric depression: A quantitative review. *Journal of Consulting and Clinical Psychology*, 62(1) 69-74.

Scogin, F. (2000). *The first session with seniors: A step-by-step guide* New Jersey: John Wiley & Sons, Inc.

Seligman, M. E. P. & Csikszentmihalyi, M. (2000). Positive psychology: An introduction. *American Psychologist*, 55, 4 – 15.

Seligman, M. E. P., Steen, T. A. & Park, N. (2005). Positive psychology progress: Empirical validation of interventions. *American Psychologist*, 60, 410 – 421.

Simões, A., Ferreira, J. A., Lima, M. P., Pinheiro, M. R., Vieira, C. M., Matos, A. P., & Oliveira, A. L. (1999). Reflexões pedagógicas, em torno do bem-estar subjectivo: A importância das metas pessoais. *Revista Portuguesa de Pedagogia, 33*(2), 61-88.

Smith, E. (2006). The strength-based counseling model. *The Counseling Psychologist,* 34, 13-79.

Snyder, C. R. & Lopez, S. J. (Eds.), (2002). *Handbook of positive psychology.* 327 – 350. New York: Oxford University.

Konstam, V.; Holmes, W., Levine, B. (2003). Empathy, Selfism, and Coping as Elements of the Psychology of Forgiveness: A Preliminary Study; *Counseling and Values*, Vol. 47, 3.

Veenhoven, R. (1997). The utility of happiness. *Social Indicators Research*, 20, 333 – 354.

Walker, D. F. & Gorsuch, R. L. (2002). Forgiveness within the Big Five personality model. *Personality and Individual Differences,* Volume 32, Number 7, 1127-1137(11).

Yalom, I. (1985). *The theory and practice of group counseling and psychotherapy*, 3rd ed. New York: Basic Books.

Zarit, S.H. & Knight, B.G. (Eds.), (1996). A guide to psychotherapy and aging: Effective clinical interventions in a life-stage context Washington: *American Psychological Association.*

In: Families in Later Life: Emerging Themes and Challenges   ISBN 978-1-60692-328-3
Editor: Liliana Sousa   © 2009 Nova Science Publishers, Inc.

Chapter 4

ELDERLY MEN ON AGEING FAMILIES

Oscar Ribeiro

SUMMARY

Elderly men on ageing families constitute a recent focus of research. Since gender and families in later life have been mostly studied in view of women's experiences, scientific reflections addressing older men's family roles, their sense of maleness and the relationships they establish with relatives remained scarce and demanding greater awareness. This chapter focuses on issues involving older men and late-life masculinities, and aims to make contributions to the ongoing debate on gender and ageing by reframing traditional research themes as that of caregiving relationships. At the outset, it takes a glance at older men's gendered lives, exploring the seemingly incompatibility of "old men" and "masculinity", and focus on the way the salience of gender ideology is revealed in specific live events as retirement, widowhood and caring for a dependent family member. Secondly, allowing for this last experience's relevance in contemporary ageing families, the chapter presents some findings from a qualitative study that looks carefully at the features that characterize the willingness of a group of men aged 65 and over to assume the "non-traditional" caregiving role and the masculinity negotiations underneath its enactment. As spouse carers differ from other family caregivers on many dimensions, particularly on the extent to which caring for an ill partner may be a "normative" part of the marriage contract and entail necessary tasks for sustaining the quality of the relationship (maintaining the independence as a couple), the significance ascribed to the experience within the marital dynamics is emphasised.

INTRODUCTION

The available evidence of adult developmental changes in gendered behaviour shows that these are mostly driven by significant adjustments in family life, physical status, social position, career or health (Hatch, 2000). All these transformations have the potential to affect in significant ways the elder's familial relationships, their senses of self and, ultimately, the conventional architecture of gender ideology. However, in part because gender categorization may become less salient than age among older adult's self definitions (Silver, 2003) and/or because the elderly are recurrently perceived as an *ungendered* group (Spector-Mersel, 2006), reflections on how men and women negotiate and navigate the gender roles and identities that are thrust upon them as they reach old age are as limited as the extent of essays in masculinity and femininity in a life course perspective. Men and women move through midlife and old age in multifaceted ways, face a wide variety of biological and psychosocial processes and experience both change and continuity through familial and work transitions, but the potential challenges to their gendered pasts are just frequently overlooked.

Particularly in the case of men in families and households, much of the recent discussion in the sociologies of the life course and family systems rely on their role as fathers (Morgan, 2003), sometimes forgetting, it would seem, that other important identities and role changes occur as men age, and that those may be associated with important gender relations. In fact, although several reviews of the literature in family gerontology put evidence to the importance given to gender issues and the way they affect family relationships in old age (e.g. mother-child relations; grandmother relations) they also have drawn attention to the lack of studies addressing old men as a research core within the family system (cf. Editorial).

Treated as if they were "invisible" (cf. Fennell & Davidson, 2003; Fleming, 1999), old men have been made peripheral in both gender studies and social gerontology, two important scientific domains that in expanding the insights about the lives and age-related experiences of older women (who undoubtedly constitute the majority of the ageing population) have basically glossed over crucial psychosocial changes and gendered experiences attached to old men, namely their embracement of the manhood ideology. Moreover, aging men have not only been insufficiently studied *as men*, as gendered beings, but have served mostly as the reference point to better understand elderly women's lives and, at the best, younger men's experiences. The numerous ways in which men may be involved in family life as they age, and specifically the cha(lle)nging gender roles they may face, demand, therefore, greater acknowledgment.

1. OLDER MEN'S GENDERED LIVES

1.1. Masculinity: Dynamics of Hegemony and Ageing

Unlike discussions of masculinity and class, ethnicity, sexuality, or religious background, rarely has aging been contemplated when masculinities are discussed. To all intents and purposes, growing older seems to be outside conceptualizations of masculinity. In most discourses one can be masculine and one can be old, but not both. (Thompson, 2004:1).

Connecting gender and ageing in the studies of older men is one of the most recent trends in gerontological research. A representative echo of such leaning is the latest special issue of the *Journal of Aging Studies* which begins with an editorial conveniently entitled "Aging and Masculinity: a topic whose time has come"[1]. There, van den Hoonaard (2007) exposes the

---

[1] *Journal of Aging Studies – Special Issue on Masculinity and Aging*, 21, 2007.

current lack of work on late-life masculinity and highlights the increasing yet limited call for new ways to theorize gender and ageing together, and particularly to focus on ageing men.

Complementarily, and in line with the tendency to treat men as if they are genderless, also research communities in men's studies have recurrently failed to study old men *as men,* maintaining the descriptions of their daily circumstances in a significant contrast with the abundance of literature on the social construction of young men's gendered lives (Thompson, 2004)[2]. Actually, in being sidelined from the burgeoning discourses on the social construction of gender, aging men have been maintained aside from the "ethnographic moment" that currently characterizes the international research on masculinities (Connell, 2000) and which has revealed, in an unwitting way, a tendency to present adult men as ageless.

Thompson's landmark publication of *Older Men's Lives* in 1994 and, more recently, Arber, Davidson and Ginn's (2003) edition of *Gender and Ageing: Changing Roles and Relationships* constituted important contributions in clarifying that older men also exhibit masculinities in their relation with others. When exposing the reasons for their invisibility, the relative comfort of their lives, and the socially constructed images of aged men, Thompson (2004) argued that the failure to connect masculinity and ageing was rooted in the fact that much of the gerontological literature has introduced older biological males by virtue of describing a sex difference in aging, failing to recognize a basic distinction between sex as fundamentally biological, and gender, like race and class, as an experience that is influenced more from social practices than from biological differences. Likewise, as the aging process also made the understanding of men's gendered lives something peripheral, he presented the insidious effect of ageism as a key element for the non-acknowledgment of older men's masculinities and age-specific gender performances. According to that author, the degendered imagery of the older men kept afloat a masculinity pattern and a discourse that sustained for the most part the lives and experiences of youthful men.

Further scholarship supported the ageism explanation by asserting that its cultural pervasiveness has maintained reflections on gender and later life aside from discussions about old men's masculinities. On one hand, it has been argued that ageism stimulates a *genderlessness* image of the elderly who are perceived as a separate (segregation) and uniform (homogenization) group (Spector-Mersel, 2006); on the other hand, since older adults are perceived as weak, infirm, lonely, senile, and unproductive, old men are not likely to be viewed as dominant, successful, engaging in risk-taking behaviours, and/or competitive. Those well-established manhood ideology characteristics, in expressing Connell's (1987, 1995) concept of *hegemonic masculinity* (a cultural ideal for men that ascribes the most important characteristics of maleness and embodies the ideals of physical ability, independence and self-reliance and the dominance of doing rather than being, activity rather than passivity), constitute a special challenge that aging men may have to face. *Hegemonic masculinity* is mostly based upon the lives and bodies of younger men, and as Kilmartin (2000:133) noted *"even those* [men] *who were `successful' in traditional masculine realms often find it difficult to live up to mainstream gender standards. Traditional masculinity is defined as very physical, work-oriented and independent, yet older men experience physical decline, retirement, and the increasing need to depend on others and ask for help."*

---

[2] The first special issue ever devoted to old men's gendered performances *as men* in a men's studies journal (and from which derives Thompson's words that introduce this section) occurred in 2004 - *The Journal of Men's Studies*, 13 (1).

Older men's contradictory social power (when compared to older women they enjoy certain benefits but their life expectancy remains appreciably lower) and potential inadequateness to the dominant constructions of maleness constitute an issue that is deeply rooted in the ambiguousness of personal beliefs and social expectations of what it is to be simultaneously "masculine" and "old". All societies have a gender order constructed by multiple ideas about what is seen as feminine or masculine, and "doing gender" is an ongoing activity embedded in everyday social interactions that vary with regard to factors such as age, social context and ethnic background (West & Zimmerman, 1987). Growing older in Western society is traditionally associated with a downward curve, with losses and decline of the body and mind, and older men may not be up to the standards of conventional manliness; moreover, they also find a lack of clear hegemonic scripts which may put them in an indefinite model of action (Spector-Mersel, 2006). In being simultaneously constrained by the influence of manhood ideology (as a legacy of previous life periods) and in an arena of outwardly normative freedom (since they are often expected to be *ungendered*), older men may have difficulties locating themselves in a specific masculine standard, in acting the "right way". Furthermore, as some research on how gender roles, attitudes and expectations develop with aging suggests that women and men become less differentiated by gender, presenting a move towards androgyny (Gutmann, 1987; Pleck, 1981), acting masculine may become less sharply defined, with older men presenting a tendency to be more affiliate and nurturant, principally in their family roles.

Regardless of the arguable gender convergence presented by the androgyny thesis, namely its usefulness and validity (cf. Hatch, 2000), what seems definite is that the blueprints of older men's masculinity are, at this time, visibly unclear. As Thompson (2006) referred when introducing his study about the commonly held images of old men's masculinity, *"neither the behavioural norms scripting later life masculinity nor the behavioural norms older men institute have been charted"*. The masculinities older men encounter or those they disclose are just yet to be better understood. And this is especially true within family life.

1.2. Acting "Old" and "Masculine" on Families in Later Life

As it has been expressed previously, theorizing masculinity in contemporary social science has mostly relied on the study of young and middle-aged men. However, when entering old age, men are more likely to experience important psychological events such as the congeners' deaths, retirement, health problems, modifications in sexual life, and changes in family status that have the potential to affect their socio-emotional condition as well as their gender ideologies and behaviours.

Allowing for the study of masculinities and family relationships, although reflections on older men and on their gender roles are not unprecedented (cf. Thompson's selected annotated bibliography on men and aging, 1996), continued experience of fatherhood, relations with siblings and grandchildren, marital relations or other family ties have not attracted as much attention as, for example, older men's health conditions. These last ones, namely sexual health, have proved to be a more "gender related" and attractive issue, a fact reinforced by the WHO's explicit efforts in delineating a conceptual framework for the health of ageing men (WHO, 2001). According to Hatch (2000), it seems that there have been only two familial changes alleged to require extensive and different gendered adaptive efforts and about which knowledge has been developed with some emphasis on elderly men: retirement and spousal bereavement. But even these two have shown sizeable gaps as early research didn't connect them to men's adaptation to gender ideologies.

Considering retirement as an important life event, some studies have emphasized the structured set of power relations by which the dominant groups (men in their prime years) are eased out of the economic dominance associated with masculinity and its entitlements to power through ageing. Both sociological discourses of older men's lives as an inexorable period of disengagement from former power-brokering statuses (spotlighting younger men's lives and masculinity) or those related to a continuity perspective (underlining the maintenance of significant roles and practices) highlight the core values of a masculinity that best fits younger employed men; what these reflections have revealed to a lesser extent are the social conditions under which different masculinities may occur (Thompson, 1994) and the way they may be brought to family life. As older men are very likely to face a loss of status, public recognition and authority in the family as they retire, such transition may be accompanied by a weakening of their sense of male identity once they are envisioned as being "outside" normal work spaces and, by default, invading their wives' space - the family home (Keith, 1994). The true is that *hegemonic masculinity*, in being significantly defined by paid work (Connell, 1995), constitutes a dominant script that does not reflect the reality of retired men who are outside the "good provider" masculine yardstick.

After an old man decides to retire, he may question the sense of authority, self-reliance and competence that he brings from years at work (Gradman, 1994). The wish to maintain respect in a traditionally feminine realm (household) along with the need to maintain a sense of masculinity have the potential to make him bring a work ethic to his new familial condition, space and routines. The importance of paid work as part of the identity of being a man and the significance of supporting the notion of the traditional male breadwinner (even when circumstances such as illness and divorce meant that some role reversal occurred) have been found among older men's sense of masculinity (cf. Emslie, Hunt & O'Brien, 2004) but the repercussion of such beliefs on other family ties than the marital one is not clear. It has been suggested, though, that along with a stereotypical understanding of the appropriate roles for men and women, they can also pervade the view of significant familial relations as grandfatherhood and the roles adopted towards grandchildren and within extended families (Wilton & Davey, 2006).

In what concerns spousal bereavement, gerontological research has made evidence that men and women experience widowhood in different ways though it is similarly a process of grieving, adjustment and self-definition. Several authors suggest that the emotional consequences of widowhood provide an emotional challenge to conventional views of what it is a manly man, in part due to the fact that the experience of bereavement increases the gap between masculine ideal and lived reality. According to Bennett (2007), to the same extent that older men are confronted with cultural beliefs about what it is "masculine", widowers find themselves up against conventional ideas of what it is to grieve: they are expected to show emotion and to withdraw, and such cultural expectations are in opposition to two dominant masculine ideals, specifically emotional control and public life. This author argues that widowed men are successful in negotiating these two social constructions (by not showing too much emotion and by moderately withdrawing from society) but their balance and timing is particularly delicate. In her opinion, the issue of remarriage would be a further particular challenge – if widowed men fail to repartner they may be seen as not masculine, if they do so too quickly they are thought not to have loved their wives enough.

According to Bennet, Hughes and Smith's (2003) examination of the traditional masculine role in older widowed men's coping strategies, men deal with loss and subsequent new demands and responsibilities by calling mostly on their notions of masculinity as being capable, strong and in control. Bennet's (2007) later study on the emotions associated with bereavement and the challenges put to men in order to live up to the masculine ideal, confirmed that men maintain their masculinity through the use of rhetorical devices of emotional control, rationality and successful action. Moore and Stratton (2003), who deeply studied a group of fifty-one senior widowers, enlightened their specific needs and services and also brought to light the influence of masculinity scripts throughout the illness and death of their spouses – from the unwillingness to seek help (self-reliance ideology), to the adjustments to female roles (housework) or the (limited) expressions of grief, all were pervaded by important notions of manhood.

To all extent and purposes, masculine ideals of conventional masculinity seem to imbue the experience of important day-to-day circumstances as that promoted by bereavement and retirement. These are not, however, the only life events that may play a pivotal responsibility in shaping aging men's identities and family ties with others, neither the only ones involving particular challenges on the ways of acting masculine in the family life. Older men in later life families have also the increased possibility of facing the onset of health problems that conduct to emerging needs and constraints like assuming day-to-day care of an ailing spouse or, on the other hand, becoming a care receiver. Although both situations comprise complex adaptations, since caring has been traditionally assigned to women, a man who assumes primary caregiving confronts challenges to his early and most fundamental self-conceptualizations (Kaye & Applegate, 1990). Caregiving is dependable on a set of cultural expectations and norms and if a man was socialized to provide and protect, was brought up to be agentic, instrumental and to emphasise cognitive over affective aspects of experience, he will meet in caregiving a series of tasks that call for close emotional involvement, making him undertake what he has come to think of as women's work.

2. MALE CAREGIVING

Men as informal caregivers have received an increased attention during the last two decades, specially as a result of the number and visibility older men have assumed in taking such responsibilities (Kramer, 2002). Indeed, men engaged as primary caregivers are, more likely than not, older husbands caring for their incapacitated wives (Kaye, 1997) which makes reasonable that the amount of information available on male caregiving relies on the unique experience of husbands on their 50s or over. With a special focus on the strains that go beyond those placed on the caregiver helping a victim of Alzheimer's disease (the most studied caregiving situation), and taking into account the gendered nature of the role, most recent efforts in understanding male's involvement with care work have assumed what is not merely a deviation from the female "normative" caregiving experience, but an occurrence that comprises a set of difficulties and outcomes that are possibly distinctive to the male caregiver (Bookwala, Newman & Schulz, 2002). This way, as a relationship of care that is fundamentally unidirectional, mainly when there's a fracturing bond due to the cognitive impairment of the dependent person, providing assistance to a dependent spouse is recognized to entail several stressful demands that are not only emotionally, physically and socially debilitating (Hoffman & Mitchell, 1998), but also closely related to the gendered nature of the role and to its potential unfamiliarity for older male cohorts.

According to Kramer (2002) and Ribeiro (2007), there are three main psychosocial challenges older male face, especially husbands, when assuming the caregiving role (see table 1). These encompass taking on new tasks and learning new skills (both domestic chores and intimate tasks), losing confiding and emotional support (as they rely mostly on their dependent wives who habitually are the sole source of emotional support) and dealing with social and health services (as they are unaccustomed to coping with welfare agencies and are less likely to seek assistance or admit their adversities). All of these challenges incorporate specific constraints and put forward the gendered nature of the role, and the salience of cultural expectations related to masculine acting scripts.

Table 1. Main psychosocial challenges for the older male carer (husbands)

Masculinities	Taking on new tasks and learning new skills • Doing/learning a set of new tasks, specifically those related to domestic life, and the development of specific caregiving competences and skills. Losing confiding and emotional support of a partner • Reduced number of significant others; primary relations frequently circumscribed to the dependent spouse. Dealing with social and health services • Self-sufficiency and the masculine ideology in help seeking behaviour; lack of gender-specific interventions and "feminization" of available services.

Despite the crosswise dimension of multiple masculinities in all the identified challenges, Thompson (2002) draws attention to the fact that few conclusions have gone beyond the traditional sex difference approach (men *vs* women) and questioned the way gender constructions, societal reactions and men's involvement and relationship configure their experience as caregivers. In fact, even though the field of male caregiving is increasing its maturity due to a noteworthy augment in quality and quantity of studies in the last two decades (cf. Carpenter & Miller, 2002) and to the increasing focus given to the centrality of gender ideals of behaviour in the organization of caregiving (e.g. Calasanti & King, 2007), the questioning and examining of late life masculinities associated to the role is slowly coming to the forefront research literature. So far, the amount of reflections on gender and masculinities have revealed some interesting findings: that older male carers do not necessarily forfeit their masculine self-image when assuming the role (Bowers, 1999), may be motivated by male stoicism (Kaye, 1997), bring to their caring responsibilities an instrumental rationality approach through the definition of their caring duties as work (Gollins, 2001) and have several difficulties expressing the emotional aspects of being a caregiver. The power retained in the caregiving relationship, as an expression of manhood, has also been pointed as an important element of the male's experience, expressly in the course of controlling and managing caregiving responsibilities (Harris, 1993). Moreover, Davidson, Arber and Ginn (2000) evidenced that older men retained power within the caring relationship whether or not they were the carers or the care-receivers, consubstantiating previous suggestions that even when being cared-for, men still attempt to remain in control (Rose & Bruce, 1995).

Considering gender as a critical factor mediating the experiences of caregiving within late-life marriage, and that it demands wider exploration in order to get a more accurate comprehension of older men's involvement with care responsibilities (Milne & Hatzidimitriadou, 2003), next section presents some findings from a qualitative study that looks centrally at the factors that condition the willingness of older men to provide care to their chronically-ill wives, and at the various gendered constructions of the role and manly identities within.

2.1. The Experience and Relationship of Older Husbands Caring for their Dependent Wives

The data on which this study is based form part of a broader research of older men's experiences of caregiving that was conducted in several Portuguese Northern districts between the years 2003 and 2006 (Ribeiro, 2007). It includes fifty-tree men aged 65 years and over who were the main carers of their dependent wives (i.e., were responsible for at least 50% of the required support in the activities of daily living), at various points of the caregiving continuum (in-home and post-placement situations). Couples were all original partners with long-lived catholic marriages. Most dyads are very old (both caregiver and care-receiver's mean age is 78 years old) and live by themselves in the community (39). The average length of the caring episode is five years and the care-receiver's dependency level is high. The majority of husbands had some help from formal services (e.g. meals) and/or had family support; approximately 1/3 of the caregivers received exclusively formal support and no help from family or friends. Main characteristics of the caregivers are displayed in table 2.

Participants were recruited from several health agencies (e.g. hospitals) and social facilities (e.g. day centres), and through the snowball technique with some study participants referring other recruits. An unstructured interview guide was used to elicit information about individual perceptions of the caregiving role and the process of "becoming" a caregiver (meanings and motivations to care), about the tasks they performed (including main difficulties and use of formal/informal support), the sources of stress and adopted coping strategies (main difficulties and adaptations to new functions) and about the perceptions participants had of themselves as men in the caring role.

The study used a qualitative, social constructivist approach (Hendricks, 1996) and the analysis made use of a coding framework which attempted to reflect both the theoretical concerns that framed the research questions and those themes that emerged directly from data, i.e., using the open coding technique (Ritchie & Lewis, 2003). QSR NUD*IST 6.0 software was used to provide auxiliary help in examining themes and their relationship with one another. Themes were set out under several main headings from which we've selected those related with the marital relationship dynamics and the salience of gender ideology within. Therefore, in this chapter we focus on a small number of coding categories.

Table 2. Main characteristics of husband caregivers (N=53)

Variable	N
Age in years	
Mean	77.73
Range	65-89
Age of wife in years	
Mean	77.62
Range	62-92
Number of years married	
Mean	52.2.
Range	35-68
Number of years in the caregiving role	
Mean	5
Range	1-15
Level of education[1]	
0-1 years	6
<4 years	10
4 years	27
>4 years	10
Living arrangement	
Lives alone with wife	39
Lives with wife and children	10
Nursing home	4
Wife's impairment level	
Mild	8
Moderate	17
Severe	28

[1] Number of year's full education.

2.1.1. Caring for the House, or the Tacit Definition of Care

The first common denominator that linked the husbands in this study was their description of the caregiving situation in light of their involvement with household chores. Their wives' illness changed their daily routines and the ways of relating that were present in their long-enduring marriages, and those first ones were recurrently reported when they assumed taking on unfamiliar chores. The great majority of the participants (41/53) started the interview with explicit references to their household routines rather than by describing their involvement in tasks closely linked to personal care or related to their wives' medical condition. Antonio[3] and Peter, aged 86 and 84, were caring for their severely dependent wives for four and two years respectively, and their words illustrate how the definition of caregiving as *"taking care of the house"* was naturally present in their discourses when unfolding both their current situation and the transition to the role:

> And then I started caring for her the best way I could... And, you see... I don't know a thing about cooking and house cleaning but I started doing whatever there was to be done... It is not easy being in my situation, you know? But I do whatever there is to be done.

> It wasn't really caring for her, because she still managed to do the housework quite well... But then she started showing difficulties and when she could no longer do the things she used to do, then I started doing them myself, taking care of the house and so... Making the possible for keeping our situation okay...

Similar definitions have already been exposed in previous research (Arber & Ginn, 1990; Dupuis, Epp & Smale, 2004) and put evidence on the traditional and cultural gendered division of household chores that are still very present among older cohorts.

Although mostly lacking domestic experience, some of the husbands reported having helped with household responsibilities in previous times of their marital relationship; even so, for the majority caregivers the spouse's frail condition meant that they were doing something new and unfamiliar. Caregiving, as they defined it, was an unexpected role (46/53) and two main reasons were presented for being so: they were older and they were men. Following this argument, they expected to be cared for, not the other way around. Paul, 89 years, and Richard, 67, clearly exemplified so by stating:

> It never crossed my mind! I always pictured that the natural thing would be getting sick before she did (...) I always thought it would be me who would be cared for, not her... It's not supposed to be like this, I'm the oldest...

> I had never expected it; I just had never expected to reach this age and having to take care of my wife... It's like having a wife and not having a wife at the same time... you know what I mean... I'm a man, a man usually doesn't do these things... And the house... the house is not the same anymore...

The scope of their instrumental definition of caregiving as "doing chores" and its intrinsic relation to household rearrangements was also found in some husband's implicit assessment of the care-receiver's dependency level, which was measured considering the extent of her participation in the housework. Alfredo's assertion exemplifies such line of reasoning and simultaneously his gendered view of the marital relationship. His wife had Alzheimer's disease and he looked after her for two years. On his situation he said:

> I know I have to adapt myself and that probably I wouldn't be doing these things I do if I had a women in her 100%... But since I don't have, I must do things I just wouldn't normally be doing. So, I am the one who now prepares the lunch and dinner, the one who does the laundry,

---

[3] Anonymity and confidentiality are closely observed in all cases therefore fictitious names are used to identify study participants.

who looks after the house... the one who does everything. As I told you before, I had never expected to do this...

Although there could be found some inadequateness when performing caregiving tasks expressed by a clear lack of proficiency, the assumption of the household chores by these husbands did not seem to constitute a major threat to their sense of masculinity. This was so partially because they didn't experienced a loss of their sense of management. Similarly to qualitative research reviewed by Milne and Hatzidimitriadou (2003), the maintenance of masculinity in assuming the responsibility of caring relied on the fact that these men saw themselves as doing something useful and important for themselves and for the dyad. Considering that older men are thought to take up gradually the responsibilities of the caring role because they have shared a household over a long period of time with the spouse, and that their "caring for" may be a natural extension of their "caring about" (Arber & Gilbert, 1989), to some extent such process can reflect the tangible representation of their marriage and the identity they prefer to assume: that of a husband rather than that of a caregiver. For men in this study, house work was neither a part of their identities nor of their expectations of themselves; but it was the most instrumental expression of their family tie towards their wives, and conjointly of their masculine accountable responsibilities as we will next see.

2.1.2. A Husband with a Sense of Duty

Recent qualitative research on older husbands as carers suggests that they are motivated to care by a combination of marital duty and reciprocal love, and that in general they appear to accept caregiving as an extension of their marital vows and the ongoing reciprocity between spouses (Miller & Kaufman, 1996; Neufeld & Harrison, 1998). In this study, an intense emotional bond between men and their wives was frequently found to be at the heart of both their caregiving role and their family life. Most participants were deeply committed to providing care for their ill spouses, and expressed it in diverse and occasionally figurative ways.

The most prevalent motivations for assuming caregiving was anchored in a perception of the role as a duty and as a commitment they had towards their wives (47/53). Themes alluding to altruistic values – the fact that she was a human being in need of care and assistance (21/53) – and to motivations rooted in feelings of love and affection (20/53) were also found to be very present. These and other motivations were occasionally found to be closely intertwined with each other in the same interview passage (table 3), but more easily found separately at some point of the husbands' discourses.

The evocative definition of the caregiving role as *"it all boils down to the 2 v's – vows and values"* (Harris & Bichler, 1997:171) illustratively synthesises the most common understanding this study's participants had about their caregiving situation. Responsibilities were mostly defined as a confluence of marital vows and ethical values that were oriented to the fulfilment and promotion of the spouse's well-being. Philip, 79 years old, married for forty-five years to his wife presently diagnosed with Alzheimer's disease explained the salience of his commitment when describing in a very structured way the reasons for having assumed the caregiving role:

Well, first of all, I married her and we made a commitment to each other, right? Secondly, she's a human being, isn't she? So I must care for her, I think it is my duty... if we got through the good days we must get through the bad ones as well...

Ed, 74 years old and caring for his severely dependent wife for four years (currently in a wheel chair due to a second stroke), expressed his thoughts about the caregiving role in similar ways, emphasising his responsibility as a man and as a husband:

It is my responsibility, of course... As a man and because we are human beings... And I have this moral obligation... she is my wife, don't you think I am right? Who else would care for her? And I'll do anything for her...

Table 3. Motivations to care (commonalities)

Themes	N[1]	Love	Duty	RA[2]	HB[3]	Job	Cross	Sport	Challg	Mission
Love	22	—	10	8	3	0	1	0	0	0
Duty	47		—	6	9	3	4	1	0	0
Recip. Act	12			—	2	0	0	0	0	0
Human B.	21				—	2	0	0	0	0
Job	11					—	0	1	0	0
Cross	9						—	0	0	0
Sport	4							—	0	0
Challenge	2								—	0
Mission	1									—

[1] Number of carers presenting each motivation;
[2] "Reciprocal Act"
[3] "Human Being"

Description of the caregiving role as an expression of reciprocity and gratitude (i.e., an opportunity to give back attention and care) included principally a reference to periods in the couple's past when their wives had cared for them, played a significant role for the family functioning or made valuable efforts in raising the children. This last positioning is present in Manuel's involvement with care work, whose main motivation was associated with worship and duty:

I must have this patience because it is my duty and because I love her. She had my children, took care of them, and was a wife beyond compare, a unique wife in all the ways you can imagine... she was [pause] ... a woman devoted to our live as a couple, to our children. A woman who lived with several economic difficulties [in managing the house] but that was always there for me. So here I am.

For another group of participants (11/53), caregiving was described in terms of a new "job" or even as a career that required setting goals, being organized and practising skills. This notion substantiates preceding findings (Harris & Bichler, 1997; Russell, 2001) and echoes a clear work identity similar to that found by Gollins (2001) in his study on the interaction between notions of masculinity and being an informal carer. Equally framed by a traditional manhood core were some husbands' interpretation of the role as a sort of "intense sport", or as a "challenge" in the sense of something they were ought to succeed the best way they could.

Less dominant frameworks for describing the nature of the involvement with caregiving work were metaphors and analogies embedded in religion that evoked to a sense of suffering and/or a major devoted purpose in life (a "cross to be carried" or a "sort of mission"). Leonard, 86 years old, was typical in his use of one such metaphor for describing his caregiving situation:

> This is a cross, a cross [silence]... but what can I do? We love each other since we were engaged, ever since we were very young... We made the promise that we will love each other until we die, and that vow has been accomplished so far. We will keep it this way even after we are dead. It all depends on God... He gave me this cross and I must carry it for as long as I can...

Apart from the distinct motivations that oriented these men's involvement with caregiving, one thing was clear all through the interviews: by reinforcing the sense of being a husband, most participants didn't define themselves as "caregivers". Such designation was not only a foreign term for them due to cultural reasons, but their prominent self-perception was deep-rooted in their manly responsibilities and marriage commitment. They saw themselves as men caring for their wives, and as individuals who were responsible for someone else's well-being. In openly expressing this, they seemed to preserve their masculine self-identity at the same time they faced the (instrumental and emotional) challenges of seeing their wives' progressive deterioration. Like in Sandberg and Eriksson's (2007) study, the importance was to maintain continuity in their relationship with their wives regardless of the adversities they were facing.

2.1.3. Managing Care and the Marriage's Identity

Most caregivers in this study reported various sources of stress resulting from their caregiving engagement. Not surprisingly, and in line with the main psychosocial challenges previously presented (see Table 1) and with the tacit definition of the caregiving role, a substantial part of the instrumental difficulties derived from taking over household tasks and helping with personal care.

Echoing a recurrent theme found in the literature on older male carers and widowers (e.g. Harris & Bichler, 1997; Moore & Stratton, 2003), among household routines preparing meals was the most challenging task, and the one more profusely evidencing the gender-differentiated division of house life that most couples had. Jack, 76 years old and in the caregiving role for two years expressed this in a very clear way. When questioned about the main difficulties felt when assuming the caring responsibilities for his cognitively impaired wife he said:

> Well, the *real* [interviewee's emphasis] difficulty was cooking! I mean... I just never had done anything like that in my entire life. That really cost me a lot, yeah, it was that, it really was that... I never entered in the kitchen, I had never learnt anything to do with that (...) It was my wife who always managed it, not me... it was *her* thing [interviewee's emphasis] you see?

Among the provision of personal and intimate care, assistance in bathing and toileting were the most exigent. They were found overtly in 17/53 interviews and combined the carer's own physical constraints with the gender-linked nature of the chore. Personal discomfort in executing the work was also occasionally observed but the lack of strength due to old age was the main reason for presenting such day-to-day tasks as being of greater difficulty. Daniel, 73 years old, explained how it was bodily hard for him to give bath to his wife (especially because she was in a wheel chair) and his reluctantly to ask for help:

> The hardest thing for me to do is... [pause] well, there aren't that much things... I can carry her from bed to the living-room; I dress her, put on her makeup... I do all that... I just don't give her bath because I have this idea that a man... [pause] well, first of all, the bathroom is too small and we can hardly be there the two of us, especially as I need to have space for helping her right... and the other thing is that I have this problem on my arm... I have no strength, and it is quite hard because she is heavy you know? So I have my daughter now to help me out with that, but only with that [peremptorily].

Even though housework and intimate care were presented as significant difficulties within their responsibilities as caregivers, for these men the wife's health progressive deterioration was by far the most common preoccupation. The suffering felt by seeing their spouses getting more vulnerable as time went by and the enduring efforts managing some of the disease's manifestations (as the behaviour and psychological symptoms of dementia) were transversal in the description of the spouses' clinical condition. On this topic, Bruno, 66 years old and married to his wife since he was 16, stated:

> What was harder for me was seeing her that way, seeing her getting worse and worse... All the rest, well, all the rest was difficult too... I didn't like the household life, the kitchen... I never enjoyed cooking, now I kind of like doing it though. But what cost me the most was that... you know, seeing her like that every day... .

When looking at these husbands' description of their daily exchanges of emotional and practical support, and in the sequence of perceiving the wife's disease as a threat to their marriage's emotional stability, the preservation of marriage identity emerged as an important category. The couple's unique history (incorporating specific habits, traditions and values) and the commitment these men made to marriage years before were often exposed when they talked about their wife's condition as well as when they referred to their efforts in managing all caregiving responsibilities and strains. Charles was one of the husbands who rooted his motivation to care in the marital vows he assumed 55 years ago (in the wedding day) and when explaining so, he said the following:

> We must think straight, right? We must ponder everything and not thinking only about ourselves but about us [couple]. It was for the good times and for the bad times we got married, and we must stick to that... If she can no longer assume her role as a wife... well... at least as she used to before this [referring to the sickness] I'll manage to keep mine as a husband. I'll manage our lives as I always did.

Being the principal caregiver served as a painful reminder of the changed marriage, and for a significant part of the interviewees the continuity of such an important tie (as it underlain their daily life) seemed to be partially achieved by sustaining a sense of rightness of caregiving and marital commitment. Furthermore, if for most husbands the tasks their wives could no longer assume determined their entrance in the caregiving role, in a subsequent point of their caregiving trajectory, having control over the situation (i.e., over the household) made their maintenance in it more "legitimate". By having some sort of authority and control that they frequently described under the designation of being "the head of the couple", they were men *in charge of care* retaining varying degrees of power over the caring and marital relationship (cf. Ribeiro, Paúl & Nogueira, 2007). They expressed it either by explicit statements, by describing the way they wanted to be single-handedly in the role and/or by evidencing the breadwinner logic of their economic responsibilities in care-work. Gabriel, 75, caring for his wife with vascular dementia, puts evidence on this last account by indirectly expressing how he always guaranteed the best for his wife:

> I'm that man who gets her whatever she needs. Just name it and I will go and buy it for her... whatever she needs. Sometimes it costs me a lot [economically], you see? But I'll go and get it, I must do it, I always did...

While evidencing their wish to maintain their marital role even if the role itself has changed, they also highlighted the importance of avoiding a move into a nursing home and the wish to keep their wives at home for as long as possible[4]. Not only doing so would prevent them from feeling lonelier (even though in some cases their wives' presence was merely physical due to dementia), but it also expressed a wish to uphold the marriage's conventional characteristics and the maintenance of their roles as husbands who ought to look after their wives no matter the circumstances.

Finally, it is important to stress that although most husbands had referred at some point in their interviews that they had some difficulties when performing their role as caregivers, some of them (15/53) explicitly said that they hadn't had any, even when directly asked about it. The reasons they exposed alluded to the fact that they had already structured a specific set of formal and informal support (operating efficient caregiving solutions), had "specific personal characteristics" (lifelong personality traits) and/or had a strong motivation to care (mostly deriving from their sense of commitment and duty). All of these husbands said that they were well adapted to their responsibilities.

3. DISCUSSION

Conceptualizing gender in late life marriage relationships, and particularly in the case of informal care provided by the male counterpart, is a complex task. First of all, most existing definitions on male care result either from formally articulated positions on caregiving or from recurrent comparisons with women's care work, the "standard" experience. The emphasis on care as household work and as an instrumental practice, rather than on intimate and/or medical tasks or as an expression of personal intrinsic characteristics assumed a

---

[4] Among the four post-placement situations considered in this study, institutionalization was transversally an unwished option; in the institutions where these couples lived all husbands maintained some sort of control over their wives' situation, either in actively participating in the routine activities of formal care (supervising them), or by substituting the staff it in specific tasks like dressing or feeding the spouse.

particular significance in this study, highlighting the importance tacit definitions of care have for the understanding of the lived experience of specific subgroups of caregivers (Wrubel et al., 2001).

Contrarily to women who tend to view much of the care work they perform to their spouses as part of their everyday routines (Davidson, Arber & Ginn, 2000), husbands are more likely to report and concentrate themselves in housework, which was the case in here. From a life course perspective, the division of household labour unsurprisingly revealed an important cohort effect and its socio-cultural and gender determined dimension: the great majority of the husbands were members of cohorts who reached adulthood between the 1930's and early '40s and experienced a common set of norms and role expectations that reinforced the homemaker role for women and paid employment for men. In this context, since housework became the most salient dimension of their responsibilities, structuring their day-to-day routines, it seemed that such centrality shaped both the meaning they had of care work and their redefinition of marital responsibilities. Concretely, these men did not simply engage in caring responsibilities in relation to a spouse; they engaged in the whole caring relationship as a way of benefitting the marriage itself, with significant efforts to maintain their marital tie as it had been before they became carers, as well as their manly defined *husband* position on it.

For the majority of participants, following a gendered marital scripting determined by marriage vows and ethic values contributed to their involvement with caregiving and, to some extent, to the social construction of their sense of masculinity. They were caught on the "shoulds" of marital ideals and the "musts" of their situation, and in responding to both these requirements they performed a gendered way of acting that was perceived as simultaneously consistent with a traditional manhood ideal and with the structure of the new marital relation pattern they were facing. This way, defining themselves as husbands (a role that included caregiving responsibilities) appeared as a sort of mediator of the ambiguity caused by carrying out tasks that do not reside within the dominant masculine discourse but were justifiable enough in light of long-lasting marriage relationship and definitions of a man's role within a couple's life.

Consistent with previous research (Calasanti & King, 2007), men in this study engaged in behaviours that draw upon their gendered repertoires of action. Caregiving was perceived as a female role and such perception was one important hurdle they had to overcome. Their use of gender as an interactional resource, making it salient throughout the explanation of their situation was clearly present in the way they conceived their marital relationship and the caring role as mentioned, but it could also be found in the description of their everyday life. In executing multiple levels of masculine scripting (by a managerial approach, by assuming control, by emphasising "doing care" rather than "being a carer", or just by defining care work as job or sport in some situations), they attended and performed their role as caregivers dealing with the potential threats to their sense of masculinity. At this specific point of these men's familial lives, caring assumed the centrality of daily living and, in general, they faced the gendered nature of the role in consistency with their structural positions as men in a new challenging household arrangement and with a decisive understanding of care as a form of practice. Caregiving gave continuity in their status as husbands and allowed them to keep on expressing their love and commitment, maintain a home and a life together with their wives. In brief, it maintained the integrity of their husband's (manly) self and caring marriage.

4. EXIT THOUGHTS

The ways in which "men" are constructed as meaning through and by reference to "age" are very recent in social gerontology, gender studies and family research, but the fact that "old" and "masculine" may not outline a so unimaginable pair advocates for new ways of conceptualizing gender and the conventional gender bipolarizations that pervade family roles and identities in later life. Suggesting that elderly men are *gendered* entails that their self-perceptions, feelings and behavioural predispositions derive from lifelong involvement with women and men, and that probably masculinity scripts are not "interrupted" but rather transformed throughout the aging process and family course. By focusing on a key transition as caregiving, we hope this chapter's study and small-scale qualitative findings provide new insights into a challenging lived experience elderly men are increasingly facing in their family lives, and stimulates further social scientific research into ageing men and the gender-related challenges of the helping experience. It is important, however, to stress that with the changing scenery of the present geriatric population, and with all the implications further cohorts bring along, men will probably (re)define and reinvent themselves (either as husbands, as carers or both) and the role itself through different ways than those presented here. Such potentially different meanings would be particularly interesting and challenging to study in light of the constantly changing patterns of marriage, divorce and remarriage experienced by men who are on the verge of entering later life. Such happenings are very likely to have different consequences for their family relationships.

ACKNOWLEDGEMENTS

This chapter presents data drawing from a research project supported by the Foundation for Science and Technology (FCT), Portugal (Grant SFRH/BD/8819/2002).

REFERENCES

Arber, S. (1996). Gender Roles. In J. E. Birren (Ed.). *Encyclopaedia of Gerontology: Age, Aging and the Aged, Volume 1* (pp. 555-565). London: Academic Press.

Arber, S., Davidson, K. & Ginn, J. (2003). Changing approaches to gender and later life. In S. Arber, K. Davidson & J. Ginn. (Eds.). *Gender and Ageing: Changing Roles and Relationships* (pp. 1-14). Buckingham: Open University Press.

Arber, S. & Gilbert, N. (1989). Transitions in caring: gender, life course and the care of the elderly. In B. Bytheway, T. Keil, P. Allatt and A. Bryman (Eds.). *Becoming and Being Old: Sociological Approaches to Later Life* (pp. 72-92). London: Sage.

Arber, S. & Ginn, J. (1990). The meaning of informal care: gender and the contribution of elderly people. *Ageing & Society*, 10, 429-454.

Bennet, K. M. (2007). "No sissy stuff": towards a theory of masculinity and emotional expression in older widowed men. *Journal of Aging Studies*, 21 (4), 347-356.

Bennet, K. M., Hughes, G. M. & Smith, P. T. (2003) "I think a woman can take it": widowed men's views and experiences of gender differences in bereavement. *Ageing International*, 28 (4), 408-424.

Black, H. K., Schwartz, A. J., Caruso, C. J. & Hannum, S. M. (2008). How personal control mediates suffering: elderly husbands' narratives of caregiving. *The Journal of Men's Studies*, 16 (2), 177-192.

Bookwala, J., Newman, J. & Schulz, R. (2002). Methodological issues in research on men caregivers. In B. J. Kramer & E. H. Thompson (Eds.), *Men as Caregivers. Theory, Research, and Service Implications* (pp. 69-96). New York: Springer.

Bowers, S. P. (1999). Gender Role Identity and the Caregiving Experience of Widowed Men. *Sex Roles*, 41 (9/10), 645-655.

Calasanti, T. (2003). Masculinities and care work in old age. In S. Arber, K. Davidson & J. Ginn. (Eds.). *Gender and Ageing: Changing Roles and Relationships* (pp. 15-30). Buckingham: Open University Press.

Calasanti, T. & King, N. (2007). Taking ⧠women's work⧠like a man⧠: husbands⧠experiences of care work. *The Gerontologist*, 47 (4), 516-527.

Carpenter, E. H. & Miller, B. H. (2002). Psychosocial challenges and rewards experienced by caregiving men: a review of the literature and an empirical case example. In B. J. Kramer & E. H. Thompson (Eds.), *Men as Caregivers. Theory, Research, and Service Implications* (pp. 99-126). New York: Springer.

Connell, R. W. (1987). *Gender & Power.* Standford, California: Standford University Press.

Connell, R. W. (1995). *Masculinities.* Cambridge: Polity Press

Connell, R. W. (2000). *Understanding Men: Gender Sociology and the New International Research on Masculinities.* Lecture held in the Department of Sociology, University of Kansas. Retrieved 2nd May 2006 http://www.europrofem.org/contri/2_04_en/research-on-masculinities.pdf

Davidson, K., Arber, S. & Ginn, J. (2000). Gendered meanings of care work within late life marital relationships. *Canadian Journal on Aging*, 19 (4), 536-553.

Dupuis, S. L., Epp, T. & Smale, B. (2004). *Caregivers of Persons with Dementia: Roles, Experiences, Supports and Coping.* Ontario: University of Waterloo.

Emslie, C., Hunt, K. & O'Brien, R. (2004). Masculinities in older men: a qualitative study in the West of Scotland. *Journal of Men's Studies*, 12 (3), 207-226.

Fennell, G. & Davidson, K. (2003). "The invisible man?" Older men in modern society. *Ageing International*, 28 (4), 315-325.

Fleming, A. A. (1999). Older men in contemporary discourses on ageing: absent bodies and invisible lives. *Nursing Inquiry*, 6, 3-8.

Gollins, T. (2001). *Male carers: a study of inter-relations between caring, male identity and age.* Sheffield Online Papers in Social Research (ShOP). Retrieved 23th January 2003 from http://www.shef.ac.uk/socst/Shop/gollins.pdf

Gutmann, D. (1987). *Reclaimed Powers: Towards a New Psychology of Men and Women in Later Life.* New York: Basic Books.

Harris, P. B. (1993). The misunderstood caregiver? A qualitative study of the male caregiver of Alzheimer's disease victims. *The Gerontologist*, 33 (4), 551-556.

Harris, P. B. & Bichler, J. (1997). *Men Giving Care: Reflections of Husbands and Sons.* New York: Garland Publishing, Inc.

Hatch, L. R. (2000). *Beyond Gender Perspectives: adaptation to aging in life course perspective*. New York: Baywood Publishing Company, Inc.

Hendricks, J. (1996). Qualitative research: contributions and advances. In R. H. Binstock and L. K. George (Eds.) *Handbook of Aging and the Social Sciences, 4th ed.* (pp. 52-72). London: Academic Press.

Hoffmann, R. L. & Mitchell, A. M. (1998). Caregiver burden: historical development. *Nursing Forum*, 33, 5-11.

Gradman, T. J. (1994). Masculine identity from work to retirement. In E. H. Thompson (Ed.), *Older Men's Lives* (pp. 104-121). London: Sage.

Kaye, L. (1997). Informal caregiving by older men. In J. I. Kosberg & L.W. Kaye (Eds.), *Elderly Men: Special Problems and Professional Challenges* (pp. 231-249). New York: Springer.

Kaye, L. W. & Applegate, J. S. (1990). *Men as Caregivers to the Elderly: Understanding and Aiding Unrecognized Family Support*. Lexington, MA: Lexington Books.

Keith, P. M. (1994). A typology of orientations toward household and marital roles of older men and women.. In E.H. Thompson (Eds.). *Older Men's Lives*. (pp. 141-158). Thousand Oaks: Sage.

Kilmartin, C. T. (2000). *The Masculine Self*, 2nd Edition. New York: McGrawHill.

Kramer B. J. (2002). Men caregivers: an overview. In B. J. Kramer & E. H. Thompson (Eds.), *Men as Caregivers. Theory, Research, and Service Implications* (pp. 3-19). New York: Springer.

Miller, B. & Kaufman, J. E. (1996). Beyond gender stereotypes: spouse caregivers of persons with dementia. *Journal of Aging Studies*, 10, 189-204.

Milne, A. & Hatzidimitriadou, E. (2003). "Isn't he wonderful?" Exploring the contribution and conceptualization of elder husbands as carers. *Ageing International*, 28 (4), 389-407.

Morgan, D. H. J. (2003). Men in Families and Households. In J. Scott, J. Treas & M. Richards (Eds.) *The Blackwell Companion to the Sociology of Families*. Blackwell Publishing. Retrieved 17th May 2008 from http://www.blackwellreference.com/ subscriber/tocnode?id=g9780631221586_chunk_g978063122158624

Moore, A. J. & Stratton, D. C. (2003). *Resilient Widowers: Older Men Adjusting to a New Life*. New York: Prometheus Books.

Neufeld, A. & Harrinson, M. J. (1998). Men as caregivers: reciprocal relationships or obligation? *Journal of Advanced Nursing*, 28 (5), 959-968.

Pleck, J. H. (1981). *The Myth of Masculinity*. Cambridge: MIT Press.

Ribeiro, O. (2007). *O Idoso Prestador Informal de Cuidados: Estudo sobre a Experiência Masculina*. [Older men as informal carers: a study on the masculine experience]. Unpublished PhD Dissertation in Biomedical Sciences. Porto: ICBAS-UP.

Ribeiro, O., Paúl, C. & Nogueira, C. (2007). Real men, real husbands: caregiving and masculinities in later life. *Journal of Aging Studies,* 21 (4), 302-313.

Ritchie, J. & Lewis, J. (Eds.) (2003). *Qualitative Research Practice: a Guide for Social Science Students and Researchers*. London: Sage.

Rose, H. & Bruce, E. (1995). Mutual care but differential esteem: caring between old couples. In S. Arber & J. Ginn (Eds.) *Connecting Gender and Ageing: A Sociological Approach*. Buckingham: Open University Press.

Russell, R. (2001). In sickness and in health: a qualitative study of elderly men who care for wives with dementia. *Journal of Aging Studies*, 15 (4), 351-367.

Sandberg, J. & Eriksson, H. (2007). 'The hard thing is the changes'. The importance of continuity for older men caring for their wives. *Quality in Ageing – Policy, Practice and Research*, 8 (2), 5-15.

Silver, C. B. (2003). Gendered identities in old age: toward (de)gendering? *Journal of Aging Studies*, 17, 379-397.

Sousa, L. (this volume). Editorial - New themes in aging families. In L. Sousa (Ed.). *Families in Later Life: Emerging Themes and Challenges*. New York: Nova Publishers.

Spector-Mersel, G. (2006). Never-aging stories: western hegemonic masculinity scripts. *Journal of Gender Studies*, 15 (1), 67-82.

Thompson, E. H. (1994). Older men as invisible in contemporary society. In E.H. Thompson (Eds.). *Older Men's Lives.* (pp. 1-21). Thousand Oaks: Sage.

Thompson, E. H. (1996). *Men and Aging: a Selected, Annotated Bibliography.* Westport, Connecticut: Greenwood Press.

Thompson, E. H. (2002). What's unique about men's caregiving? In B. J. Kramer & E. H. Thompson (Eds.), *Men as Caregivers. Theory, Research, and Service Implications* (pp. 20-47). New York: Springer.

Thompson, E. H. (2004). Editorial. *The Journal of Men's Studies*, 13 (1), 1-4.

Thompson, E. H. (2006). Images of old men's masculinity: still a man? *Sex Roles*, 55, 633-648.

van den Hoonard, D. K. (2007). Aging and masculinity: a topic whose time has come. *Journal of Aging Studies,* 21 (4), 277-280.

West, C. & Zimmerman, D. (1987). Doing gender. *Gender & Society*, 2, 125-151.

WHO. (2001). *Men, Ageing and Health: Achieving Health across the Life Span.* Geneva: World Health Organization.

Wilton, V. & Davey J. (2006). *Grandfathers – Their Changing Family Roles and Contributions.* Blue Skies Report No 3/06. Retrieved 1st July 2008 from http://www.nzfamilies.org.nz/download/blueskies-davey.pdf

Wrubel, J., Richards, T. A.; Folkman, S. & Acree, M. C. (2001). Tacit definitions of informal caregiving. *Journal of Advanced Nursing*, 33 (2), 175-182.

In: Families in Later Life: Emerging Themes and Challenges   ISBN 978-1-60692-328-3
Editor: Liliana Sousa   © 2009 Nova Science Publishers, Inc.

Chapter 5

REINVENTING FAMILY CAREGIVING: A CHALLENGE TO THEORY AND PRACTICE

Daniela Figueiredo

SUMMARY

Caring for an elderly dependent relative has been described mainly as a burden or a stressful experience which has a significant impact on the health of family carers and other aspects of their lives. Over the past two decades, researchers have examined the effects of several types of intervention designed to reduce the stress and burden associated with the caring role. The findings, however, are varied and inconsistent and no single intervention has been completely successful in responding to all the needs and problems of carers. The relative failure of intervention outcomes can frequently be attributed to the methodological weakness of intervention research studies. This chapter provides a summary of the interventions designed to reduce the stress and burden for carers and an overview of their (in)effectiveness. It emphasises the need to consider other reasons beyond methodological issues in order to understand the mixed picture provided by research findings. It also underlines the need to move beyond the burden paradigm emphasised in the idea of the "biomedicalization of caregiving".

INTRODUCTION

More than 30 years ago Fandetti and Galfand (1976) published one of the first articles about family caregiving in a historic and prestigious scientific American journal dedicated to gerontology - *The Gerontologist.* The authors studied a sample of Italian and Polish residents to ascertain their attitudes toward caring for aged relatives. Since then, there has been a massive expansion of interest in family/informal carers as a main source of support for elderly dependents and an "explosion" in literature and research on caregiving, which continues to be one of the most extensively researched areas in the field of gerontology.

The result has been a growing body of evidence suggesting the negative effects of caregiving on the carer's physical, psychological or emotional health, social life, leisure and finances, which is defined as the caregiver burden or stress. Conceptualizing family care in terms of burden and stress has led to interventions based on a biomedical model of care. The relevance of the stress/coping paradigm is indisputable in any understanding of the complexity of family caregiving and it has unquestionably become a major theoretical framework for gerontological research and practice. Consequently most forms of support and intervention have been developed in terms of relieving the carer burden. A growing number of supportive, psycho-educational, respite-based and psychotherapy interventions designed to reduce the carer burden have been published, but no clear conclusions can be made as to their effectiveness, which still needs to be established. While it seems evident that, as a group, carers may experience a variety of problems, the fact that these impacts are not the same for all individuals concerned is often overlooked.

This chapter aims to provide a critical overview of the main forms of support and services and their (in)effectiveness and to open up new approaches to (re)understanding the caregiving experience.

1. FAMILY CAREGIVING: THE CHALLENGE OF A NORMATIVE AND STRESSFUL PROCESS

A longer life expectancy has been one of the greatest achievements of humanity, leading to more opportunities for personal development. However, ageing has also been a cause for special concern, since the ageing process increases the likelihood of physical and mental deterioration. Elderly people are the group most severely affected by incapacitating chronic diseases, often leading to a loss of functional capacity. Recent data shows that approximately 20% of the European population aged over 65 is dependent to some extent, most of whom are looked after by informal carers within the family (Carretero, Garcés & Ródenas, 2007). Caring for an elderly relative can last for a short period of time or van, more commonly, extend over years, and has become a normative "life event challenge" (Cavanaugh, 1998: 131).

During the past 30 years, "family care" has become a major topic of interest in gerontological research, and has been conceptualized as a complex and multidimensional experience, primarily explained in terms of stress, burden and physical and mental health outcomes (Zarit, Reever & Bach-Peterson, 1980; George & Gwyther, 1986; Pearlin et al., 1990; Vitaliano, Scanlan & Zhang, 2003). The impact of the caregiving process on the carer has been described in terms of the "carer burden", a concept that encompasses multiple and inconsistent definitions and indicators. Theory and research has tended to conceptualize this burden either in terms of the stress factors affecting the carer (the objective burden) or as an appraisal of caring as a stressful experience (the subjective burden). Research into intervention has tended to view the burden as an outcome, often treating it as a phenomenon similar to depression or other psychological symptoms (Knight, Fox & Chou, 2000).

Despite these variations, the impact of caregiving on the physical and psychological health of carers, family relationships, finance, work, and social and leisure spheres has been well documented, particularly in relation to those caring for dementia patients (dementia being considered one of the most stressful experiences). Carers experience poor immune system functioning (Kiecolt-Glaser & Glaser, 1994), report poor health status perception (Thompson & Gallagher-Thompson, 1996) and suffer more from chronic diseases (Haley *et al.*, 1996). In terms of mental health, carers frequently display symptoms of depression and anxiety (Schulz & Williamson, 1994) as well as low levels of life satisfaction (Figueiredo & Sousa, 2007). As Schulz and Williamson (1994) emphasise, the co-morbidity of physical and mental problems is the rule rather than the exception. In addition, carers often abandon or severely modify certain aspects of their social life, for example by cutting down on time spent on leisure and recreational activities or missing out on opportunities to socialize with friends, have a holiday, take regular exercise or have time to themselves (Bedini & Phoenix, 1999). The financial impacts are felt in the form of medical and paramedical expenses, hospitalisation and the rising costs of medicine and equipment (Borgemans, Nolan & Philp, 2001). In addition, caregiving often results in family strain and conflict and has a negative impact on work performance (Aneshensel et al., 1995).

Given the potential negative outcomes of caregiving for family members, the person who provides care for the impaired elderly has been called the "hidden patient".

Summary: Negative impacts of caregiving

Physical Health	• Poor functioning of immune system • High blood pressure • Relatively high levels of use of psychotropic drugs • Sleep disorders • Poor health status perception • Greater prevalence of chronic diseases • Fatigue
Psychological Health	• Depression • Anxiety • Low levels of life satisfaction • Feeling burdened • Fear • Guilt
Family relations	• Family conflicts • Marital strain • Abuse of the elderly
Work and finance	• Productivity negatively affected • Less working time • Sense that performance is affected • Absences from work • Giving up work • Promotion denied • Increased expenses due to care
Social life and leisure	• Social isolation • Loss of privacy • Fewer leisure time activities

1.1. Conceptualizing the Caregiving Role: The Stress/Coping Model

The experience of caring for an elderly member of the family has been conceptualized within the context of transactional models of stress, defining stress as a result of interaction between individuals and their environments within which potential stressors are understood in terms of their ability to cause harm. In general, research based on conceptual models of stress and coping aims to understand (Kinney, 1996):

- How family carers face potential stressors.
- The extent to which potential stressors affect the carer's personal resources, self-esteem or skills.
- How carers select coping strategies or mobilize resources to deal with stressors and demonstrate certain levels of adaptation.

Amongst conceptual models of stress and coping, the stress process model developed by Pearlin et al. (1990) is one of the most widely used frameworks for understanding the caregiving experience, as it provides a comprehensive approach and enables the carer's demands and resources to be identified.

In recent decades, these conceptual models, together with findings on the impact of caregiving, have led to research into support services and interventions aimed at reducing the carer burden. However, the effectiveness of the existing services and interventions is still not clear despite these efforts (Hanson et al., 2006). Moreover, no single carer intervention has been identified as a panacea for all the stresses and burdens of caregiving (Dupuis, Epp & Smale, 2004). This topic will be explored later.

2. COPING WITH THE CAREGIVING ROLE: HOW (IN)EFFECTIVE ARE INTERVENTIONS?

In order to enable elderly dependents to remain in their homes, carers are offered a range of different forms of support and services. Some interventions and resources (principally respite care, educational and skills training, counselling or support groups) are well developed and widespread in certain European countries (e.g. Denmark, Sweden, the United Kingdom, France, Belgium, Germany, the Netherlands) and North America, whereas in others (such as Portugal, Spain, Italy, Greece, Poland or Slovenia) any form of provision is rare or in the initial stages of development (Mestheneos and Triantafilliou, 2005).

There have been some reviews of support services and interventions and their effectiveness for in-home carers (Kennet, Burgio & Schulz, 2000; Acton & Kang, 2001; Schulz et al., 2002; Sörensen, Pinquart & Duberstein, 2002; Dupuis, Epp & Smale, 2004; Visser-Meily et al., 2005). Generally, these reviews suggest that efforts to intervene with family carers have not been highly successful or long lasting. To date, no single carer intervention has been identified as completely effective for all the burdens of caregiving. Moreover, researchers have only identified small-to-moderate statistically significant effects on a wide variety of outcomes such as depressive symptoms, burden or well-being (Sörensen, Pinquart & Duberstein, 2002; Schulz et al., 2003).

Based on reviews of research literature (Sörensen, Pinquart & Duberstein, 2002; Dupuis, Epp & Smale, 2005), a brief description of the formal caregiver support systems follows, underpinned by a discussion of their use and effectiveness.

2.1. TYPES OF INTERVENTION

Approaches to carer intervention can be divided into two main groups (Sörensen, Pinquart & Duberstein, 2002): i) those aimed at reducing the objective burden or amount of care provided by caregivers (respite, interventions to improve the skills of care recipients); ii) those aimed at improving the carer's well-being and coping skills, generally called psychosocial interventions (psycho-educational programmes, psychotherapy, support groups). More recently, an integrated approach has emerged, which combines a range of intervention strategies and is classified as multi-component.

Psycho-educational Interventions

Psycho-educational interventions usually involve structured programmes designed to provide information about the illnesses suffered by those receiving care (symptoms, causes, and progression) and the resources for support and services that are available. They also aim to train caregivers to respond effectively to disease-related difficulties, such as memory and behaviour problems in dementia patients or depression and anger in cancer patients. The format of the intervention generally includes lectures, group discussions and written materials and it is guided by a trained leader. This type of intervention may include a support slope, but this is secondary to the educational content.

Research into this type of intervention suggests it has moderate effects in terms of delaying the institutionalisation of those receiving care and improving the psychological well-being of the carer (Kennet, Burgio & Schulz, 2000). Psycho-educational interventions showed consistent short-term effects on a wide range of outcome indicators (carer burden, depression, well-being and capabilities, and the symptoms of care recipients) (cf. Sörensen, Pinquart & Duberstein, 2002). A recent intervention study found a significant reduction in health-risk behaviour and improvements to self-care and psychological well-being in family carers following a psycho-educational program (Won et al., 2008). Another recent piece of research reported positive effects on burden and satisfaction for those providing care to dementia sufferers after they had taken part in a psycho-educational programme (Andrén & Elmstal, 2008). Other significant improvements in the self-efficacy, emotional well-being, and self-care of caregivers were also observed after a psycho-educational programme (Boise, Congleton & Shannon, 2005).

Psychotherapy

Intervention involves establishing a therapeutic relationship between the carer and a trained professional. Most psychotherapeutic interventions with carers adopt a cognitive-behavioural approach (Sörensen, Pinquart & Duberstein, 2002) in which therapists (*a*) aim to improve self-monitoring, (*b*) challenge negative thoughts, assumptions and appraisals underlying the carer's unhealthy behaviour, (*c*) help carers develop problem-solving skills by focusing on time management, overload, and management of emotional reactions and (d) help the carer re-engage in enjoyable activities and positive experiences. Some studies reveal that this type of intervention is successful in reducing depressive symptomatology and dysfunctional thoughts about caregiving in family carers of dementia sufferers, as well as in modifying their appraisal of their relative's behaviour problems (Márquez-González et al., 2007).

The meta-analysis carried out by Sörensen and her colleagues (2002) found that, as with psycho-educational interventions, psychotherapeutic interventions have the most consistent short-term effects over different types of outcomes.

Supportive Interventions

These interventions include both professionally-led and peer-led unstructured support groups which focus on building up a rapport amongst participants and developing opportunities to share experiences of caregiving. In these groups, peers provide emotional support and encouragement as well as insights into successful strategies for dealing with several aspects of the caregiving role. Support groups rely strongly on peers to provide empathy and insight into shared problems, encourage the exchange of effective coping strategies and promote the sharing of concrete information on the needs of those receiving care, how problem behaviour can be managed and how services can be accessed. In contrast to psycho-educational programmes, these interventions are seldom standardized and education is not their primary focus.

In terms of their effectiveness, Sörensen and her colleagues (2002) found that support groups had a significant impact on reducing the carer burden and led to a greater ability/understanding of how to cope with the caregiving role, but had no effect on other outcome variables (caregiver depression and well-being and the symptoms of care recipients). In addition, Dupuis, Epp and Smale (2004) reported that whilst some studies have found that support groups have modest but positive effects on caregiver depression and other psychiatric symptomatologies in addition to other positive outcomes, other studies suggest that the effect on the caregiver's physical or mental health is minimal or nil.

Respite Interventions

Respite interventions focus on reducing carer distress and long-term care costs by preventing or delaying institutionalisation. These types of services are designed to relieve the carer for short or longer periods of time.

The main types of respite intervention include (Zarit, 2001; Dupuis, Epp & Smale, 2004):

a) *In-home respite*, which provides relief in the home in the form of workers with suitable qualifications and training. In-home respite services may include companionship, help with personal care or housework, and/or recreation/focused programmes. Accordingly to Zarit (2001), this is the type of respite service most widely used by family carers.

b) *Adult day care services/programmes*, a structured, comprehensive community-based program that provides a variety of health, social and related support services in a protective setting during part of the day.

c) *Overnight respite services*, which provide care for a night, weekend or longer in a residential care facility or official nursing home. Some programmes focus on taking the carer, rather than the care recipient, out of the home temporarily for a rest whilst 24-hour care is provided in the home (Olshevski, Katz & Knight, 1999). This type of respite service is the least available and the least studied (Zarit, 2001)

d) *Institutional respite and vacation/emergency respite*, which includes round-the-clock substitute care, usually used for longer, continuous periods of time, often when carers need to be away for short periods of time (e.g. when they need a holiday, become temporarily ill, or in emergency situations such as a death in the family). This type of respite is the least frequently used by carers (Dupuis, Epp & Smale, 2004).

In general, the studies show that many carers do not use respite services, or use them too little and too late in the caregiving trajectory (Zarit, 2001; Dupuis, Epp & Smale, 2004). There is little evidence to suggest that respite delays placement or provides cost-savings. This may be because caregivers use respite late in the caregiving process or because it may not, in itself, address the main causes of placement. Adult day care services and overnight respite might facilitate institutionalisation, since they provide the emotional distance that caregivers need (Zarit, 2001). There is also little evidence that respite care has significant long-term benefits for the well-being of caregivers, particularly in terms of burden, psychiatric or physical health (Acton & Kang, 2001; Dupuis, Epp & Smale, 2004; Carretero, Garcés & Ródenas, 2007). Some studies reveal its effectiveness in terms of the caregiver burden, depression and well-being (Sörensen, Pinquart & Duberstein, 2002), but not in relation to the care recipient. Thus, even though respite services may be helpful to carers, they are underused, or used only in crisis situations, which may reduce their effectiveness.

Interventions to Improve Care-receiver Skills

These interventions are targeted at care receivers and may include memory clinics for dementia patients or activity therapy programmes developed to improve involvement and everyday skills. The Sörensen, Pinquart and Duberstein (2002) meta-analysis found that training care recipients was effective in enhancing the carer's subjective well-being and reducing the care receiver's symptoms, although the impact on caregiver burden, depression, and skills/knowledge was not statistically relevant. Another study based on an intervention program for cognitively able elderly care receivers aimed at helping care recipients to effectively manage their own care and optimize relationships with carers found significant effects in terms of improved relationships with carers, self-care strategies, loneliness and quality of life (Cox et al., 2007).

Multi-component Interventions

Multi-component interventions include several combinations of strategies (psycho-educational, psychotherapy, supportive, respite) and target multiple outcomes. Several studies have illustrated the benefits for carers of combining various strategies and programmes (cf. Dupuis, Epp & Smale, 2004). For example, Donaldson and Burns (1999) reported on an Alzheimer's programme that combined interventions for carers (group therapy, management skills training and educational interventions) and patients (memory retraining, reminiscence therapy, environment reality orientation). This intervention resulted in reduced psychological morbidity in carers.

Thus, multi-component interventions seem to be more effective in improving the well-being of carers and relieving their stress and burden in comparison to the more narrowly targeted interventions (Sörensen, Pinquart & Duberstein, 2002; Schulz et al., 2003; Dupuis, Epp & Smale, 2004).

Carers can rely on a several formal services and interventions designed to help them look after elderly dependent relatives in the community and to cope with the caregiving role. A growing number of psycho-educational, respite, support or psychotherapy interventions have been published. However, intervention studies designed to reduce stress and burden present a conflicting picture and have shown only modest success. No single intervention is completely successful in responding to all the needs and difficulties of carers and care receivers, an extremely important factor since the desirability of carers receiving/participating in several support interventions when they are already burdened with the demands of caregiving may be questionable. Nevertheless, individual interventions seem to be more effective in improving carer well-being, whereas group interventions are more useful in improving the symptoms of care receivers. Moreover, some interventions (psychotherapy, psycho-educational programmes, multi-component interventions) seem to have broad, non-specific effects over several outcomes, whilst others have more specific effects on targeted outcomes (support groups, respite) (Sörensen, Pinquart & Duberstein, 2002). The results also suggest that multi-component interventions can be more effective than interventions with more limited goals and strategies. Interventions aimed at individual carers and their families, including the care receiver, are more likely to attenuate the caregiver burden than those focussing only on carers. Additionally, the length of the intervention appears to be an important success factor, since carers and care receivers can benefit more from more frequent and longer interventions.

A number of authors have discussed the possible reasons why research findings on caregiver intervention have been inconsistent (Acton & Kung, 2001; Sörensen, Pinquart & Duberstein, 2002; Schulz et al., 2003). The explanations are essentially related to research design and a number of methodological issues. Some argue that the outcome indicators used may be sensitive to change to greater or lesser degrees (e.g. the caregiver burden appears to be less changeable than well-being). In addition, studies frequently include inappropriate or unrelated outcome indicators that do not match the intervention goals: certain skills and knowledge might be expected to change after a psycho-educational programme, but not the burden, which might only alter after a respite-based intervention.

Others identify a misapplication of intervention approaches borrowed from medical and psychotherapeutic trials. Carers do not usually fall into single syndromal clinical categories that lend themselves to a clearly targeted intervention but instead generally have problems in multiple interrelated domains existing at varying, but not extreme, levels of intensity (Schulz et al., 2003).

However, many factors related to intervention characteristics, the caregiving situation or research design can mediate the effectiveness of intervention, such as (i) the amount and length of the intervention sessions; (ii) the amount of care provided (by respite interventions, for example.); (iii) individual intervention as opposite to group intervention; (iv) the characteristics of care receivers, e.g. interventions with carers of dementia patients are less successful than those designed for other caregivers; (v) the relationship with the care receiver (adult-child interventions as opposed to interventions involving spouses); (vi) the extent to which participants adhere to the intervention (regularity of attendance or dropout rate); (vii) a number of research design features such as random assignment or reliability and the validity of outcome indicators (for example, randomized control trials revealed fewer effects than non-randomized trials and interventions using the Geriatric Depression Scale revealed fewer effects than studies using the Beck Depression Inventory).

The overriding message from this overview is that caregiving presents a complex range of challenges that are not easily addressed. As a result, findings from intervention studies are confused and conflicting. Despite the conceptual and methodological reasons discussed above, other possible explanations that extend beyond methodological debate may exist. These processes will be discussed in the following section.

3. Moving beyond Methodological Limitations

The relative failure of interventions designed to relieve the carer burden has been attributed to the methodological weaknesses of research into intervention, as previously discussed. However, the "burden" of intervention disappointment also demands a close attention to the approach of researchers, practitioners, governments and society as a whole to the caregiving experience.

Research has conceptualised informal caregiving as a stressful event associated with a deterioration in the health of the carer and an increased risk of morbidity. Based on this approach, various burden indicators have been created and findings have revealed that many carers experience high levels of burden, as well as depression, anxiety, social isolation, financial strain and other negative outcomes. In the light of this assumption, researchers, policy-makers and professionals have become interested in developing a variety of intervention programmes and services to relieve the carer burden. In addition, carers have been valued as an important component in total care, leading to a political discourse based on the creation of "partnerships" between services and carers.

In the light of this framework – based on the notion that caregiving is a negative and dysfunctional experience – the relative incongruence of the findings of intervention studies may not be limited to methodological issues. The answers to the question "why don't programmes and services work?" may extend beyond the use of inadequate outcome indicators, weak experimental design or questionable sampling and randomization strategies to include the mismatch between practitioners/services and cares/users or the conceptual models underlying interventions and practices. Obviously, these reasons are connected and interrelated, but each will be discussed separately in order to facilitate analysis.

3.1. The Mismatch between Services and Carers

An overview of carers' reasons for not using services may provide an insight into the dilemma concerning the effectiveness of intervention.

Little has been published on the reasons why caregivers do not use services. Nevertheless, different studies provide some explanations (Nolan et al., 2003; Dupuis, Epp & Smale, 2004; Brodaty et al., 2005) that appear to be consistent and relevant, namely: (i) carers do not view services as relevant to their needs; (ii) the inflexibility of the services and their complex eligibility requirements; (iii) feelings of guilt and duty; (iv) concerns/doubts about the quality of official care; (v) lack of information about availability of services; (vi) feelings of being imposed upon by official helpers or professionals.

The Importance of a "Real" Needs Assessment

The fact that caregivers do not view services as relevant to their needs is of extreme importance. Services, especially home respite, focus mainly on providing help in performing instrumental activities for the dependent person, personal care and household tasks. This type of support is therefore targeted mainly at the elderly care receiver, based on the assumption that if the elderly person receives formal care, caregivers will be relieved or feel less burdened. However, this is not unreservedly confirmed by research findings. Therefore, it may be suggested that the ineffectiveness of services may be due, in part, to a failure to accommodate the real needs of carers to the type of support provided by the services. Services are needed but tend to be reductionist by addressing mainly the objective aspects of care. This underlies the importance of a "real" needs assessment in order to identify the outcomes that carers see as important, in terms of the complexities of each caregiving situation, and to move beyond the objective burden of care. In this sense, a regard for the positive aspects of caregiving and a strengths-based approach is also desirable (this idea will be discussed later).

However, this also encompasses the significance of combining different types of support targeted at different goals and outcomes, such as multi-component interventions i.e., an approach relying strictly on "packaged" programmes or services such as respite, which may be helpful in addressing certain outcomes (usually the objective burden) but is likely to be ineffective overall. As Aneshensel et al. (1995, 310 and 311) emphasise, "assessments (and, consequently, interventions[1]) should identify the unique constellation of issues found within a particular family", therefore "broad and comprehensive interventions are needed" and, as "not all the caregivers have the same problems and concerns, we should use multiple criteria to evaluate interventions"

Professionals and Carers: Challenges to Interaction Patterns

Another reason for failing to use services is the fear of being imposed upon by professionals. On the one hand, this assumption reflects the generally-held view of

---

[1] Our comment.

researchers and professionals as experts who define solutions, whilst also underlining the fact that the needs of carers should be recognized and valued by formal systems in terms of the role they play and their skills, as well as constituting an important element in decision-making processes. Therefore, creating effective services also involves a change in the patterns of professional-carer interaction, based on a more balanced relationship, promoting a sense of partnership in which carers are seen as co-partners rather then "subordinates" and professionals as facilitators and enablers rather than "executers" or providers. Assessment can provide an opportunity to put this into practice.

In fact, the nature of the interaction between clients (in this case, carers) and professionals is largely determined by systematic beliefs or myths which, in turn, affect the intervention process. Sousa and Eusébio (2007) have identified some of these myths, stressing their decisive role in the success of interventions. One of the most common beliefs is that professionals are "the" experts and are therefore responsible for the effectiveness of the intervention. Thus, professionals tend to adopt a biomedical approach by defining "treatments" for client problems and clients are expected to obey the professionals' advice. In this sense, collaborative interventions, based on the recognition of client/carer skills and knowledge and promoting subsequent adjustments and negotiations between "partners", are often underestimated. Another significant myth is that a polite approach facilitates intervention and leads to positive outcomes. However, as emphasised by Sousa and Eusébio (2007), those using the polite approach avoid saying what they think and fail to see that more assertive attitudes are often needed, often omitting to discuss important issues and proposals.

These myths, to a certain extent, underlie some of the models often used in the assessment process in which decisions about service provision are usually made, namely the questioning model and the procedural model (Smale et al., 1993 in Hanson et al., 2006). In the questioning model, the assessor is the "expert" who asks questions that are answered by the carers, and has the "power" to determine the appropriate services based on carer responses. The procedural approach is based on relatively fixed eligibility criteria which determine whether the carer has a "right" to services and ensures that power remains in the hands of the professional. In fact, one of the most consistent reasons for not using services is the complex eligibility requirements.

These types of approaches to the assessment process rely on unbalanced interactions in which professionals are seen as powerful and carers as powerless, resulting in services/interventions that often do not match carer needs. It is here that an exchange model is needed. Based on the assumption that all parties (professionals and users) have knowledge, skills and expectations, this approach is more likely to ensure that services and interventions are negotiated and agreed as a result of all parties sharing their expertise and knowledge.

Acceptability of Services

Inflexibility of services, complex eligibility requirements and concerns/doubts about the poor quality of care often create consistent barriers to the use of support services. In terms of the quality of services, Nolan et al. (1996) argue that this can be viewed as a continuum ranging from the *facilitative* (those that make efforts to be sensitive and respond to the caregiving dynamic and carer point of view) to the *obstructive* (seen by carers as at odds with their own goals and quality standards and usually quickly rejected) and including the *contributory* (sometimes complementing the carer's efforts, but more as the result of fortuitous circumstances than negotiation and agreement) and the *inhibitory* (rarely achieving the status of facilitative support but sometimes accepted out of necessity or desperation)

More recently, Nolan and colleagues (2003; Hanson et al., 2006) have suggested that two other relevant factors help determine whether services are acceptable or not: the degree of *symmetry* (the degree to which there is agreement between the carer and the service providers on the intended goals and outcomes) and *synchronicity* (reflecting the importance of the temporal dimensions of care, since support must be consistent with carer needs at different stages in their caregiving "career"[2]). Therefore, when there is agreement on the intended goals and outcomes of the services and when support is delivered "on time" (this is, taking into account the characteristics and dynamics of each stage of the caregiving role), services have a greater chance of being facilitative and readily accepted. Conversely, when neither of these criteria is met, the services are likely to be seen as obstructive and unwanted.

3.2. Time to Change Paradigms

There is one fact in the traditional informal caregiving "history" that is often forgotten or undervalued. Despite the negative costs that informal caregiving may involve, many carers choose to care and to continue to care even when the burdens of caring become obvious. It may be wondered why this is the case, yet the reasons have been insufficiently explored. Some would argue that this is because, in general, carers are not really free to choose, due to the questionable quality, availability, adequacy and accessibility of services. However, it is debatable whether the barriers created by services/programmes are a sufficient motive.

It may be that stronger and more intrinsic reasons exist that need to be explored more deeply. For example, caregiving can be a way of finding meaning in life and a sense of usefulness through being given the opportunity to help and care for a dependent relative. An interesting study developed by Brouwer et al. (2005) found that while some informal carers gain considerably from being relieved of their caregiving demands, others would loose a major part of their total happiness if forced to give up caregiving. Consideration should also be given as to whether adopting a caregiving role could be a means of keeping the family together or a means of spiritual development.

It would appear that there is a need for more research into how individuals take on the caregiving role. It would be interesting to discover whether these kinds of reasons/motives – such as finding meaning, a sense of usefulness, a willingness to keep the family together and so on – are associated with the different impacts of various types of intervention. For example, could the growing consensus in literature on the subject that psychosocial interventions (e.g., providing knowledge through psycho-educational programmes, specific therapeutic skills training, enhancing problem-solving skills) are more effective than respite services be associated with the willingness of the carer to provide care? In other words, could carers simply want to provide care for a loved and dependent relative?

Moreover, the traditional concepts of caregiving – mainly as a stressful and negative event – may be negatively affecting other forms of thinking about the caregiving experience. The pathogenic approach to caregiving often excludes/forgets those carers who feel healthy,

---

[2] For a detailed discussion and understanding of the importance of the temporal perspective of caregiving - the caregiving "career" -see Aneshensel et al. (1995) and Nolan, Grant and Keady (1996).

energetic, have a sense of complete well-being, are not depressed, are satisfied with their life and are happy. A biomedical approach hinders the search for the origins of health and well-being in carers. There is a lack of research into happy and healthier caregivers which could identify which variables are associated with happiness, well-being and quality of life in general. Whereas the relationship between the demands of caregiving and burden and negative outcomes (such depression, anxiety, poor health perception) has been well documented, much less is known about the factors and processes associated with positive well-being and happiness.

Furthermore, this pathological approach has ignored any opportunities to find out about the positive aspects of care and to promote them. There is, however, growing evidence (Farran et al., 1999; Ayres, 2000; Tarlow et al., 2004; Kuuppelomäki et al., 2004; Andrén & Elmstahl, 2005) that it is possible for positive outcomes or rewards to be derived from caregiving, such as a sense of reciprocity and personal growth, despite the stressful situation. Moreover, as Nolan, Grant and Keady (1998) stress, the rewards and satisfactions of caregiving are associated, amongst other things, with improved carer well-being, successful coping or a more positive attitude towards the future. Thus, considering the positive aspects when assessing carer needs is extremely important, since directing supportive efforts only towards burden relief may aggravate the caregiving relationship by ignoring the opportunity to enhance the satisfaction gained from the relationship. Moreover, exhausted carers who derive satisfaction from their role may require a different kind of intervention from those who do not experience this (McKee et al., 2003). In this sense, the benefits and rewards of the caring process seem too important to be ignored.

The traditional pathogenic approach to the stress/coping paradigm has also led to interventions based on a deficit approach in which carers are assumed not to have the necessary resources, skills and competences to cope with their stressful situations. In contrast, a more salutogenic approach provides a focus on strengths rather than on burdens and deficits, recognizes carer skills and competences, and has the potential to empower carers and help them to develop healthier lifestyles.

Considering caregiving from a salutogenic or wellness perspective requires a change in professional practice by valuing and considering the strengths, competences and opportunities of individuals in order to enhance resilience and personal empowerment (Cadell, Karabanow & Sanchez, 2001). In this sense, recent findings suggest that carer well-being can be enhanced if interventions emphasize resources rather than limitations and treat the caregiving burden through a focus on strengths rather than on a mental and physical pathology (Kurylo, Elliot & Shewchuck, 2001; Myers, 2003).

Moreover, the biomedical paradigm for caregiving creates a reductionist approach, as it mainly emphasises individuals in their carer role and neglects the person-carer as a whole. As a consequence, policies and services often focus on the provision of care in an effort to relieve the carer burden and ignore innovative forms of intervention that focus on other dimensions of the carer's life, such as social, professional and leisure aspects. A wellness perspective considers the interactive nature of the various dimensions of the caregiving experience, so that change in one area (e.g. greater flexibility at work or the activation of informal networks) contributes towards changed in other areas as well.

4. PATHWAYS FOR THE FUTURE:
MOVING BEYOND THE "BIOMEDICALIZATION OF CAREGIVING"

It is currently assumed that the most serious implication of demographic ageing for societies, and particularly for the welfare and care systems, is the increasing number of chronic diseases related to greater life expectancy. In both developing and developed countries, chronic diseases play a significant role and are frequently the cause of disability and reduced quality of life in older people.

There is also a general expectation that the burden of disease and disability in later life will grow in the future. However, some argue that severe disability is declining in older people at a rate of 1.5% per year in developed countries. For example, United States estimates predict the number of severely disabled older people will fall by half between 2000 and 2050 if current trends continue (WHO, 1999). This scenario has important implications for societies heavily defined by economic rules and directed by and towards production, as it demolishes the stereotype of the elderly as frail, dependent and a burden and gradually allows for them to be recognised as persons with individual interests, desires and choices who do not necessarily have to be economically and socially unproductive.

It would, however, be prudent to not engage in a wave of "geronto-optimism" and to recognize that, despite individual diversity, as individuals age, chronic diseases become the leading causes of morbidity, disability and mortality across the world (WHO, 2002). Informal carers, mainly family members, provide the bulk of support and care for older adults who need assistance, accompanied by a political discourse of deinstitutionalisation. It has been argued that informal carers (who are often older people) must be recognized and supported too, unless they are to become one more patient in the care system. Consequently, formal interventions and resources have been designed to support family carers, although the effectiveness of existing interventions has been questioned.

However, despite all the theoretical, methodological and practical considerations, effective interventions appear to share several characteristics. For instance, multi-component interventions which include a combination of skills building (both for carers and care receivers), knowledge, problem solving and counselling and target a range of carer needs have been observed to be more effective. Moreover, interventions that view the carer as a person, allowing him/her to identify the problems that need to be addressed and the type, timing, amount and frequency of support/intervention are more likely to be successful than interventions relying on an "expert" model defining what, when, how and who will be supported. In addition, carers who derive a sense of mutual benefit from services (i.e., a sense that the services benefit both themselves and the care reviver) are more likely to use them.

As a final word, the view of caregiving as a negative, stressful and burdensome event has encouraged societies to think about and understand the caring experience in pathological terms, seeking desperately for solutions to "cure" the negative outcomes of care provision. On the basis of Estes' and Binney's (1989) concept of the "biomedicalization of ageing", this "biomedicalization of caregiving" has fostered a tendency to view informal care negatively and to normalise formal responses as expert, necessary and appropriate. On the basis of the argument that it is in the interests of older people to live as long as possible in the community (usually, in their homes, within their families), an emphasis has been placed on the carer as the support/co-partner for the dependent elderly person who, in turn, needs help to continue in this role, but neglects the carer as a "person". This position has prevented policy-makers, researchers and practitioners from understanding the complexity of caring and from seeking innovative and balanced solutions to the needs of the family and the elderly.

REFERENCES

Acton, G. & Kang, J. (2001). Interventions to reduce the burden of caregiving for an adult with dementia: A meta-analysis. *Research in Nursing & Health*, 24, 349-360.

Andrén, S. & Elmstahl, S. (2005). Family Caregivers' subjective experiences of satisfaction in dementia care: aspects of burden, subjective health and sense of coherence. *Scandinavian Journal of Caring Sciences*, 19, 157-168.

Andrén, S. & Elmstal, S. (2008). Psychosocial intervention for family caregivers of people with dementia reduces caregiver's burden: development and effect after 6 and 12 months. *Scandinavian Journal of Caring*, 22, 98-109.

Aneshensel, C., Pearlin, L., Mullan, J., Zarit, S. & Whitlatch, C. (1995). *Profiles in Caregiving. The Unexpected Career.* San Diego, CA: Academic Press.

Ayres, L. (2000). Narratives of family caregiving: The process of making meaning. *Research in Nursing & Health*, 23, 424-434.

Bedini, L. A. & Phoenix, T. L. (1999). Addressing leisure barriers for caregivers of older adults: A model wellness program. *Therapeutic Recreation Journal*, 33 (3), 222-240.

Boise, L.; Congleton, L. & Shannon, K. (2005). Empowering family caregivers: the powerful tools for caregiving. *Educational Gerontology*, 31, 573-586.

Borgermans, L., Nolan, M. & Philp, I. (2001). *Europe.* In I. Philp (Ed.), *Family Care of Older People in Europe* (pp. 2-25). Amsterdam: IOS Press.

Brodaty, H., Thomson, C., Thmpsoon, C. & Fine, M. (2005). Why caregivers with dementia and memory loss don't use services. *International Journal of Geriatric Psychiatry*, 50, 537-546.

Brouwer, W., Excel, N., Berg, B., Bos, G. & Koopmanschap, M. (2005). Process utility from providing informal care: the benefit of caring. *Health Policy*, 74, 85-99.

Cadell, S., Karabanow, J. & Sanchez, M. (2001). Community, empowerment and resilience: Paths to wellness. *Canadian Journal of Community Mental Health*, 20(1), 21-35.

Carretero, S.; Garcés, S. & Ródenas, F. (2007). Evaluation of the home help service and its impacts on the informal caregiver's burden of dependent elders. *International Journal of Geriatric Psychiatry*, 22, 738-749.

Cavanaugh, J. C. (1998). Caregiving to adults: A life event challenge. In I. H. Nordhus, G. R. VandenBos, S. Berg and P. Fromholt (Eds.), *Clinical Geropsychology* (pp. 131-136). Washington, DC: American Psychological Association.

Cox, E., Green, K., Hbart, K., Jang, L:, & Seo, H. (2007). Strengthening the late-life care process: Effects of two forms of a care-receiver efficacy intervention. *The Gerontologist*, 47 (3), 388-397.

Donaldson, C. & Burns, A. (1999). Burden of Alzheimer's disease: Helping the patient and caregiver. *Journal of Geriatric Psychiatry and Neurology*, 12, 21-28.

Dupuis, S. L., Epp, T. & Smale, B. (2004). *Caregivers of persons with dementia: Roles, experiences, supports, and coping.* Ontario: University of Waterloo.

Estes, C. L. & Binney, E. A. (1989). The biomedicalization of aging: Dangers and dilemmas. *The Gerontologist*, 29, 587-597.

Farran, C., Miller, B., Kaufman, J., Donner, E. & Fogg, L. (1999). Finding meaning through caregiving: Development of an instrument for family caregivers of persons with Alzheimer's disease. *Journal of Clinical Psychology*, 55(9), 1107-1125.

Fandetti, D. V & Gelfand, D. E. (1976). Care of the aged: attitudes of white ethnic families. *The Gerontologist*, 16: 544-549.

Figueiredo, D. & Sousa, L. (2007). Caregiving stressors and life satisfaction: family carers of demented and non-dementes elderly. *International Association of Gerontology and Geriatrics VI European Congress: Healthy and Active Aging for All Europeans*, Saint Petersburg, Russia (5th-8th July).

George, L. & Gwyther, L. (1986). Caregiver well being: A multidimensional examination of family caregivers of demented adults. *The Gerontologist*, 26, 253-259.

Haley, W., Rrothe, D., Coleton, M., Ford, G., West, C., Collins, R. & Isobe, T. (1996). Appraisal, coping and social support as mediators of well-being in black and white family caregivers of patients with Alzheimer's disease. *Journal of Consulting and clinical Psychology*, 64 (1), 121-129.

Hanson, E.; Nolan, J., Magnusson, L., Sennemark, E., Johansson, L. & Nolan, M. (2006). *COAT : The Carers Outcome Agreement Tool.* Getting Research into Practice (GRiP) Report No 1, University of Sheffield.

Kennet, J., Burgio, L. & Schulz, R. (2000). Interventions for in-home caregivers: A review of research 1990 to present. In R. Schulz (Ed.), *Handbook on dementia caregiving: Evidence-based interventions for family caregivers* (pp. 61-125). New York: Springer.

Kiecolt-Glaser, K. & Glaser, R., (1994). Caregivers, Mental Health, and Immune Function. In E. Light, G. Niederehe e B. Lebowitz (Eds.) *Stress effects on family caregivers of Alzhemier's patients* (pp. 64–75). New York: Springer Publishing Company.

Kinney, J. (1996). Home care and Caregiving. In J. Birren (Ed.) *Enciclopedia of Gerontology. Age, Aging, and the Aged.* San Diego: Academic Press, Vol. I, 667- 678.

Knight. B. G., Fox, L. S. & Chou, C. (2000). Factor structure of the burden interview. *Journal of Clinical Geropsychology*, 6(4), 249-258.

Kurylo, M., Elliott, T. & Shewchuck, R. (2001). FOCUS on the family caregiver: A problem-solving training intervention. *Journal of Counseling & Development*, 79, 275-281.

Kuuppelomäki, M., Sasaki, A., Yamada, K. Asakawa, N. & Shimanouchi, S. (2004). Family carers for older relatives: sources of satisfaction and related factors in Finland. *International Journal of Nursing Studies*, 41, 497-505.

Márquez-González, M., Losada, A., Izal, M., Pérez-Rojo, G. & Montorio, I. (2007). Modification of dysfunctional thoughts about caregiving in dementia family caregivers: Description and outcomes of an intervention programme. *Aging and Mental Health*, 11(6), 616-625.

McKee, K., Philp, I., Lamura, C., Prouskas, B., Öberg, B., Krevers, B., Spazzafumo, L., Bien, B., Parker, C., Nolan, M. & Szczerbinska, K. (2003). The COPE index – a first stage assessment of negative impact, positive value and quality of support of caregiving in informal carers of older people. *Aging and Mental Health,* 7(1), 39-52.

Mestheneos, E. & Triantafillou, J. (2005). Supporting Family Carers of Older People in Europe – The Pan-European Background Report. Münster: Lit Verlag.

Myers, J. E. (2003). Coping with caregiving stress: A wellness-oriented, strengths-based approach for family counselors. *The Family Journal: Counseling and Therapy for Coumples and Families*, 11(2), 153-161.

Nolan, M., Grant, G. & Keady, J. (1996). *Understanding family care.* Buckingaham: Open University Press.

Nolan, M., Grant, G. & Keady, J. (1998). *Assessing the needs of family carers. A guide for practitioners.* Brighton: Pavilion Publishing.

Nolan, M., Keady, J., Grant, G. & Lundh, U. (2003). Introduction: why another book on family care?. In M. Nolan, U. Lundh, G. Grant & J. Keady (Eds.), *Partnerships in family care: Understanding the caregiving career* (pp. 1-14). Maidenhead: Open University Press.

Olshevski, J. L., Katz, A. D. & Knight, B. G. (1999). *Stress reduction for caregivers.* Philadelphia: Brunner/Mazel.

Pearlin, L., Mullan, J. , Semple, S. & Skaff, M. (1990). Caregiving and the stress process: An overview of concepts and their measures. *The Gerontologist*, 30(5), 583-594.

Schulz, R. & Williamson, G. (1994). Health effects of caregiving: prevalence of mental and physical illness in Alzheimer's caregivers. In E. Light, G. Niederehe & B. Lebowitz (Eds.), *Stress effects on family caregivers of Alzhemier's patients* (pp. 38-75). New York: Springer Publishing Company.

Schulz, R., Burgio, L., Burns, R., Eisdorfer, C., Gallagher-Thompson, D., Gitlin, L. & Mahoney, D. (2003). Resources for Enhancing Alzheimer's caregiver health (REACH): Overview, site-specific outcomes, and future directions. *The Gerontologist*, 43 (4), 514-520.

Schulz, R., O'Brien, A., Czaja, S., Ory, M., Norris, R., Martire, L., Belle, S., Burgio, L., Gitlin, L., Coon, D., Burns, R., Gallagher-Thompson, D. & Stevens, A. (2002). Dementia caregiver intervention research: In search of clinical significance. *The Gerontologist*, 52(5), 589-602.

Sörensen, S., Pinquart, M. & Duberstein, P. (2002). How effective are interventions with caregivers? An updated meta-analysis. *The Gerontologist*, 42 (3), 356-372.

Sousa, L. & Eusébio, C. (2007). When multi-problem poor individuals' myths meet social services myths. *Journal of Social Work*, 7(2): 217-237.

Tarlow, B., Wisniewski, S., Belle, S., Rubert, M., Ory, M. & Gallagher-Thompson, D. (2004). Positive aspects of caregiving: Contributions of REACH Project to the development of new measures for Alzheimer's caregiving. *Research on Aging*, 26(4), 429-453.

Visser-Meily, A., van Heugten, C., Post, M., Schepers, V. & Lindeman, E. (2005). Intervention studies for caregivers of stroke survivors: a critical review. *Patient Education and Counseling* 56, 257-267.

Vitaliano, P., Scanlan, J. & Zhang, J. (2003). Is caregiving hazardous to one's physical health? A meta-analysis. *Psychological Bulletin*, 129 (6), 946-972.

WHO – World Health Organization (1999). *Ageing. Exploding the myths.* World Health Organization.

WHO - World Health Organization (2002). *Active Ageing.* World Health Organization.

Won, C., Fitts, S., Favaro, S., Olsen, P. & Phelan, E. (2008). Community-based "powerful tools" intervention enhances health of caregivers. *Archives of Gerontology and Geriatrics*, 46, 89-100.

Zarit, S. H. (2001). *Respite Services for Caregivers*. Washington, DC: National Family Caregiver Support Program, Selected Issue Brief. Available form: http://www.aoa.gov/prof/aoaprog/caregiver/careprof/progguidance/background/program_issues/zaritmonograph.pdf

Zarit, S., Reever, K. & Bach-Peterson, J. (1980). Relatives of the impaired elderly: Correlates of feelings of burden. *The Gerontologist*, 20, 649-655.

In: Families in Later Life: Emerging Themes and Challenges   ISBN 978-1-60692-328-3
Editor: Liliana Sousa   © 2009 Nova Science Publishers, Inc.

Chapter 6

QUALITY OF LIFE, FAMILY ROLE AND CHRONIC ILLNESS IN ELDERLY PEOPLE INSTITUTIONALIZED AND LIVING AT HOME

Carlos F. Silva, Rosa Martins, Isabel M. Santos and Jorge Costa

SUMMARY

Significant increases in life expectancy over the last decades, with the consequent increase in the number of people suffering from chronic illnesses, started to raise new concerns regarding the elderly. At the same time, demographic and lifestyle changes contribute to a lower availability of the family to provide care. Thus, measures to improve the quality of life of elderly people are now a major priority in main research and governmental programs. Here we report the findings from a study with a sample of the Portuguese population, from the interior centre town of Viseu, which is situated in a transition area between the coast and the interior, and between north and south, and which is characterised by large asymmetries and inequalities. The study aimed to investigate the characteristics of chronic illnesses, quality of life, functional dependence in daily activities and family support in this population. Elderly people were subdivided in two samples: those still living at home (either by themselves or with family members) and those institutionalized. Statistical analyses compared the main aspects of interest between the two groups and these are discussed in detail. In general, it can be concluded that the characteristics of this sample are comparable to those observed in other studies. Loneliness, low retirement pensions, family rejection and social exclusion are the most significant factors compromising the quality of life of the elderly from this region. Measures to deal with the significant ageing of the population and its consequences worldwide must take into account the need for independence and social support for a longer period of time, and the financial and personal costs of caregiving.

INTRODUCTION

The increase in the number of chronic illnesses that is recently observed is a direct consequence of the increase in life expectancy (Hirschfeld, 2003). At the same time, demographic trends suggest that family members may not be available to provide care when needed and that seniors may be suffering from a chronic illness when they are needed as a family caregiver (Grunfeld, Glossop, McDowell and Danbrook, 1997; Vitaliano, Young & Zhang, 2004). Therefore, improving the quality of life of elderly people is currently one of the strategic lines assumed by the European Union (E.U.) both through research and through the elaboration of community intervention plans.

EU research and innovation in this area has already a successful track record in creating innovative Research & Development solutions for elderly people (Carvalho & Patrícia, 2006). Two good examples are MobilAlarm, a tracking service allowing older persons to initiate an alarm call and get support whenever and wherever they need or want to do so, and heating systems, microwaves and washing machines more accessible for people with physical or cognitive impairments (7thSpace, 2007). Greater online accessibility is at the same time one of the objectives of the Commission action plan "Ageing Well in the Information Society" (IP/07/831) (European Comunitties Commission, 2005a).

These projects of the EU are very important, because it is estimated that by 2020, 25% of the EU's population will be over 65 years (INE, 2002). To face this growing demographic challenge, the Council of Ministers approved on 14th June 2007 a Commission plan to make Europe a hub for developing digital technologies designed to help older people to continue *living independently* at home, providing some additional funding to a new European Joint Research Program. Through this new program companies can develop highly innovative digital products and services to enhance security at home, such as user friendly interfaces for those with impaired vision or hearing, and to improve the quality of life of elderly people, their careers and families (7thSpace, 2007).

Portugal is one of the countries participating in this new EU Joint Research Program, because the number of elderly persons in Portugal in 2001 (last national census) was superior to a million and a half (1,511,950) and corresponded to 16.4 % of the total population (10,355,824 individuals, 4,999,964 males e 5,355,860 females) (INE, 2002). In 2001, in the region of Viseu, in the interior central region of the country, the number of elderly people was 69,790 and represented around 17% of the total population (INE, 2002). This meant that in this region the ageing rate of the population was superior to the national level. The projections presented by the National Institute of Statistics (2001) estimate that in 2020 there will be 112 elderly for each 100 youths. Most of these elderly will be women and the elderly will be the poorest population sector of the country (Gonçalves, 2001; Paúl, 2006;). On the other hand, the index of total demographic dependency ({[0-14yr]n + [>65yr]n} / [15-64yr]n) will go from 49% in 2005 to 66% in 2030 (INE, 2001). These data show that we are faced with a demographic phenomenon with strong social and economical implications in Portugal, namely in what concerns Social Security, Health and Education.

In this society of consume, specialized labour, stratification and optimisation of production, the elderly is often excluded from work. In this context, elderly people feel that they have lost their role as knowledge transmitters across generations, they tend to isolate themselves and to become dependent of others (Pimentel, 2007). On the other hand, retirement pensions in Portugal do not provide enough means to guarantee a good quality of life (Guimarães, 1999; European Committees Commission, 2005a). To worsen the situation, Portuguese families have great difficulties in providing the necessary support, especially if they do not live in the same house as the elderly (Lage, 2005; Sousa, Figueiredo & Cerqueira, 2006), similarly to what happens in other countries (Crane *et al.*, 2005). The institutionalization of the elderly has been a way of warranting this support, and of ensuring well-being levels that are favourable to a better social and economical integration, therefore, influencing the quality of life of elderly people who do not have the necessary conditions to live alone (Firmino, Falcão & Rodrigues, 2006).

The paradigmatic and structural changes in the family also contribute to worsen the problem. There is a progressive diminution of the communication between people and generations in the families (Sousa, Figueiredo & Cerqueira, 2006). As a matter of fact, intergenerational communication is generally reported to be more problematic than intragenerational communication (Giles *et al.*, 2003). On the other hand, in 2001, there were 3,650,612 traditional families living in Portugal, representing an increase of 16%, between 1991 and 2001, variation which doubled the one observed between 1981 and 1991 (7.6%) (INE, 2001).

Thanks to the steady increase in life expectancy, there is a strong world growth of very elderly people (80+) – 17.1% between 2005 and 2010 and 57.1% between 2010 and 2030 – which will then be around 34.7 million against the around 18.8 million that exist currently (INE, 2002). The proportion of isolated people will increase, especially in the case of women, as a result of the larger number of female widowers that derives from the difference in longevity of both sexes (INE, 2002). As a consequence of the increase in life expectancy, the number of chronic illnesses will also increase, diminishing the quality of life (Heidrich, & Powwattana, 2004; Luskin & Newell, 1997).

Families will not be able to solve alone the issue of caring for the elderly, whether they are dependent or autonomous. However, it is predicted that in the future elderly people will be autonomous for increasingly longer periods of time and will want to stay in their respective homes (Paúl, Fonseca, Martin & Amado, 2005). "Intense" care will be increasingly focused at the end of life, but there will also be more people that will feel the need for caregiving as a result of their loss of autonomy (Morss *et al.*, 2008; Motta *et al.*, 2008).

Either way, it will be necessary to ensure adapted care. Nowadays, this care is in many countries warranted by the families and mainly by women. Nevertheless, women are increasingly more employed, with the aggravating condition that many children, when reaching adulthood, live apart from their parents (Arno, Levine & Memmott, 1999). The compatibility of family and career will play an important role in Europe's future economic and social development, mainly in what concerns chronic illnesses. In an effort to meet these challenges, the EU heads of state and government decided to establish a *European Alliance for Families* in May 2007 to create impulses for more family-friendly policies through exchanges of ideas and experience in the various State Members and to foster cooperation and fruitful learning from each other in the European Union (European Committees Commission, 2005b).

In the near future, families will need more support than they currently get. This is the role of the social services and of the solidarity and care networks in the framework of the local communities (European Committees Commission, 2005a). Until now there are no exact data on the number of elderly people who are institutionalized, nor prospective studies on the future evolution. Nevertheless it is estimated that, according to the last census undertaken in Portugal (2001), the proportion of elderly people living in institutional families was 3.6% of the total resident population over 65 years old (Gonçalves, 2001). There are, nonetheless, indicators that the requests for institutionalization will increase in the future (Hirschfeld, 2003), which makes the foster housings a crucial structure for elderly support (Carvalho & Patrícia, 2006). However, in a country such as Portugal, where there are many cultural and socio-economic differences, the institutions for elderly people are also heterogenic in what concerns service patterns, quality of the structure, financial organization and population accepted (Firmino, Falcão & Rodrigues, 2006; Gonçalves, 2001).

Linked to the precarious family relations and the inappropriate residential and social-economic conditions, the chronic illnesses and the physiologic changes that come with age increase the probability of physical limitations and of incapacities in elderly people (Paschoal, 2002), as well as changes in what concerns their psychological well-being, as a consequence of the lower quality of life of these patients (Fonda, Wallace & Herzog, 2001; Kay, Beamish, & Roth, 1964; Schnittker, 2005). Nevertheless, we also know that if the individuals grow old with autonomy and independence, with good physical health, with a satisfactory family relationship, carrying out some social roles, remaining active and enjoying sense and personal meaning (active aging), the quality of life can be nearly optimal (Socías & Cerdà, 2007; Paúl, 2006; Wickrama, Conger & Abraham, 2005).

The answers can only be found if we take into account the risk of considering the elderly in his/her biological, psychological, sociological, cultural and ethical dimensions, elements which are part of human lives and that should be valued (Serra, 2006). However, only a global, integrative and comprehensive thinking, which gathers the different interactions between phenomena, will truly enable us to understand the issue of family caregiving (Harper, 2004). A new paradigm is needed, a *family-focused approach* to manage the chronic disease in sharp contrast to the traditional *patient-focused approach* (Ellenwood & Jenkins, 2007; Fisher, Karen & Weihs, 2000). This new approach adopts an ecological perspective, shifting the focus from the patient and disease to the social setting in which disease management typically takes place.

The chronic disease is a very significant problem to patients, their families and community, with economic impact. For example, the cerebrovascular disease, arthritis and coronary artery disease are the best predictors of the functional limitation in the elderly (Boult *et al.*, 1994). In a study by Foley *et al.* (2003), 83% of 1,506 community-dwelling men and women aged 55-84 years in the U.S.A. reported one or more of 11 medical conditions, and ¼ of the elderly persons (aged 65-84 years old) had major co-morbidity (one or more medical conditions): depression, heart disease, bodily pain, memory problems, obesity, arthritis, type 2 diabetes, stroke, osteoporosis and sleep problems.

These illnesses trigger processes of adaptation within the families which are not always successful. Many chronic diseases require repetitive, tedious and invasive management procedures that produce enormous changes in family lifestyle (Ellenwood & Jenkins 2007). Some family caregivers develop protective behaviours against negative disease management outcomes, such as family closeness and connectedness, problem-focused family coping skills, clear family organization and decision making, and direct communication among family members regarding the chronic disease. But many others develop hostility, criticism, perfectionism and rigidity and, in many cases, psychopathology (Fisher, Karen & Weihs, 2000). These negative behaviours operate pathological changes in the immunological and hormonal systems of elderly persons with chronic diseases and their families through homeostatic adjustments and increases in allostatic load (Vitaliano, Young & Zhang, 2004).

On the other hand, *"the distress that family caregivers experience may affect their ability to care for the patient"* (Weitzner *et al.*, 1999: 55). According to these authors, caregiving has a considerable impact on the caregiver's quality of life because informal caregivers experience increased symptoms of anxiety, insomnia, depression, organic disturbances associated with psychological distress, restrictions of roles and activities, strain in marital relations and poor health perception. Brito (2002) carried out a study with a sample of 41 Portuguese caregivers of the elderly. It was observed that 29.3% of the caregivers showed symptoms of mild depression and 26.8% showed signs of moderate or severe depression. In fact, caring for an elderly family member with chronic illness at home create a chronic stress with adverse effects on the caregivers (Grunfeld *et al.*, 1997). On the other hand, the family caregivers have substantial financial losses associated with the caregiving, direct out-of-pocket expenses and lost wages because of time taken off work.

These research data point out for the need to implement support services for the family caregivers (Hirschfeld, 2003) based on the identification of the instrumental resources necessary to manage a person with a chronic disease at home, on the determination of the type and size of the burden involved and on the assessment of the behaviours leading to successful management of overwhelming stress.

In Portugal there are few studies on elderly persons with chronic illness and their families. For this reason, one of the authors (Rosa Martins) decided to study empirically the problem of elderly people, their families and chronic diseases. To conduct this research, the author chose the region of Viseu, in the centre and interior region of Portugal (Figure 1), because it is, as Gomes (2000) states, a region situated on the brim of the oppositions seaside/interior and north/south, with visible asymmetries and inequalities (characteristic of interior areas), producing negative impacts on the lives of the people.

Seeing the "quality of life of the elderly" as a multidimensional concept referenced to social-normative and intra-personal criteria (Veríssimo, 2006), linked with current, past and prospective relationships between the elderly person and his/her environment, as well as with the chronic illnesses and their limitations (Haas, 2007; Felce & Perry, 1995), our research problem is enunciated by these four questions:

What kind and with which frequency do the elderly people of Viseu show chronic illnesses?

What quality of life do the elderly people of Viseu show?

Do the elderly who live in their homes show better quality of life than those who are institutionalized?

Amongst several factors (personal, situational, leisure activities, family relationships, social support, economical situation, health/disease situation and degree of autonomy/dependence,) is the family going to have a predictive value of the quality of life of the elderly?

Figure 1. Map of Portugal with the Districts of Viseu and Coimbra highlighted.

1. METHODS

Objectives

Taking into account our research question, we have defined the following objectives:

1. Characterise socio-demographically the elderly population of the region of Viseu;
2. Compare a group of elderly people living at home with a group of elderly people living in residential institutions;

3. Characterise the chronic illnesses of this group and the perception that elderly people have of familiar and social support;
4. Assess the levels of functional independence in the performance of daily activities and instrumental activities;
5. Characterise the quality of life of the group of elderly people living at home and institutionalised;
6. Assess the relative role of the family in predicting the quality of life of the population under study.

Variables

In our study, the dependent variable (criterion variable) is the «quality of life of elderly persons». To define it, we adopted some operational criteria (according to WHO and the Portuguese Government):

*   Elderly person – "Every person aged 65 years-old or more".
*   Quality of Life – "It is the individual or group's perception that their necessities are met and that no opportunities to reach a state of happiness and personal fulfilment are denied, in search of a quality of existence above mere survival".

Obviously, the quality of life will have an inverse relation with the presence of chronic illness and with the perception of the suffering and limitations resulting from them. For that reason, we will use an instrument for assessment of the quality of life that comprises items related to chronic illnesses and their limitations (Haas, 2007).

According to the objectives and revised literature, the independent variables (factors) in our study are: age, gender, marital status, education, retirement situation, economic resources, living at own home (or with family) or in protected institutions, living conditions at home, perception of own health/illness condition, dependency/autonomy levels in performing daily activities, leisure occupational activities, perception about the relationship with family relatives, and social support.

Hypotheses

We hypothesise that:

3. The elderly people from Viseu have chronic illnesses that are similar to the ones referred in the literature and with similar frequencies.
4. The group of elderly people that live at home have higher levels of quality of life than the group of elderly people that are institutionalised.
5. The group of elderly people that live at home have lower levels of functional dependence in performing daily activities than the group of elderly people that are institutionalised.

6. The level of family functionality is a significant predictor of the level of quality of life in elderly people.

Table 1. Structure of the Questionnaire

Study domains	Section	Questions
Personal factors	I	1 – 7
Situational factors in HOME group	IIa)	1 – 8
Situational factors in INST group	IIb)	1 – 11
Health perception	III	1 – 23
(In)dependence in daily life activities (Katz Index)	IV	1 – 6
Leisure activities (Leisure Index)	V	1 – 9
Perception of current life	VI	1 – 4
Perception of future life and necessities	VII	1 – 10
Social support (Social Support Scale)	VIII	1 – 16
Family functioning (Family Apgar)	IX	1 – 5
Quality of Life (Assessment scale of QOL)	X	1 - 7

Materials

We used a questionnaire elaborated by us, including several scales adapted to the Portuguese population. The questionnaire is composed by some items common to the two different sub-groups (HOME – the group living at home; INST – institutionalized group) and other items specific to each sub-group (Table 1).

Section I: *Socio-demographic factors*
This section contains seven questions, of which six are closed and one is open. It provides personal information, such as age, sex, marital status, education, economic situation, retirement situation and level of satisfaction with the pension value.

Section II a): *Situational factors of the HOME group*
This section assesses the situational characteristics of the elderly group that lives at home. These characteristics include housing, with who does the elderly usually lives, number of descendants and their place of residence. There are eight questions in this section, from which seven are closed with various response alternatives, and one is open, being related to the number of descendants, which is later transformed into an interval variable.

Section II b): *Situational factors of the INST group*
It consists of eleven questions, three open and eight closed, to assess the residential context of the elderly person: the motives for becoming a resident, who took the initiative, timing and preferences, perception of the institutional relationships (residents and staff), privacy, food, visits, exits and level of satisfaction with the residential institution.

Section III: *Health perception*

It is a scale about health perception (which already existed), and five additional questions pertaining to health vigilance. Regarding health perception, the referred scale ("Minha Saúde" – "My Health" – adapted to the Portuguese population by Ribeiro, 1993) consists of eighteen 5-points Likert scale, which assesses the general health perception. The scores can oscillate between 18 and 90, with the average global score for the Portuguese population being 62.73 (SD=9.16) for men, and 61.07 (SD=8.96) for women. The higher the obtained score, the better is the individual's health perception. It has four factors: "perception of current health" (PCH), "perception of past health" (PPH), "concerns with health" (CH), and "concerns about going to the doctor" (CGD). The five additional questions assess the quantity of medication that the individuals take daily, the costs of that medication, the annual number of doctor appointments, the reasons for not going if that is the case, and the diseases that most afflict them.

Section IV: *Assessment scale of daily life activities (Katz Index)*

The scale of daily life activities (modified Katz index, Katz, Downs, Cash and Grotz, 1970; Katz and Akpom, 1976) assesses the degree of dependence/autonomy of the elderly person: the bath, getting dressed, going to the toilet, mobility, continence, and feeding. The scoring varies between 0 and 6, allowing to rank the individuals in three groups: those with scores 0-2 are classified as "important dependency", scores 3-4 are "partial dependency", and scores 5-6 are considered "independency".

Section V: *Index of leisure activities*

This section includes nine questions that assess the activities of reading, watching TV, listening to music, going for a walk, gardening, horticulture, knitting, card playing, and talking with friends, with 5 alternative answers. The scoring of the index varies between 0 and 36, and we have defined three groups ($\overline{X}$ ± SD): none or few leisure activities (scores 0 to 15.71), moderate number of leisure activities (scores 17.72 to 28.29) and many leisure activities (scores higher than 28.29).

Section VI: *Perception of current life*

Section VI consists of four questions, three closed and one mixed ("do you like to live?", "how do you feel in relation to the way you lived before?", "what pleases you most in life?" and "do you feel discouraged in relation to life?") and is related to the perception that the elderly person has about his/her current life.

Section VII: *How the elderly person faces the future and felt necessities*

This section consists of 10 open and closed questions. It assesses the feelings of the elderly people towards the present, the future and their perceived needs: what they consider necessary to improve their daily life; if they schedule tasks and make plans for the future; how they face the possibility of a serious illness and/or death; if they feel sadness and loneliness; how do they feel that elderly people should be taken care of, and also what are the biggest problems that the elderly person faces.

Section VIII: *Perception of social support*

The social support scale (SSS) was developed by Matos and Ferreira (2000), with 16 Likert-type questions. The scoring varies between 16 and 80, with the averages score for the Portuguese population being 64.87 (SD=8.32). It has and alpha of Cronbach of 0.849 for a sample of 214 individuals and a test-retest correlation of 0.957, for a minimum interval of one month. It has three factors (49.88% of shared variance): information support, emotional support and instrumental support.

Section IX: *Perception of family relationships*

To assess family functionality, we used a family Apgar scale developed by Smilkstein (1978) and adapted to the Portuguese population by Azeredo (1998), with five questions that assess the quality of the relationships between the individuals and their family relatives. The global result in this scale is obtained by adding the scores attributed to each of the questions, and it varies between 0 and 10. A global score between 7 and 10 in indicative of a "highly functional family"; scores between 4 and 6 are indicative of a "family with moderate dysfunction", and scores between 0 and 3 indicate a "family highly dysfunctional". We also included an additional question related to the periodicity of the visits of the family relatives and friends, given that we verified that this was an issue that the individuals associated to their assessment of the family relationships.

Section X: *Assessment scale of the quality of life of the elderly person*

To determine the quality of life we used the assessment scale to calculate the IQL index (Instrumental Quality of Life) that was proposed and tested in the Portuguese population by the General Health Division (Direcção Geral de Saúde, 1995). The scale assesses seven basic components of adult life: (1) affective and social isolation/communication; (2) mobility; (3) daily life activities; (4) occupational activities; (5) leisure activities; (6) family relationship; and (7) financial resources. Each of these components is divided in classes with scores that vary between 0 and 8, with the IQL index varying between the minimum score of 3 and the maximum score of 50. There is quality of life with scores equal or greater than 23.

Participants

We selected our participants through a convenience sampling method. To calculate the number of subjects we used the formula to finite populations:

$$n = \frac{\sigma^2 p.q.N}{e^2(N-1) + \sigma^2 p.q}$$

n = sample size; σ^2 = number of standard deviations; p = % of observable phenomena; q = additional %; N = population size; e^2 = maximum error allowed.

Considering that in 2001 the elderly population of the district of Viseu consisted of 69,790 persons (INE, 2001; INE, 2002) and that this age group corresponds to 17% of the total population, the equation to calculate the sample is as follows:

$$n = \frac{4 \times 17 \times .83 \times 69790}{9 \times (69790 - 1) + 4 \times 17 \times 83}$$

$$n = 622$$

Accepting a confidence level of 95% (two deviations) and an error of up to 3%, the sample should include a minimum of 622 elderly persons. As inclusion criterion, the participants' age should be 65 years old or more, and they should be able to participate in the interview process (being able to answer the questions verbally and to orient themselves in space and time).

Our sample includes 673 elderly persons, 336 living at home (HOME group) and the remaining 337 living in residential institutions (INST group). From the total sample, 56.8 % is female and only 43.2 % is male. The predominance of females is accentuated in the institutionalised group, which is consistent with the national statistical data published by INE (1999).

The average age is 77 years old (minimum 65 and maximum 100 years-old), the median is 77, the mode is 69 and the standard deviation is 7.3 years. In the HOME group, the average is slightly lower (75 years old, median 74, mode 69 and standard deviation 6.9 years). The higher percentage of elderly people belongs to the first age group (65-75) for the HOME group (49.4 %) and to the second age group (75-85) for the group INST (45.1 %). Still for the INST group, there are a significant number of elderly people (18.4 %) that occupy the third age group (85-94).

Regarding the marital status, being a widower is the most common in our sample (mode = widower) with 52.3 %, followed by married with 32.2 %, and in third place are the single persons, with 13.7 %. Analysing the marital status by groups, we find some differences: thus, the majority of the elderly persons of the HOME group are married (48.2 %) and widowers (12.3 %), whereas in the INST group, the majority (62.3 %) are widowers and 19.6 % are single. Despite being a small percentage, it is worth noting that there are 12 cases of divorce in our sample, which reinforces the divulged idea that in the 90's, the divorce rates in elderly people in Portugal had a positive evolution, both for men and women (INE, 1999). With regard to the marital status as a function of gender, we verified that the higher frequency of the married status belongs to the men (20.1 %), whereas 35.4 % of the women are widowers. As we referred previously, these results are also in accordance with the released national characteristics.

The low education level of the elements of our sample is a notorious characteristic: 42.1 % are illiterate (the mode), 27.7 % "know how to read and write", and 24.7 % have four years of education. These results were not surprising, given that they are consistent with the statistical data published in 2001 about the Portuguese elderly population.

Concerning the economic situation, 71.5 % of the elderly people in our sample earn a monthly income between 200 and 350€, 14.1 % earn less than 200€, and the remaining people receive higher values. The individuals in the HOME group report lower monthly incomes.

For the majority of the elderly people, the monthly income derives from retirement pensions. In both groups, the majority of the individuals receive a pension for reaching the retirement age limit (45.5 % in the HOME group and 49.6 % in the INST group). The "social pension" (from the non-contributory scheme) represents the second type of retirement pension, also in both groups, followed by the "infirmity pension". 8.6 % of the individuals receive a pension for death of spouse. Consistent with previous data, 72.4 % of the respondents manifest themselves dissatisfied with the pension values, but it is in the HOME group that the dissatisfaction (83.3 %) acquires greater relevance.

With regard to housing and its characteristics in the HOME group, the majority (75.9 %) lives in their own private house, mostly detached or semi-detached houses (90.5 %), with staircases (83.6 %) and sanitation, water and electricity (84.5 %) (Table 2). These results are in line with data released by INE (2001) which refers that the majority of the elderly live in independent houses (with spacious areas), but have worse infrastructures than the remaining population.

Analysing the answers to the question "with who do you usually live?" (Table 3), the majority lives with the spouse (44.6 %) or alone (28.9 %). Only 21.4 % live with their descendants. In reality, there is still a significant number of elderly persons living alone. However, the majority lives amidst of the so-called "traditional families", which reinforces the theory that these continue to be a relevant (informal) support group. Considering that the support that sons and daughters can give to their progenitors depends more on the proximity of the residence than on their number, we found that 32.1 % of the inquired have their sons/daughters living in the same village/town, 18,5% in the same district and 24.8 % in the same country. As expected, as a result of the strong migration flows that took place in previous decades, 10.1% of the elderly have descendants living abroad.

Table 2. Housing characteristics of the HOME group

	Male		Female		Total sample	
	N	%	N	%	N	%
HOUSING						
Own	123	80.4	132	72.1	155	75.9
Rented	15	9.8	24	13.1	39	11.6
Lent	15	9.8	27	14.8	42	12.5
TYPE						
Detached /Semi-det.	143	93.5	161	88.0	304	90.5
Flat	8	5.2	18	9.8	26	7.7
Room	2	1.3	4	2.2	6	1.8
STAIRCASES						
Yes	123	80.4	158	86.3	281	83.6
No	30	19.6	25	13.7	55	16.4
SANITATION						
Yes	128	83.7	156	85.2	284	84.5
No	25	16.3	27	14.8	52	15.5
Total	**153**	**100.0**	**183**	**100.0**	**336**	**100.0**

Table 3. Characteristics of the household of the HOME group

	Male		Female		Total sample	
	N	%	N	%	N	%
Usually lives with:						
Spouse	101	66.0	49	26.8	150	44.6
Son/daughter	24	15.7	48	26.2	72	21.4
Brother/sister	5	3.3	8	4.4	13	3.9
Friends	0	0.0	4	2.2	4	1.2
Alone	23	15.0	74	40.4	97	28.9
Number of descendants						
No descendants	13	8.5	36	19.7	49	14.5
1 to 3	81	52.9	88	48.1	169	50.3
4 to 6	50	32.7	44	24.0	94	28.0
7 to 9	9	5.9	7	3.8	16	4.8
10 or more	0	0.0	8	4.4	8	2.4
Residence of descendants						
No descendants	13	8.5	36	19.7	49	14.5
Same village/town	41	26.8	67	36.6	108	32.1
Same district	22	14.4	40	21.8	62	18.5
Same country	56	36.6	27	14.8	83	24.8
Abroad	21	13.7	13	7.1	34	10.1
Total	**153**	**100.0**	**183**	**100.0**	**336**	**100.0**

To the question "if you live alone, who does usually visit you?" the majority (58.6 %) chooses to not answer; 19.6 % says that they are visited by their sons/daughters, followed by brothers/sisters, close relatives, neighbours and friends (for 18.2 % of them). 3.6 % says that nobody visits them.

In the group of elderly living in residential institutions (INST group), 33,5 % attributes the institutionalisation to the difficulty in taking care of themselves (this reason being prevalent in the females), 28.8 % refers that it was their own choice to live in an institution, despite having family, and 13.4 % said they did it because they lacked family support. Not having family or not having a good family relationship (only for men) was the central motive for institutionalisation in 9.2 % of the elderly. The lack of economic resources and housing conditions are also reasons given by 13.3% of the elderly. Noting the reasons given by the respondents as a function of gender, we find that the choice for institutionalisation is more linked to family reasons and lack of economic resources for men, whereas women's choices are more related to incapacity in self-care and poor housing conditions.

The initiative for the internment was attributed to the elderly in 64.1 % (216) of the cases. 31.5 % (106) were brought to the institution by relatives, and unlike the results from other studies (Santos, 1995), only 3 persons were institutionalised by intervention of social service workers. Regarding the duration of the internment, we observed that more than half of the elderly in this sample (75.3 %) have been in the institution for less than 6 years (with a prevalence of 2 to 4 years) and only 5.1 % of the participants have a period of permanence in the residence larger than 12 years.

Table 4. Aspects related to the internment that were mentioned by the elderly

	Male		Female		Total Sample	
	N	%	N	%	N	%
Motives						
Difficulty in self-care	22	15.9	91	45.8	113	33.5
Lack of economic resources	17	12.3	3	1.5	20	5.9
Lack of housing conditions	9	6.5	16	8.0	25	7.4
No family	12	8.7	13	6.5	25	7.4
Bad relationship with family	6	4.4	0	0.0	6	1.8
Lack of family support	24	17.4	21	10.6	45	13.4
Preference for the residence	42	30.4	55	27.6	97	28.8
Health difficulties	6	4.4	0	0.0	6	1.8
Iniciative						
Auto-initiative	88	63.8	128	64.3	216	64.1
Family	44	31.9	62	31.2	106	31.5
Friends	6	4.3	6	3.0	12	3.6
Social workers	-	-	3	1.5	3	0.9
Duration (years)						
0 – 2	27	19.6	51	25.6	78	23.2
2 - 4	34	24.6	78	39.2	112	33.2
4 – 6	30	21.7	34	17.1	64	19.0
6 – 8	8	5.8	12	6.1	20	5.9
8 - 10	12	8.7	9	4.5	21	6.2
10 -12	15	10.9	10	5.0	25	7.4
≥ 12	12	8.7	5	2.5	17	5.1
Preferred residence						
With relatives / friends	28	20.3	42	21.1	70	20.7
Own house	80	58.0	149	74.9	229	68.0
Day care centres	30	21.7	8	4.0	38	11.3
Total	**138**	**100.0**	**199**	**100.0**	**337**	**100.0**

Various authors have described the entry into homes for the elderly as being a mix of voluntary and compulsory (Townsend, 1981). Thus, we asked them "if you could live somewhere else, what would be your choice?". The answers that we obtained, which are shown in Table 4 demonstrate that the majority (68.0 %) of the elderly would go back to their own house, 20.7 % would choose to live with relatives and friends, and there is still a small group (11.3 %) that would prefer to go to day care centres. Comparing the answers as a function of gender, we note that the female preferences are more related to the house (seeing in it their privileged place of well-being and security), whereas men were divided between home and day care centres (where sociability and leisure are more intense).

Regarding the perception of the elderly about their experiences in the institution, 50.4 % (170) considers that the workers in the centre are quite concerned with them, and 24.6 % (83) considers that they are really very concerned. The relationships that they maintain with the other residents are perceived by the majority (64.7 %) as "good". 24.3 % consider that they are "very good" and only 10.4 % thinks that they are "not good or bad". Regarding the relationships they establish with the staff of the centre, 62.9 % of the elderly classify it as "good", 27.0 % as "very good" and the rest of the residents evaluate it in a less positive way. In respect to privacy, 35.0 % of the residents thinks it is "not good nor bad", 3.6 % classified it as "bad" and "very bad", and the remaining individuals considers that privacy is "good" or "very good". Concerning the "isolation from the exterior world", 33.2 % of the inquired leaves the institution weekly, 32.0 % leaves monthly and the remaining (34.8 %) leave less often, which in some way confirms the isolation previously referred. Women remain in the centre for longer periods and leave less frequently. Still in the institutionalised group, for 24.9 % of the elderly there is nothing that displeases them in the centre, 19 % feel and suffer from "missing their relatives and friends", and 13.4 % refers lack of autonomy.

Thus, the majority of the difficulties manifested by the institutionalised elderly group are from the personal and affective domain (lack of relatives, friends, personal objects and privacy). Globally, the mentioned dissatisfaction reinforces, in our opinion, the view defended by Paúl (1997) that the institutions for the elderly withdraw (in many cases) the privacy of their users and subject them to the control and dependence on the internal rules.

Procedures

We have sent several letters to the entities responsible for some residential homes for the elderly, from which we mention the following: *Provedoria das Misericórdias de Viseu* (which are responsible for the *Lar de Acolhimento de Idosos de São Caetano* and *Residência Rainha D. Leonor de Viseu*), and the Residential Homes for the Elderly of Mangualde, Penalva do Castelo, Santa Comba Dão and Vouzela. These letters requested permission to apply the data collection instruments to the elderly living the institution. Similarly, permission was sought from the Directorate of the Health Sub-Region of Viseu, to collect data on the Health Centres One and Two of Viseu, Mangualde, Tondela, Santa Comba, Penalva do Castelo and Vouzela from elderly persons living in their own houses. In these requests, we indicated the name of the person responsible for the research project, explained the objectives and interests of the study, guaranteed confidentiality regarding the results, and promised to avoid disruption in the operation of services and institutions. We obtained informed consent from the elderly to participate in this research. The interviews took place during a period of 4 months, in the institutions indicated above.

Data Analysis

We used descriptive and analytical statistics: absolute frequencies (N) and percentages (%), means (M), medians (Md), modes (Mo), standard deviations (SD) and variation coefficients (cv). Regarding analytical statistics, we determined the Pearson correlation coefficients (r) and carried out t-tests to compare means, multiple regression analyses using the stepwise method, analysis of variance for independent samples and Tuckey tests. Statistical analysis was carried out with the software SPSS (Statistical Package for the Social Sciences) and Excel for Windows.

Table 5. Chronic illnesses

	Home		Institution		Total sample	
	N	%	N	%	N	%
Oncologic	56	16.7	40	11.9	96	14.3
Blindness	17	5.1	17	5.0	34	5.1
Deafness	8	2.4	79	23.4	87	12.9
Infirmity	19	5.7	50	14.8	69	10.3
All kinds	27	8.0	56	16.6	83	12.3
Stroke	68	20.2	15	4.5	83	12.3
Diabetes	9	2.7	8	2.4	17	2.5
Rheumatism	39	11.6	33	9.8	72	10.7
Varicose veins	16	4.8	20	5.9	36	5.3
Hypertension	32	9.5	3	9.0	35	5.2
Osteoporosis	4	1.2	-	-	4	0.6
Psychological	8	2.4	-	-	8	1.2
Anaemia	6	1.8	-	-	6	0.9
None	6	1.8	-	-	6	0.9
No answer	21	6.3	16	4.7	37	5.5
Total	**336**	**100.0**	**337**	**100.0**	**673**	**100.0**

2. RESULTS

In the first hypothesis, we admitted that *the elderly from Viseu have chronic illnesses and respective frequencies similar to the ones reported in the literature*. The chronic illnesses most frequently reported by the elderly belonging to HOME group are (1) strokes, (2) cancer, (3) arthritis, and (4) hypertension. In the INST group, the most frequent illnesses are mainly deafness and cancer (Table 5). Overall, these results are in agreement with what various authors point out as the prevailing illnesses in this age group (Wolff, Starfield & Anderson, 2002).

The *number of medicines* consumed is related to the illnesses that afflict them: 19.4 % of the respondents take 6 or more different medicines per day, 18.7% takes 2 different medicines per day, and 29.5 % take daily 3 to 4 medicines. The elderly in the INST group are the ones that take more medication (Table 6). A relevant aspect also related to the intake of medication is the amount of money spent monthly: the majority (64.4%) does not know exactly how much they spend. This is an understandable situation, given that in some institutions this task is assumed by the staff, and in the case of the elderly that live with their relatives, these are the ones doing it. This situation represents a paradox, in the sense that, while the largest expenses are reported by the elderly people living at home, the largest number of medication is consumed by the institutionalised group. The explanation for this probably lies in the fact that the residents in institutions do not control the expenses themselves.

Approximately half of the elderly from our sample (49.6%) goes to an average of seven of more medical appointments per year, being also the INST group the one that seeks consultations more often. Regarding the hypothesis that *the elderly living at home have higher quality of life than the elderly that are institutionalised*, independent samples t-tests suggest that the HOME group shows in fact higher levels of quality of life (M= 33.29; SD= 9.63) than the INST group (M= 31.65; SD= 9.72), and these differences are statistically significant (t = 2.201; p = 0.028), confirming our hypothesis. Moreover, these results agree with findings from other studies (Griffin & McKenna, 1998).

The *affective and social relationships* that were evaluated show that from 673 elderly people in the region of Aveiro, 34.2% considers to have a functional family integration, 47.4% perceive an emotional and social link involving an aid relationship, and 18.4% refer not having any relation with their relatives. The elderly from the HOME group are those that report a better family relationship.

The *economic resources* reported by our participants show that, in fact, many of the elderly in Viseu live close to the poverty limit, given that 23.3% considers that the amount of money that they have available per month is not sufficient and therefore it does not meet their basic needs. The great majority (66.3%) classifies their economic situation as sufficient and only 10.4% declares having an economic situation beyond their basic needs. Even though there is a larger number of elderly in the HOME group reporting insufficient funds, the difference between the two groups is negligible.

Table 6. Characteristics of medical care in the two elderly groups

	Home		Institution		Total Sample	
	N.º	%	N.º	%	N.º	%
Quantity of medication						
Does not take	51	15.2	36	10.7	87	12.9
One	37	11.0	21	6.2	58	8.6
Two	73	21.7	53	15.7	126	18.7
Three	60	17.9	40	11.9	100	14.9
Four	40	11.9	58	17.2	98	14.6
Five	16	4.8	14	4.2	30	4.5
Six or more	59	17.6	115	34.1	174	19.4
Expenses with medication						
None	36	10.7	44	13.1	80	11.9
Does not know exactly	127	37.8	239	55.8	336	64.4
< 25 €	83	24.7	9	2.7	92	13.7
25 to 100 €	84	25.0	36	10.7	120	17.8
> 100 €	6	1.8	9	2.7	15	2.2
Nr. of consultations /year						
Does not go to consultations	23	6.8	9	2.7	32	4.8
One to two	56	16.7	21	6.2	77	11.4
Three to four	69	20.5	42	12.5	111	16.5
Five to six	50	14.9	69	20.4	119	17.7
Seven or more	138	41.1	196	58.2	334	49.6
Total	**336**	**100.0**	**337**	**100.0**	**673**	**100.0**

Table 7. Results of the multiple regressions for QOL in the HOME group

Dependent variable – Quality of life of the elderly living at home				
Regression analysis summary				
R	**R²**	**Adjusted R²**	**SE of the estimate**	**R² Change**
0.876	0.768	0.764	4.677	0.005

Analysis of variance					
Source	**S.S.**	**df**	**M.S.**	**F**	**P**
Regression	23,854.547	5	4,770.91	218.083	0.000
Residual	7,219.283	330	21.88		
Total	31,073.830	335			

Coefficients				
Model	**B**	**β**	**t**	**P**
(Constant)	-7.717	-	-5.071	0.000
Informational support	1.522	0.750	24.291	0.000
Leisure activities	0.202	0.140	4.614	0.000
(In)dependence in DLA	0.617	0.094	3.329	0.001
Perception past health	0.314	0.072	2.621	0.009

Regarding the hypothesis that *the elderly living at home have less functional dependence in performing their daily life activities*, statistical analysis demonstrated that the elderly from the HOME group show higher levels of independence – Katz index (M = 5.37; SD = 1.46) than the INST group (M = 4.70; SD = 1.58), and this difference is highly significant (t = 5.639; p = 0.000).

Daily life activities (considered essential to life quality maintenance and the wellbeing of the individual) are performed autonomously by 55.4% of the elderly. The remaining individuals manage to perform them with technical help (24.1%) and with the help of others (11.3%). It is noteworthy that 9.2% of our sample is totally unable to perform these activities. In this matter, as in the previous ones, we still observed greater levels of dependence in the INST group.

Cultural and leisure activities are observed only in 23.8% of the cases. For 45.3%, leisure activities are practiced regularly and 30.9% refers not practicing that kind of activity. Contrary to what has been observed for the anterior components, leisure activities are more common in the INST group (which is understandable, if we consider that these are part of the "established programs" in these care centres).

Regarding the hypothesis that *family functionality predicts the quality of life of the elderly*, in the regression model only the factors informational support (from social support), leisure activities, independence in daily life activities (DLA) and past health perception (PHP) emerged as significant. Thus, the variable family functionality was excluded from the model, given that it was not a significant predictor of the quality of life. The correlation coefficient for the HOME group is 0.876, and the proportion of variance in QOL explained by the model is 76.4% (Table 7). The regression equation has a highly significant predictive ability (p=0.000) and the standardised beta coefficients suggest that the elderly that show higher levels in the variables included in the model are those that tend to show better levels of quality of life.

Table 8. Results of the multiple regression for QOL in the INST group

Dependent variable – Quality of life of the institutionalised elderly					
Regression analysis summary					
R	**R²**	**Adjusted R²**	**SE of the estimate**		**R² Change**
0.881	0.777	0.774	4.624		0.003
Analysis of variance					
Source	**S.S.**	**df**	**M.S.**	**F**	**P**
Regression	24,648.086	5	4,929.62	218.083	0.000
Residual	7,076.293	331	21.38		
Total	31,724.380	336			
Coefficients					
Model	**B**	**β**		**t**	**P**
(Constant)	-20.006	-		-6.168	0.000
Informational support	1.446	0.680		22.762	0.000
Leisure activities	1.678	0.273		9.588	0.000
(In)dependence in DLA	0.280	0.121		4.161	0.000
Perception past health	0.255	0.055		2.012	0.045

Table 9. Results of the multiple regressions for QOL in the total sample

Dependent variable – Quality of life of the elderly from the total sample					
Regression analysis summary					
R	**R²**	**Adjusted R²**	**SE of the estimate**		**R² Change**
0.875	0.765	0.763	4.722		0.002
Analysis of variance					
Source	**S.S.**	**df**	**M.S.**	**F**	**P**
Regression	48,401.402	6	8,066.90	361.780	0.000
Residual	14,850.340	666	22.30		
Total	63,251.741	672			
Coefficients					
Model	**B**	**β**		**t**	**P**
(Constant)	-13.633	-		-5.732	0.000
Informational support	1.496	0.720		33.170	0.000
Leisure activities	1.071	0.172		8.519	0.000
(In)dependence in DLA	0.209	0.125		5.725	0.000
Perception past health	0.336	0.075		3.846	0.000

In the case of the institutionalised elderly, as we can see in Table 8, the results were slightly different from the HOME group. The observed correlation coefficient is 0.881 and the variance in QOL explained by the model is 77.4%. The variable with higher predictive value was also factor 1 (informational support) from social support, explaining 68.0% of the

QOL variance in the INST group, followed by the independence level to perform DLA, leisure activities and finally the factor PSP from health with 5.5%. The variable family functionality was again a non-significant predictor in this model. The regression equation has again a highly significant predictive value (p=0.000) and the standardised beta coefficients indicate that the higher the informational support, independence in DLA, leisure activities and past health perception, the better the quality of life.

The multiple regression analysis for the total sample (Table 9) shows that, similarly to what was observed before, the family functionality is still not a predictor of the QOL in the elderly. The regression coefficient is 0.875 and the proportion of QOL that is explained by the model is 76.3%. This is again a highly significant regression equation (p=0.000) and the standardised beta coefficients lead us to think that the higher the levels of the independent variables that entered the regression model, the higher is the quality of life that the elderly enjoy.

Thus, we conclude that the hypothesis regarding the variable family functionality is rejected.

3. DISCUSSION

The analysis of the distribution of elderly people through age groups and living place suggests that elderly people who live at home are predominantly of the lower age group (65-74 years old), while the elderly that are institutionalized tend to be older, on average. These data strengthen the theoretical supposition that, as age increases, the elderly population living in institutions raises significantly (Townsend, 1981).

Widower is the most representative marital status (52.3%) in our sample. The family dissolution, essentially by death of one of the members of the couple, acquires in this population group a growing importance that is not seen in younger age groups (Ekerdt et al., 2004). On the other hand, the HOME elderly group are mainly married, while the institutionalized are essentially widowers and single. These data reinforce the idea that institutionalization is primarily a solution for the elderly with no family or for those who suffer from isolation (in the inexistence of an interaction network). There are more married males and more female widowers, which is also in conformity with the national statistics, since the wedding rates of elderly people are higher in men (second marriages) and the widower condition is higher in women.

The low levels of school education observed in our sample did not surprise us, since the national data show "that most of the elderly population did not complete any level of formal instruction". Moreover, the illiteracy rates in the region of Viseu in 2001 were around 15.3%. The "illiteracy", predominantly feminine, is also understandable in the socio-cultural framework that prevailed in our society for a large number of years.

The economic situation of the majority (71.5%) of the elderly people in the region of Viseu suggests that there are a great number of people on the threshold of poverty. Having monthly incomes around 200 and 350€ means not having the economic capacity to satisfy the basic needs and to live with dignity. These basic needs are, in many cases, worsened by the additional expenses associated with chronic illnesses. The costs of the internment in institutions are high and between 22 and 70 hours per week are spent in caregiving at home with patients with Parkinson and Alzheimer's disease (Wolff, Starfield & Anderson, 2002).

The retirement pensions are the most important component of the incomes of elderly people. The largest group (47.5%) has a retirement pension that results from the age limit (of the contributory regime). There is also a significant proportion of income that results from social pensions and from the death of the spouse, mainly in the case of females. These data are also in agreement with the social politics that were in use in previous decades. Women had mostly domestic activities for which they received no income, being therefore exposed to economic frailties with strong implications for their quality of life.

The dissatisfaction with the pension values was a feeling expressed by 72.4% of the enquired elderly, which was predictable, bearing in mind the amount of money that most of them earn. The predominance of dissatisfaction in the HOME group is also understandable, since this group is faced with an increased range of expenses (for example, the maintenance of the dwelling, equipment, and so on) which do not constitute reason for concern for those who are institutionalized.

Analysing the information about the family setting of the elderly, we conclude that 44.6% live with a spouse and 21.4% live with their direct descendants. Men live mostly with the spouse while a higher number of women live alone, which we once again think might be related with the shorter life expectancy of men and definitive female celibacy. Most of the elderly who live alone remained silent when asked about whom usually visits them, which suggests (as many authors refer) that there is a diminution of the relationship circle. Nevertheless, the direct descendants, close relatives and friends still constitute an important network of social support that goes from emotional support, opportunity to socialize and even material support (Paúl, 1997).

The conclusive aspects of many studies on the institutionalization of elderly people take us to the idea of dwellings for a marginalized old age, as the last form of managing elderly age for most of the guests and, therefore, entering these institutions when it is no longer possible to live somewhere else (Paúl, 1997).

The results of our study show a broader perspective and diverge from what has been said in some aspects. As an example, we can see that some of the reasons pointed out by the elderly regarding the motives for institutionalization are related to the difficulties in the self-care, lack of family support (whether having family or not), inexistence of good housing conditions and lack of economic resources. However, the second largest percentage of answers (28.8%) attributes this choice solely to their personal preference for living in an institution. These are data that reflect the existence of different social views about institutions, which are no longer necessarily associated with negative aspects, but are regarded as a residential alternative which can bring advantages to the elderly. From this point of view, it is understandable that 64.1% of the elderly people went to the institution on their own initiative. Nevertheless, 31.5% holds the family responsible for the decision, suggesting that, in these cases, entering the institution was a "mix of voluntary and compulsory" (Paúl, 1997).

Even though many of the elderly people stated that they entered the institution on their own initiative, when questioned about their favourite place of living (with equal conditions), the majority does not hesitate to answer "in my own home" or "in the house of my relatives". These results are in accordance with those of Gomes (2000) when this author refers that among the elderly "it was said vehemently that as long as they could, they would continue with their lives at home, the institution being only a faraway alternative and only for when they could not take care of themselves". It was curious to see that the elderly have favourable opinions regarding the institutions. They frequently said sentences such as "they are very good to us" or "they help us a lot". These evaluations reinforce the idea defended by Fernandes (1995) that, currently, the institutions are already concerned with the training of their staff.

The isolation from the external environment, which is so frequently associated with living in an institution, is still present in the opinions of the elderly from our sample: of the 337 elderly persons that are institutionalized, 33.2% leaves the institution every week, and about 30% do it only on a monthly basis. The rest of the elderly answered that they leave the institution in alternatives that range from every 3 months to one year. This scenario reinforces the view of Goffman (cit. by Born & Boechat, 2002) which considers the institutions as "clusters of individuals in a similar situation, separated from the society (…) and which lead a closed and formally administrated life". The commentary we feel we need to make, when faced with the set of concerns and problems expressed by the elderly people, is that, if on the one hand we see the structural and conceptual changes in some residential centres for the elderly (as mentioned before), on the other hand, there is still in some centres the symptoms of depersonalized mass, places that gather in the same location individuals of different age groups, different beliefs and education, and with problems of diverse origins.

Regarding the self-characterization of the health profile made by the elderly we have enquired, the HOME group show greater levels of health than the institutionalized elderly. This piece of information is easily explained if we bear in mind, on the one hand, that the age average of the INST group (78 years old) is higher and, on the other hand, that the institutionalization is in many cases due to the difficulties of the family in taking care of an elderly with chronic illness. The diseases that concern the elderly the most are distributed across a wide range of pathologies (Wolff, Starfield & Anderson, 2002). Nevertheless, the oncologic diseases, the brain vascular diseases, arthritis and a cocktail of several illnesses stand out the most. These diseases, even though with certain specificities that are characteristic of this geographical and cultural context, are broadly consistent with those described by several authors as the "most prevailing in individuals of this age group" (Ermida, 1999; Isaacs, 2000).

Nevertheless, we should not underestimate the feelings expressed by 13.7% of the elderly that state that they "don't like to live". In these expressions there is also the underlying presence of the "black filters" that society nowadays is giving to the elderly, inhibiting the perception of the positive aspects, making this stage of life a "period of fears and anguishes" (Reis, 2000). Probably for these very same reasons, there is a significant number of elderly people that feels discouraged before life and shows several levels of (di)satisfaction regarding the way in which their lives unfolded. The fact the HOME elderly are those who most refer that they do not enjoying living is still a paradox. These opinions (and contradictions) lead us to believe that, actually, the adaptation to new situations is influenced by multiple human experiences, by the passing of time, by the strategies chosen, by the crises that they faced throughout life and by the personal strengths that each one has (Berger, 1995).

The "fears and anguishes" usually associated with old age are also visible in our study. In both groups there is the fear of suffering (51.1%) and of bothering others. Nevertheless, it is in the HOME group that these feelings show greater relevance. However, we have to highlight the contrast between the feelings of anger shown by the HOME elderly and the tranquillity expressed by the INST elderly. These data lead us to conclude that, in spite of the separation from their family and social milieu, the institutionalized elderly feel a kind of support that gives them greater stability and less uncertainties regarding the future and the satisfaction of their needs. Another possibility is that the elderly who still live on their own dwellings or with family members do not easily grasp the idea of one day being institutionalized, and, as such, live in the fear of a situation of even greater dependence that will lead them to burden their closest family members even more.

The greater problems that the elderly in both groups are faced with nowadays are, from the least important to the most important, loneliness, low pensions, family rejection and social exclusion (Holmén & Furukawa, 2002). To overcome these negative factors, the elderly suggest that they should be treated with tenderness and respect, patience, humanity and in the best way possible. Further, the elderly add that their daily routines could be improved if better living conditions, such as "more homes for the elderly", "better care", "greater independence", "to do what I like" and "to be able to do what I did at home" (in the INST group) and "better housing conditions and social support" (in the HOME group), were granted to them.

The importance of the family, of the solidarity network and of the interweaving of affections has been pointed out as predictors of living satisfaction in the elderly (Carvalho & Patrícia, 2006). Despite the problems that have recently been felt in family networks, most of our elderly consider their families as highly functional. Regarding the evaluation of the quality of life of the elderly in the region of Viseu, 84.5% express a positive evaluation. The immediate optimism that these results may cause should not undervalue the still significant number of elderly (15.5%) whose perception points out to a life without quality.

Despite the regional specificities that characterise our sample, the data obtained in this study are in accordance with the what has been found (using the same evaluation scale) in other regions of the country (North, Centre and South), being different only in what comes to gender, since in similar studies men are those who are usually found to have a life with higher quality (INE, 2002).

In our sample the elderly who live in their own homes present better levels of quality of live than those who live in institutions. These results are similar to those of other Portuguese studies (Cruz, 2001; Dinis, 1997; Direcção Geral de Saúde, 1995; Gonçalves, 2002) that show that living in their own house and/or with family is a situational variable relevant in the determination of the quality of life of the elderly. Institutionalization takes the elderly away from his/her environment and increases the perception of loss, which is not favourable to life satisfaction. Social support is seen as positive (creating the perception that the elderly are valued and that others care for them) and is a predictor of quality of life, which is also in agreement with other studies that show its undeniable role in the well-being and quality of life (Barron, 1996). Nevertheless, family functionality was not a predictor of the quality of life of the elderly of our sample. However, it is possible that the type of methodology that was used in the present study was not sensitive enough to accurately determine the contribution of this variable. Thus, we should be careful to not completely dismiss the role of the family in the management of the chronic disease in the elderly and to not rule out the possible importance of family functionality to the quality of life of the elderly.

Finally, and even though in this study we have not evaluated the impact of caregiving to the family itself, we mention another study carried out by the first author (Carlos Silva), in the district of Coimbra (see Figure 1), with a Portuguese version of the *Caregiver Reaction Assessment Scale* (Given *et al.*, 1992), and a sample of 112 families of caregivers (elderly persons with arthritis, coronary disease and dementia, aged 65 to 83 years old). Families in this sample obtained an average score of 2.93 in the sub-scale of disruption in the daily activities (SD=0.74), 3.52 in the sub-scale of financial problems (SD=0.46), 1.36 in the sub-scale of absence of family support (SD=0.97), 1.83 in the sub-scale of health problems (SD=0.77) and 3.61 in the sub-scale of self-consideration (SD=0.51). Bearing in mind the mean and standard-deviation values that Nijboer *et al* (1999) found, we can conclude that in this sample from Coimbra, the family caregivers present disruption of the daily activities and financial problems, but also family support, above the average, and health problems and self-consideration problems within the normal range.

CONCLUSIONS

In summary, the majority of the elderly people involved in the present study report a positive assessment of their quality of life. Nonetheless, factors such as loneliness, low retirement pensions, family rejection and social exclusion pose significant threats to this quality of life and should be taken into serious consideration in governmental and EU measures regarding elderly people. Adequate support for the families needs to be carefully considered, as it stands out that one of the main predictors of the quality of life and wellbeing in the elderly is social support, interest and care from the close ones. Additionally, a need for independence seems to be also relevant, particularly in the institutionalized group, which reports comparatively lower levels of quality of life. It is also evident from our study that the institutionalized group reports higher levels of chronic illness, which may or may not be related to the potential psychological implications of a higher perception of abandonment. This and possible confounds of age, which was higher in this group, should be investigated in future studies.

Altogether, it seems that a large percentage of the elderly perceive a certain level of abandonment, loss of independence and lack quality of life. From their opinions, maybe things could be different if the family could be more supportive (King & Wynne, 2004). However, as a recent study with the Portuguese population highlights, being a caregiver also involves high costs for the caregiver itself, with significant disruption of daily activities and financial problems. The balance is thus hard to achieve and possible answers most likely will have to encompass global measures to deal with two different issues. On the one hand, there is the need to develop new technologies aimed at helping older people to maintain their independence and live at home longer (Sörensen, Pinquart & Duberstein, 2002), which seems to be a priority in the EU at the moment. On the other hand, it is also necessary to find support measures for the family (Ballard & Morris, 2005; Colvin, Chenoweth, Bold & Harding, 2004) and the elderly people themselves (Braun, 2000) that will enable them to face the costs of caregiving and access these new technologies.

REFERENCES

7thSPACE (2007).*European Joint Research Programme*. Retrieved July 23, 2008, from http://7thspace.com/headlines/285182/ageing_well_european_commission_unleashes_60 0m_for_development_of_new_digital_solutions_for_europes_elderly_people.html.

Arno, P., Levine C. & Memmott, M. (1999). *Health Affairs, 18 (2)*, 182-188.

Azeredo, Z. & Matos, E. (1998). Avaliação do relacionamento do idoso em medicina familiar. *Geriatria 2 (20)*, 28-30.

Ballard, S. & Morris, M. (2005). Factors influencing midlife and older adults attendance in family life education programs. *Family Relations*, 54 (3): 461-472.

Barron, A. (1996). *Apoyo social: aspectos teóricos y aplicaciones*. Madrid: Siglo Veinteuno.

Berger, L. (1995). Cuidados de enfermagem em gerontologia. In L. Berger and D. Mailloux-Poirier (Eds.), *Pessoas idosas: uma abordagem global* (pp. 11-19). Lisboa: Lusodidacta, p. 11-19.

Born, T. & Boechat, N. (2002). A qualidade dos cuidados ao idoso institucionalizado. In E. Freitas (Ed), *Tratado de Geriatria e Gerontologia* (pp. 768-777). Rio de Janeiro: Guanabara Koogan.

Boult, C., Kane, R., Louis, T., Boult L. & McCaffrey, D. (1994). Chronic conditions that lead to functional limitations in the elderly. *Journal of gerontology, 49 (1)*, 28-36.

Braun, B. (2000). Spiritual resiliency in older women. *Family Relations*, 49(3): 353-353.

Brito, L. (2002). *A saúde mental dos prestadores de cuidados a familiares idosos*. Coimbra: Quarteto.

Carvalho, P. & Patrícia, A. (2006). Legislação e Programas de Apoio para o Idoso. In H. Firmino (Ed.), *Psicogeriatria* (pp. 201-214). Coimbra: Psiquiatria Clínica.

Colvin, J., Chenoweth, L., Bold, M. & Harding, C. (2004). Caregivers of older adults. *Family Relations*, 53 (1): 49-60.

Crane, M., Byrne, K., Fu, R., Lipmann, B., Mirabelli, F., Rota-Bartelink, A., Ryan, M., Shea, R., Watt, H. & Warnes, A. (2005). The causes of homelessness in later life. *The Journals of Gerontology Series B: Psychological Sciences and Social Sciences*, 60: S152-S159.

Cruz, E. (2001). *Estudo da relação entre a qualidade de vida relacionada com saúde e o bem-estar psicológico*. Master Dissertation in Sócio-Psychology of Health, Instituto Superior Miguel Torga. Coimbra.

Dinis, C. (1997). *Envelhecimento e qualidade de vida no concelho de Faro*. Master Dissertation. Faculty of Medicine, University of Coimbra.

Direcção Geral de Saúde (1995). *Estudo da qualidade de vida do idoso: aplicação de um instrumento de avaliação*. Lisboa: Direcção Geral de Saúde.

Easter, P., Roberto, K. & Dugar, T. (2006). Intimate partner violence of rural aging women. *Family relations*, 55 (5): 636-648.

Ekerdt, D., Sergeant, J., Dingel, M. & Bowen, M. (2004). Household disbandment in later life. *The Journals of Gerontology Series B: Psychological Sciences and Social Sciences*, 59: S265-S273.

Ellenwood, A. E., & Jenkins, J. E. (2007). Unbalancing the Effects of Chronic Illness. *The American Journal of Family Therapy, 35*, 265–277.

Ermida, J. (1999). Processo de envelhecimento. In M. Costa (Ed.), *O idoso : problemas e realidades* (pp. 41-50). Coimbra : Formasau.

European Communities Commission (2005a). *Green Book: Uma nova solidariedade entre gerações face às mutações demográficas.* Retrieved July 21, 2008, from http://ec.europa. eu/employment_social/news/2005/mar/comm2005-94_pt.pdf .

European Communities Commission (2005b). *The European Alliance for families.* Retrieved July 21, 2008, from http://ec.europa.eu/employment_social/families/european-alliance-for-families_en.html

Felce, D. & Perry, J. (1995). Quality of Life: Its Definition and Measurement. *Research in Developmental Disabilities, 16 (1),* 51-74.

Fernandes, A. M. (1995). *Velhice: envelhecimento demográfico e relações intergeracionais.* Dissertação de Doutoramento. Faculdade de Ciências Sociais e Humanas da Universidade Nova de Lisboa.

Firmino, H., Falcão, D., & Rodrigues, T. S. (2006). O Registo de Dados em Instituições. In H. Firmino (Ed.), *Psicogeriatria* (pp. 531-540). Coimbra: Psiquiatria Clínica.

Fisher, L., Karen, L. & Weihs, M. (2000). Can addressing family relationships improve outcomes in chronic disease? *The Journal of Family Practice, 49,* 561-566.

Foley, D., Ancoli-Israel, S., Britz P. & Walsh, J. (2003). Sleep disturbances and chronic disease in older adults. *Journal of Psychosomatic Research, 56 (5),* 497-502.

Fonda, S.; Wallace, R. & Herzog, R. (2001). Changes in driving patterns and worsening depressive symptoms among older adults. *The Journals of Gerontology Series B: Psychological Sciences and Social Sciences,* 56: S343-S351.

Giles, H., Noels, K., Williams, A., Ota, H., Lim, T., Hung Ng, S., Ryan E. & Somera, L. (2003). Intergenerational communication across cultures. *Journal of cross-cultural gerontology, 18 (1),* 1-32.

Given, C., Given,B., Stommel, M., Collins, C., King S. & Franklin, S. (1992). The caregiver reaction assessment (CRA) for caregivers to persons with chronic physical and mental impairments. *Research in Nursing & Health, 15 (4),* 271-283.

Gomes, M. (2000). *Prospectiva do envelhecimento demográfico na região de Viseu.* PhD Dissertation in Sociology. New University of Lisbon.

Gonçalves, C. (2001). As pessoas idosas nas famílias institucionais segundo os Censos. *Revista de Estudos Demográficos, 34,* 41-60.

Gonçalves, L. (2002). *Qualidade de vida dos idosos.* PhD Thesis. Faculty of Education, University of Extremadura, Spain.

Griffin, J. & McKenna, K. (1998). Influences on Leisure and Life Satisfaction of Elderly People. *Physical & Occupational Therapy in Geriatrics, 15, (4),* 1-16.

Grunfeld, E., Glossop, R., McDowell, I. and Danbrook, Ch. (1997). Caring for elderly people at home. *Canadian Medical Association Journal, 157 (8),* 1101-1105.

Haas, B (2007). Clarification and Integration of Similar Quality of Life Concepts. *Journal of Nursing Scholarship, 31 (3),* 215 – 220.

Harper, S. (2004). *Families in Ageing Societies.* Oxford: Oxford Institute of Aging.

Heidrich, S. M., & Powwattana, A. (2004). Self-Discrepancy and Mental Health in Older Women with Chronic Illnesses. *Journal of Adult Development, 11*(4), 251-261.

Hirschfeld, M. (2003). Home care versus institutionalization: family caregiving and senile brain disease. *International Journal of Nursing Studies, 40,* 463-469.

Holmén, K. & Furukawa, H. (2002). Loneliness, health and social network among elderly people. *Archives of Gerontology and Geriatrics, 35 (3),* 261-274.

INE (1999). *As gerações mais idosas*. Série de Estudos n.° 81. Lisboa, Instituto Nacional de Estatística.

INE (2001). *Censos 2001 – Resultados Provisórios*. Retrieved July 23, 2008 from http://alea.ine.pt/html/actual/pdf/actualidades_27.pdf

INE (2002). *Envelhecimento em Portugal: Situação Demográfica e Socio-Económica recente das pessoas idosas*. Lisboa: Instituto Nacional de Estatística.

Isaacs, B. (1996). *The giants of Geriatries. Inaugural Lecture delivered in the University of Birmingham*, UK.

Katz, S. & Akpom, C. (1976). A measure of primary sociobiological functions. *International Journal of Health Services, 6* (3), 493-508.

Katz, S., Downs, T., Cash, H. & Grotz, R. (1970). Progress in development of the index of ADL. *Gerontologist, 10 (1)*, 20-30.

Kay, D., Beamish, P. & Roth, M. (1964). Old age mental disorders in Newcastle upon Tyne. *British Journal of Psychiatry, 11*, 146-158.

King, D. & Wynne, L. (2004): The emergence of "family integrity" in later life. *Family Process*, 43 (1): 7-21.

Lage, I. (2005). Cuidados familiares nos idosos. In C. Paúl & A. Fonseca (eds.), *Envelhecimento em Portugal* (pp. 207-234). Lisboa: Climepsi.

Luskin, F. & Newell, K. (1997). Mind-body approaches to successful aging. In A. Watkins (Ed.), *Mind-body medicine: a clinician's guide to psychoneuroimmunology* (pp. 251-268). New York: Churchill Livinstone.

Matos, A. & Ferreira, A. (2000). Desenvolvimento da escala de apoio social. *Psiquiatria Clínica, 21 (3)*, 243-253.

Morss, S., Shugarman, L. R., Lorenz, K. A., Mularski, R. A., & Lynn, J. (2008). A Systematic Review of Satisfaction with Care at the End of Life. *Journal American Geriatrics Society, 56*, 124–129.

Motta, M., Ferlito, L., Magnolfi, S. U., Petruzzi, E., Pinzani, P., Malentacchi, F., et al. (2008). Cognitive and functional status in the extreme longevity. *Archives of Gerontology and Geriatrics, 46*, 245–252.

Nijboer, Ch., Triemstra, M., Tempelaar, R., Sandermanc, R. & van den Bos, G. (1999). Measuring both negative and positive reactions to giving care to cancer patients. *Social Science & Medicine, 48 (1999)*, 1259-1269.

Paschoal, S. (2002). Qualidade de vida na velhice. In E. Freitas (Ed.). *Tratado de Geriatria e Gerontologia* (pp. 78-84). Rio de Janeiro: Guanabara Koogan.

Paúl, C. (1997). *Lá para o fim da vida: idosos, família e meio ambiente*. Coimbra: Globo.

Paúl, C., Fonseca, A. M., Martin, I., & Amado, J. (2005). Satisfação e Qualidade de Vida nos idosos Portugueses. In C. Paúl & A. M. Fonseca (Eds.), Envelhecer em Portugal (pp. 75-95). Lisboa: Climepsi.

Paúl, C. (2006). Psicologia do Envelhecimento. In H. Firminio (Ed.), *Psicogeriatria* (pp. 43-68). Coimbra: Psiquiatria Clínica.

Paúl, M. (1994). Panorama demográfico dos idosos em Portugal. *Geriatria, 7 (70)*, 21-26.

Pimentel, L. (2007). *O Lugar do Idoso na Familia* (2ª ed.). Lisboa: Quarteto.

Reis, J. (2000). Para um prolongamento da esperança de vida e saúde no novo milénio. *Geriatria*, 13 (127): 127.

Ribeiro, J. (1993). *Características de Saúde em Estudantes, Jovens, da Cidade do Porto*. Dissertação de Doutoramento. Universidade do Porto.

Santos, P. (1995). *A depressão no idoso*. Master Dissertation, Faculty of Education, University of Extremadura, Spain.

Schnittker, J. (2005). Chronic illness and depressive symptoms in late life. *Social Science & Medicine, 60*, 13–23.

Serra, A. (2006). Que Significa Envelhecer? In H. Firmino (Ed.), *Psicogeriatria* (pp. 21-33). Coimbra: Psiquiatria Clínica.

Socías, C. & Cerdà, M. (2007). Envejecimiento, educación y calidad de vida. *Revista Española de Pedagogia, 237*, 257-274.

Sörensen, S. Pinquart, M. & Duberstein, P. (2002). How effective are interventions with caregivers? *Gerontologist*, 42: 356-372.

Sousa, L., Figueiredo, D. & Cerqueira, M. (2006). *Envelhecer em Familia* (2ª ed.). Porto: Ambar.

Townsend, P (1981).The Structured Dependency of the Elderly. *Ageing & Society, 1 (1)*, 5-28.

Verissimo, M. T. (2006). Avaliação Multidimensional do Idoso. In H. Firmino (Ed.), *Psicogeriatria* (pp. 489-498). Coimbra: Psiquiatria Clínica.

Vitaliano, P., Young, H. & Zhang, J. (2004). Is Caregiving a Risk Factor for Illness? *Current Directions in Psychological Science, 3*, 13-16.

Weitzner, M., Jacobsen, P., Wagner, H., Friedland J. & Cox, C. (1999). The caregiver quality of life index-cancer (CQOLC) scale. *Quality of Life Research, 8*, 55-63. Wickrama, K., Conger, R. & Abraham, W. (2005). Early adversity and later health. *The Journals of Gerontology Series B: Psychological Sciences and Social Sciences*, 60: S125-S129.

Wolff, J., Starfield, B. & Anderson, G. (2002). Prevalence, Expenditures, and Complications of Multiple Chronic Conditions in the Elderly. *Archives of Internal Medicine,*162 (20), 2269-2276.

In: Families in Later Life: Emerging Themes and Challenges   ISBN 978-1-60692-328-3
Editor: Liliana Sousa   © 2009 Nova Science Publishers, Inc.

Chapter 7

CONSTRUCTING FAMILY INTEGRITY IN LATER LIFE

Liliana Sousa, Ana Raquel Silva,
Filipa Marques and Liliana Santos

SUMMARY

The intention of this book is to introduce new themes that may enable theoretical frameworks for families in later life to be constructed or redefined. It seeks to go beyond ageism, so to create a view that does not focus only on health problems, functional and mental decline and family caregiving. Adopting a normative perspective, means to construct a way of thinking about families in later life that creates a sense of purpose, diminishes the fear of ageing, and enables us to view later life as another phase in life. This goal may be ambitious, but we would like to sow the seeds that will lead to the rediscovery of ageing.

In this final chapter we hope to contribute towards extending our understanding of one of the few theoretical frameworks that offers a normative and developmental perspective on families in later life: family integrity (King & Wynne, 2004). Whereas there is a vast amount of literature on the early stages of the family life cycle, relatively few theoretical contributions cover family processes in later life (King & Wynne, 2004). Therefore, "a normal life course perspective of family development and ageing is needed, emphasising the potential for growth and meaning as much as negative aspects of change" (Walsh, 2005: 310). This study has been developed in order to deepen our understanding of the process of constructing family integrity, as opposed to disconnection or alienation.

Keywords: Families in later life; family integrity; family disconnection/alienation

1. CONCEPTUALIZING FAMILY INTEGRITY[1]

King & Wynne (2004) introduced the concept of "family integrity" as a normal developmental challenge for the elderly which is influenced by factors within the family system. Family integrity (versus disconnection and alienation) indicates that the older adult's efforts to achieve ego integrity are inextricably linked to the larger process of constructing meaning and relational development within the family system. With meaning, family members are more able to gain a sense of control and find order in chaos (Nadeau, 2001). The authors distinguish three possible routes:

- Family integrity constitutes the ultimate, positive outcome of the older adult's developmental striving toward meaning, connection, and continuity within his or her multigenerational family. It is a normal developmental challenge, fundamental to the wellbeing of elderly people and influenced by factors within family systems.
- Disconnection is used to describe families in which there is infrequent contact and lack of meaningful communication, resulting in a prevailing sense of isolation or disconnection between family members.
- Alienation refers to a state in which the level of disconnection results in a lack of common values, beliefs, and family identity; this isolation may reach the point of estrangement or alienation between individuals and/or generations.

Family integrity involves processes at different levels of social organization (King & Wynne, 2004), namely: the individual, based on the elderly individual's experience of satisfaction or displeasure within the family context; the family, with reference to the family relational competencies which help create a sense of belonging and connection in members of the extended family; the social, involving the transmission of values and rituals which have an impact on other levels.

An elderly person's ability to achieve family integrity depends on three vital functions or competencies of the family system (King & Wynne, 2004, 9) (Table 1):

- The transformation of relationships across time in a manner that is dynamic and responsive to the changing life cycle needs of family members.
- Resolution or acceptance of past losses, disappointments, or conflicts, with the dead as well as the living.
- The creation of meaning and legacy by sharing stories, themes, and family rituals within and across generations

The process of building family integrity starts in the previous stages of individual and family life cycles but can only be concluded in later life, as this is the period of "grand generativity" (Erikson & Kivnick, 1986) in which elderly people assume the role of "keeper of meaning" (embodying the traditions of the past, thus providing vital family and social links between the past, present and future) (Vailland, 2002).

---

[1] See Chapter 2.

Table 1. Family integrity vs. disconnection and alienation

Domains	Family integrity	Disconnection and alienation
General	A feeling of being at peace; acceptance of and/or satisfaction with present, past and future family relationships; sense of belonging and sharing; valuing and finding meaning in life.	Absence of common values and beliefs and no sense of family identity.
Transformation of relationships	Mutuality (the ability to maintain long-term commitment to family relationships and to reinvent them over time in the face of life cycle transitions) and filial maturity (a type of intergenerational maturity achieved when adult offspring grow by providing care and support for ageing parents, and ageing parents, in reciprocal fashion, become more able and willing to accept input and help from their children) convey the adaptable, dynamic nature of successful relationships during the different stages of life. This transformation depends on the family's ability to renegotiate intergenerational power hierarchies and attain adult-to-adult relationships between parents and grown children. Contrary to the notion of role reversal, mutuality enables older adults to offer various forms of support and assistance to their families.	Absence of mutuality and, consequently, filial maturity. Individuals remain set in old roles and relationship patterns that no longer fit life cycle needs. Disengagement or cutting-off. Avoidance of contact or criticism and isolation.
Resolution of past losses/conflicts	On an individual level, people may start to recognize that there is s limited amount of time left to "right old wrongs", resulting in old grievances, estrangements or mourned losses being addressed with greater urgency. Other family members may be less willing to engage in such difficult or painful discussions because they are involved in other activities consistent with their own life cycle stage. Alternatively, younger family members may intentionally leave elders out of important family discussions (for example about divorce or impending death) in an attempt to protect them from emotional pain or discomfort. The ability to grieve and eventually let go of attachments that cannot be restored or made whole is crucial to the meaningful integration of family experiences.	Denying problems, avoiding confrontation; lack of integration of past experiences (for example, pathological grieving).

Table 1. Continued

Domains	Family integrity	Disconnection and alienation
Creation of meaning and legacy	Involves the coherent integration of personal life stories and family themes, so that elders maintain a meaningful sense of their own place in a connected and continuous multigenerational family. This process also benefits members of younger generations who inherit a family legacy to help sustain their own ageing process. Accomplished through family storytelling, the passing on of shared interests, life themes and values and involvement in shared family activities and rituals. Transmission prepares younger generations for their own ageing process by helping them to define their unique position in the ever-unfolding sequence of human lives.	There is no one to pass the legacy on to; it is not important to build a legacy; no one is interested in the legacy.

Based on: King & Wynne (2004).

2. CONSTRUCTING FAMILY INTEGRITY VS. DISCONNECTION OR ALIENATION

As family integrity is one of the few normative and developmental approaches of families in later life, in this exploratory study we aim to extend our knowledge of the process of constructing family integrity, as opposed to disconnection or alienation. The results are important in terms of acquiring a greater understanding of family tasks in later life and in identifying some intervention strategies. In our study, the sample questions for discussing aspects of family integrity in clinical or research settings were taken from the appendix to King and Wynne (2004). Portuguese versions of the questions were checked and used on a trial with three individuals to assess comprehensibility (appendix 1). A sample consisting of elderly people (aged over 64) living in the community (i.e., not permanently institutionalized) was recruited using the following procedures: permission was requested from four community institutions for the researchers to contact their elderly users to ask if they would collaborate in the research; after obtaining the consent of the institution, the researchers approached the elderly people at random, explaining who they were, the kind of collaboration they were requesting and why the individual had been chosen; all the individuals agreed to collaborate and signed an informed consent agreement; the interview was scheduled during this first meeting. All meetings and interviews took place in private settings. The interviews lasted between 22 minutes and 45 minutes. The interviewees could easily understand and respond to the questions although they felt that all the questions on the resolution of conflicts and losses led to the same answer. The sample consisted of 8 participants, 5 of whom were females, whose ages ranged from 65 to 78 years (Table 2).

Table 2. Sample

Case	Sex	Age	Residence	Marital status	Socioeconomic status (Graffar's Index)	Functional status (Barthel's Index)
1	Male	69	Rural	Widowed	Middle	Independency
2	Female	74	Rural	Widowed	Middle -low	Independency
3	Female	78	Urban	Married	Middle -low	Independency
4	Female	78	Rural	Married	Middle -low	Independency
5	Female	76	Rural	Widowed	Middle	Independency
6	Male	65	Urban	Married	High	Independency
7	Female	78	Urban	Widowed	Middle	Slight dependency
8	Male	77	Urban	Married	High	Slight dependency

All the interviews were taped, transcribed and submitted to content analysis by the authors, with the support of N-Vivo 7 software. There were two stages to the process: i) characterisation of emerging categories and subcategories; ii) classification of the interviews into the previously defined categories in order to construct tree diagrams showing routes towards family integrity or disconnection/alienation.

The first stage focussed on the creation and testing of a categorisation system using a process of successive refinement. It involved four independent judges (the authors). Each judge read the interviews and developed a list of categories and subcategories. Then the judges met to compare and discuss the proposals until an agreement was reached. After this, each judge categorised two interviews in order to confirm that the categorisation system was adequate. Finally, a list of categories and sub-categories was drawn up (table 3). In the second stage, the judges independently developed the trees, then met to discuss and analyse how they had matched the cases. Finally, the trees were organized (figures 1 and 2). On the basis of previous findings, the authors also classified each case as evolving towards family integrity (6 cases) or family disconnection/alienation (2 cases).

2.1. Families in Later Life: Multigenerational

Our findings, which are consistent with those of others (e.g. King & Wynne, 2004; Carter & McGoldrick, 2005), suggest that it is more accurate to consider the multigenerational family as the unit of analysis for families in later life. The participants emphasised that:

"The family is not just this household where I live; it is more than me, my wife and my son!"

Table 3. Categories and subcategories: family integrity

Sub/categories	integrity	Disconnection and alienation
General		
(Dis)satisfaction with life	**Satisfaction and valuing** of family and individual life: sensation of peace and fulfilment.	**Dissatisfaction** with family and individual life: sense of family disconnection due to conflicts, misunderstandings; sense of discontentment with own life.
(In)existence of emotional proximity in family relationships	**Emotional proximity:** sense of connection with members of the multigenerational family, even if geographically distant and/or involving some past conflicts. Involves feelings of belonging, sharing, protection and safety.	**Absence of emotional proximity**: sense of disconnection with members of the multigenerational family. Involves feelings of lack of availability, disinterest and apathy.
Identity and life philosophy	**Identity readjustment supported by a life philosophy:** reflects wisdom; allows for acceptance of self and of others; permits integration of life events as positive and leading to growth, even when they have some less desirable outcomes; constitutes a script that guides attitudes, behaviours and values.	**Identity in readjustment**: the individual shows difficulty in accepting self and others; no life philosophy is defined, making it difficult to integrate life events meaningfully.
Life projects centred on the past/future	**Life projects centred on the future:** the elderly have life goals for the future, which acknowledge recreating a sense of value and usefulness.	**Life projects centred on the unresolved past:** the elderly have goals that focus on resolving the unresolved past; the bond with the past makes it difficult to focus on the present or future and creates a sense of uselessness and lack of value.
Transformation of relationships across time		
(Dis)continuity in family relationships	**Continuity:** family commitment is maintained throughout life transitions. Relationships evolve and mature (strengthen), but there is a sense of stability and continuity. Invisible and visible loyalties exist, characterized by mutuality and reciprocity (including filial maturity).	**Discontinuity:** ruptures, conflicts, geographical distance and other sources of discontinuity occur throughout the life cycle, leading to weaker bonds and less commitment. Can be described as non-acceptance of normative life transformations or of some family members' life courses. Breakdown in intergenerational continuity (for instance, by not being a grandparent), experienced as devastating. Mutuality usually absent: for example the elderly person gives support and wants to receive help, but does not want to ask for it (feeling of inferiority).

Table 3. Continued

Sub/categories	integrity	Disconnection and alienation
Resolution or acceptance of losses or conflicts		
(Non)acceptance of past or present conflicts	**Acceptance and/or resolution of past and present conflicts:** there are/were no relevant conflicts; past and the present conflicts are irrelevant and easily resolved.	**Non-acceptance of conflicts:** individuals describe feelings of anxiety about past and/or present conflicts (non-acceptance). Problems/conflicts sometimes resolved through dialogue, but generally this is intended rather than accomplished .
(Un)finished business with family members	**Sense of "finished business" with family members:** the individuals feel that all issues and tasks are finished.	**Sense of "unfinished business" with family members:** some tasks or issues still need further discussion to reach closure. In some circumstances this is now impossible (for example, one participant stated that what he really wanted was to discuss some problems with his wife, but she had died so he now feels it will be very difficult to close the issue).
(In)existence of regrets	**No regrets:** individuals feel they have a "clear conscience" and a sense of peace and well-being towards the different family members. Unpleasant events (past or present) are usually mentioned, but described as irrelevant ("little things" or "unimportant things"). The elderly person feels able to cope with negative events and forgives (him/her self and others) for any unpleasantness.	**Regrets:** individuals refer to feelings of guilt and regret for past mistakes; they mention feelings of sorrow and a desire to change behaviour and attitudes. The elderly person feels that they will never be forgiven and/or cannot forgive him/herself; there is usually difficulty in forgiving others and receiving their forgiveness.
Creation of meaning and legacy		
(Dis)satisfaction with the transmission of a legacy	**Satisfaction with legacy:** the elderly person experiences feelings of satisfaction with the legacy they have passed on, whether it is accepted by family members or not. The individuals feel they have "done their duty" and have made a contribution to future generations.	**Dissatisfaction with legacy:** the elderly person experiences feelings of dissatisfaction and frustration and a sense of being undervalued because his/her legacy is not received well or not valued.
(Not) respected in the family	**Respected in the family:** the elderly person feels they have a respected and meaningful place in the family and believes this is associated with their own attitudes, namely by accepting other people's life choices and not trying to control the lives of others.	**Having a less respected place in the family:** the elderly person feels his/her place in the family is not meaningful, and not greatly respected. Some elderly people display feelings of superiority towards family members and/or a tendency to control the lives of others.

Table 3. Continued

Sub/categories	integrity	Disconnection and alienation
(In)congruent construction of family memory	**Congruent:** the elderly person feels that after their death family members will have a memory of them that is consistent with their desires; individuals show serenity in face of death and accept that they will be remembered as family members wish.	**Incongruent:** the elderly person wishes to be remembered in a way that is not valued by family members and experiences difficulty in accepting this; shows anguish in the face of death.

Note: This description of categories and subcategories should be understood as complementing those provided by King and Wynne (2004) (Table 1).

The family life cycle is usually described as focusing the nuclear family, although connections between various households within the extended family are emphasised. In families in later life, the unit of analysis (comprehension and intervention) should be the multigenerational family (as proposed in Chapter 1). Since the elderly person or elderly couple are a focal point in the family, there are several other interrelated family nuclei (such as children, grandchildren, siblings, nephews, and cousins), and even close and significant friends should be considered. Although they highlighted certain family members (particularly their children and spouse), the participants in this study mentioned the multigenerational family as the focus of their integrity. The concept of "linked lives" (Mitchell, 2006) (lives that are not lived in isolation, but experienced interdependently) is experienced strongly and concretely by elderly persons and families in later life.

2.2. Pathways to Family Integrity

The emerging categories allow us to obtain a deeper understanding of the process of constructing family integrity. The tree diagram (figure 1) shows the paths towards family integrity, although it is essential to emphasise that a person classified as being in route to family integrity may not present all the characteristics of integrity i.e., they may stress feelings of peace and satisfaction with their individual and family life but not yet be positive about other areas.

Family Integrity

Constructing family integrity in later life is a process of striving towards meaning, connection and continuity within the multigenerational family (King & Wynne, 2004). The participants identified as evolving towards family integrity described feelings of satisfaction with their relationships within the multigenerational family: "*I feel very positive; relationships in my family are very good!*" This satisfaction is strongly combined with a feeling of family connection (affective proximity): "*We get on well, sometimes little things happen, but we get over them ... even with my siblings, who live far away, we feel close!*"

The interviewees simultaneously revealed the experience of a well-defined identity ("*I know who I am*") sustained by a philosophy of life ("*I have a philosophy of life ...*"). Together these constitute a guide for reviewing and integrating life, as well as for organising everyday living and planning for the future, operating as a *manual* that determines how life is perceived and reflecting a form of integration within the family. For instance, one participant defined his philosophy of life as "*there's no point in nurturing problems*" and explains:

"I have my own way of looking at life; I don't care about certain things. If, for any reason, something displeases me, I turn my back on it! I keep out of conflicts! Because I feel life is so beautiful … Everyday when I wake up, I go to the balcony and I say good morning to the sun! I think it is a sign that I am still alive! As I feel good about life, I think there's no point in nurturing problems!"

Identity and philosophy of life seem to involve an acceptance of self and of others:

"We must accept others for what they are, not what we would like them to be! We also must also accept ourselves for what we are!"

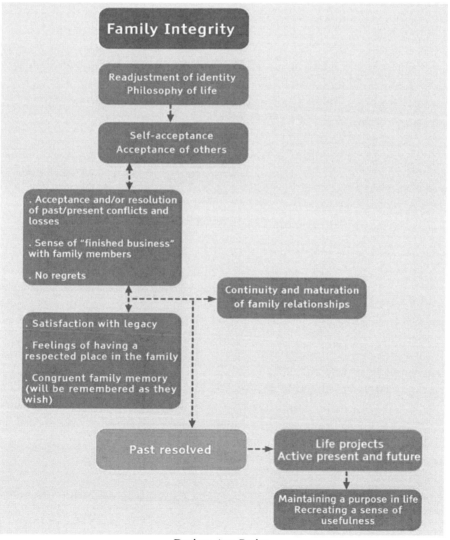

Design: Ana Petim.

Figure 1. Pathways to family integrity.

Life projects centre on the present and future and emerge when the past is resolved; they include the recreation of life purposes and a renewed sense of value and usefulness. Elderly people moving towards family integrity seem to have two time scales for life projects:

i)   The youngest of the elderly people organize more instrumental and practical goals.
      "I find pleasure and a sense of achievement in life when I have some concrete objective
      for each day. For example, today I have a class, and tomorrow I'm having dinner with
      some friends!"
ii)   The oldest of the elderly and/or those experiencing more severe health problems refer
      to more spiritual goals.
      "I have not yet achieved that plenitude. But I think that as the years go by I will get
      there. It is not just well-being in general; it is also a sense of continuity in life that makes
      us more mature in facing difficulties and becoming more flexible!"

Transformation of Family Relationships

Transformations in family relationships occur throughout family and individual life. In later life they are described by the elderly evolving towards family integrity as occurring with continuity and maturity: *"there have always been changes, the normal changes in life, but they were always for the good; the guidelines were always the same, but they got better each time"*. At the same time, the elderly person and his/her family accept individual, family and social changes. For instance:

"I have a granddaughter who has a very different lifestyle from the one I would like her to
have, very different from the routine I had at her age. But she is a good girl and a good
student. She likes to go out at night and comes back very late; during the day she is always
sleepy. There are things like this ... we disagree, but it is just a different way of living!"

Or,

"I prefer to live alone; I like solitude because I don't feel lonely: I can read a book or watch a
good TV programme or listen to music. When my husband died I carried on living alone in
my home. My daughter lives nearby. She asked me to go and live with her ... it would be
better for her, she would be more relaxed about me and wouldn't feel the need to come here
so often. But I prefer it like this and she respects that!"

Help and support occurred mutually and reciprocally within the family: the elderly person felt that the family was available and willing to support them, and had no inhibition or difficulty in asking for help. At the same time, the elderly individuals helped in whatever way they could and felt that family members knew they can ask for what they needed, although they stressed that their health problems prevented them from doing many things. They also realised and accepted that some situations were beyond their capabilities:

"I help in any way I can, but many things are beyond me. I have a nephew who is a drug
addict and I don't know how to help with that!"

Resolution or Acceptance of Conflicts and Losses

An identity and a philosophy of life which allow for acceptance of self and others facilitate the acceptance of past conflicts (even if unresolved) and losses and the attainment of a sense of "finished business" in relation to family members, leading to the removal or inexistence of regrets. In any family, varying degrees of serious conflict occur over the years and whilst some are resolved others persist. The elderly people in the processing of achieving family integrity showed an acceptance of the fact that some conflicts would never be resolved and accepted them even when they remain unresolved by the parties involved:

> "For me everything has been resolved, but not for them. The fact that two of my children don't get on makes things complicated. Time has made me forget! In myself, the situation resolved, they have made their choices, but I feel obliged to talk to both of them!"

In consequence, they felt that there were no unfinished tasks or issues: *things are the way they are* and *when you die, you die, and that's it, they have to cope with it*. And there were no regrets:

> "I haven't done anything bad intentionally, not on purpose, and now everything is resolved and I don't have any regrets!"

Creation of Meaning and Legacy

The participants described their legacies as including material goods (land, houses, money and items of material value) and symbolic goods (education and values). Regardless of the material values the elderly possessed, they always recognised that a legacy had been passed on (voluntarily or involuntarily) during their lives and that this was still taking place. Moreover, they accepted that this legacy may or may not be (or have been) well received by the recipients.

> "I have passed on good advice and values. They don't always accept it, but that's not my business!"

Even when the values that were passed on were not accepted, the elderly person assumed a respected and meaningful place within the family by accepting the others non-acceptance. Family members recognised that the elderly person had made a contribution to family life and acknowledged their respect for the choices made by others:

> "They respect me and like me! But I contribute to that, I live my life without intruding on other people's lives; I just want them to be well!"

These elderly people have achieved a sense of the congruent construction of memory. It was not necessarily important for them to be remembered as they wanted to be; the elderly people evolving within family integrity were not, in fact, really worried about how they would be remembered since they knew they would be remembered (after death) in *the best way*:

> "They will remember me, I don't know how! I would like them to remember me as I am! Let them do it the way they see fit!"

Acceptance of social change also emerges here:

"They will not remember me in the same way as I remember people who have died, because the generations are different!"

2.3. Pathways to Family Disconnection or Alienation

Figure 3 shows the tree diagram that was constructed on the basis of interviews with two participants classified as moving towards disconnection or alienation. As with the pathways to family integrity, the elderly people here also revealed experiences involving subcategories associated with both integrity and disconnection. However, they referred feeling dissatisfied with life and mentioned more subcategories associated with disconnection.

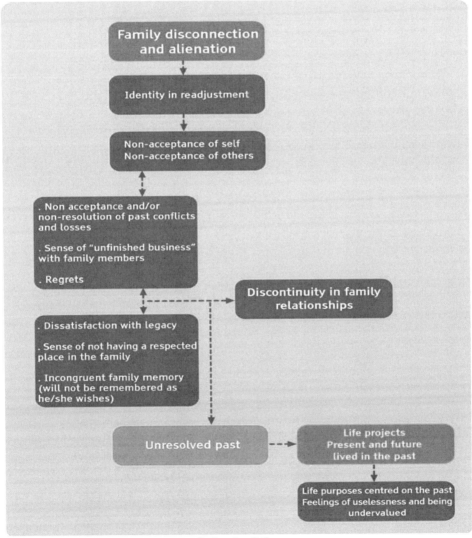

Design: Ana Petim.

Figure 3. Pathways to family disconnection and alienation.

Family Disconnection or Alienation

The elderly people classified as moving towards family disconnection/alienation emphasised their dissatisfaction with life and the lack of connections within the family. They had a tendency to focus on certain family problems or conflicts which were causing them anxiety. Their discourse emerged as centred on these (sometimes apparently irrelevant) constantly repeated issues, which they used to justify their dissatisfaction with life:

> "More than anything else, what upsets me most and makes me feel most at odds with the world is smoking [some family members are smokers]. That's what I feel is harmful to me. When I say that smoking is dangerous, they say: my grandfather was a heavy smoker and he lived until he was 97! It drives me mad when they say that. If I felt like it, I would say: well I know a bloke that had a stroke at 40 and died because he smoked".

Family detachment was associated with illness, geographical distance, past events ("stories from the past") or discontentment ("they don't pay attention to what I say, I give good advice and they just carry on as usual").

People moving towards family disconnection or alienation seem to be in the process of redefining their identity, mainly because they tend to describe themselves in comparison with others ("I am more intellectually advanced than all the other people in this room"), in comparison with what they have been in the past ("I was an extrovert and I still am") or in terms of other people's opinions ("everyone in the family says I am a fusspot, but they say it with affection"). No philosophy of life emerged in these cases, so there were no guidelines to unify and forge connections between life actions and experiences. In consequence, it was more difficult for them to review and integrate their past life and this may be why stories from the past were endlessly repeated: it was almost as if it was a struggle to integrate the stories. This suggests that these elderly people were not (yet) able to accept themselves or others: they tended to rethink their past options and blame others for some problem or wrong decision (there was constant criticism of others in an attempt to show the self in a positive light). For example:

> "My relationship with my children is distant; I have difficulty in expressing myself to them! They don't care about what I say! I think they were told bad things about me. When they were little, my wife's family told them bad stories about me!"

Within this context, past conflicts and losses were not resolved and there was difficulty in constructing meaning and a legacy. Family relationships were therefore developed in discontinuous fashion and present and future life projects focussed on resolving past issues, thus leading to feelings of being undervalued (at times disguised by attitudes of self promotion). For instance:

> "My brothers are not as good as me, at least in intellectual terms! Economically they are better off, but I feel sorry for them and I would like to help them!"

Transformation of Family Relationships

Family relationships were described in terms of discontinuity, due to various conflicts, ruptures and even geographical distance, which disengaged family members and weakened bonds. The elderly people described these situations in terms of non-acceptance and criticism of others, whilst tending to minimize their own contributions to the problems (probably as a way of disguising their non-acceptance of self): *"my children don't listen to my advice and then things go wrong for them!"*

The older people experiencing family disconnection/alienation showed difficulty in asking others for support and help, especially those with whom they had experienced some conflict or towards whom they felt some regret. They also felt that it might be hard for others to ask them for help or support, although they could not understand why because they believed they had done all they could.

Resolution of Conflicts and Losses

The participants moving towards family disconnection/alienation revealed that in the process of reviewing and reintegrating life they were not able to accept and/or resolve certain past events. One of the participants mentioned conflicts with his deceased wife, emphasising that he had not been the only one to blame: he had felt the need to discuss this with his children for some time and had thought a lot about doing so but had never taken the initiative (*"it's negligence on my part"*). Issues or tasks were felt to be unfinished: sometimes they were explicitly mentioned (*"I still have to talk to my children about that row we had"*) and at other times were disguised as other issues (*"we still have inheritances to organize, but our conflicts limit the progress we can make on that score"*). In these circumstances, the elderly person felt regret and remorse for past and/or present "faults" and a need to change behaviour and attitudes. It was often impossible to resolve the situation in the way they wanted, usually because the people concerned had died, and it was therefore difficult for them to forgive themselves or be forgiven by other(s):

> "I had several conflicts with my deceased mother-in-law! I feel sorry because I didn't care for her as I should have done. I would like to talk to her about that!"

This non-acceptance or non-resolution of past conflicts contributed towards maintaining the life projects of these elderly people centred on the past, in a struggle to resolve what was often impossible to resolve: the only available solution seemed to be self-forgiveness, which they seldom remembered or considered. Consequently, a certain loss of esteem also emerged, usually disguised by a measure of arrogance and superiority:

> "I am more capable than anyone else in this day centre. I am the only one who can help organise activities. The suggestions the others make are so boring!"

Creation of Meaning and Legacy

These elderly people felt that they had transmitted a legacy, but experienced dissatisfaction when it was not accepted or valued and therefore attempted to transmit what they wanted:

> "When my family do not accept what I want to pass on to them there is some frustration. I would like to pass on my experience and life story, but my family thinks it is useless. My children don't let my grandchildren read what I write. But I am writing down everything to leave to them and maybe one day they will value it!"

Consequently, they felt that (despite being respected) their place in the family was unimportant. Again, feelings of superiority emerged (*"I have more to pass on than them"*) and attempt to control others (*"sometimes they don't behave properly and I notice and point it out to them"*). Inevitably the elderly person felt that he/she would not be remembered after death in the way they wanted to be and this created obstacles to their acceptance of death and of life as it was and is:

"I would like to be remembered for the stories I tell, but they're not important to my family!"

In these circumstances the sense of being undervalued is accentuated and death seems to mean not only a physical end, but also an emotional and relational closing point. Death is therefore distressing and not easy to face and accept.

Discourse

The participants classified as moving towards disconnection or alienation gave longer interviews: for example, the individual who showed signs of being the most alienated gave an interview that lasted 45m and consisted of 6148 words whereas the individual with the greatest indications of family integrity gave a 2159 word interview lasting 22m (this data was consistent with all the interviews). These findings suggest that people moving towards disconnection or alienation speak more and are repetitive and boring since they always want to talk about the same issue or event, without advancing its resolution. The stereotype of the elderly person who is boring, monotonous, repetitive and centred on the past probably originates in people who are not evolving towards family integrity. In fact, those approaching family integrity are concrete, concise and refer the past only when asked; moreover they prefer to speak about the present and do not generally complain.

2.4. Forgiveness, Acceptance and Meaning

The construction of family integrity seems to be anchored on three closely related processes developed by the elderly person which require the family's support and which are relevant to intervention: forgiveness, acceptance and meaning. These topics, in particular forgiveness, were developed in Chapter 3 and we therefore only intend to refer briefly to the processes here.

Forgiving (Self and the others) versus Blaming others

Although no consensus exists on what constitutes forgiveness, it is commonly held that interpersonal forgiveness involves a reduction in negative responses (e.g., retaliation, estrangement) and an increase in positive responses (e.g., conciliation) towards the transgressor and that both types of response are evoked and expressed in terms of behaviour, affectivity and cognition (Tse & Cheng, 2006). Self-forgiveness seems to be determined by each individual's ability to forgive others. In fact, our data suggests that when an individual receives forgiveness from others but is still not capable of self-forgiveness, family integrity encounters obstacles. For instance, one participant mentioned a past episode involving an argument he had had with his wife:

"We argued in front of other people. But then we went to our bedroom and talked. I ask for her forgiveness and she forgave me! In fact, other people were to blame, not me! I still think about that: I shouldn't have done what I did, but my mother-in-law was responsible for that argument!"

This also indicates that blaming others emerges when the individual is unable to accept him/her self and/or others, and constitutes a process that leads towards family disconnection or alienation

Accepting (Self and the others) versus Controlling others

Self-acceptance can be defined as a positive attitude toward oneself (e.g. Ryff, 1989; Gough & Bradley, 1996). In general, a high level of self-acceptance indicates that an individual has a good opinion of him/herself, acknowledges and accepts the various aspects of their character, including good and bad qualities, and feels positive about the past. Conversely, low levels of self-acceptance indicate self-doubt, dissatisfaction with self and disappointment with what has occurred in the past. Self-acceptance allows the elderly person to live with whatever he/she has done for good or for bad in life and therefore facilitates their journey towards family integrity. Accepting others emerges as a concomitant process, since individual well-being leads towards understanding others. Those who experience difficulty in accepting their lives showed a tendency to control other people, leading to disconnection or alienation:

"My children and grandchildren don't value my experience of life! But when they beat their heads against the wall, I tell them: I was right; you should have listened to me!"

Meaning (Self and the others) versus Trivialising others

Self-worth (the sense of living a meaningful life) is associated with the experience of having a meaningful and respected place in the family and the community ad serves almost as an authorisation to value others and map out family integrity. The feeling that one has an insignificant and/or less important status within the family seems to lead to trivialising (devaluing) others and to family disconnection and alienation:

"My siblings don't know how to read or write and don't pay attention to what I say because they can't understand it. Sometimes they ask me: where did you learn so much? And I answer: I didn't learn much, but you know nothing!"

3. REFLECTIONS AND IMPLICATIONS

3.1. Assigning a Future to the Elderly and to Families in Later Life

One important finding in this study concerns the emergence of elderly people's life projects. The interview centred mainly on the past, while the future was only referred in relation to the creation of meaning and legacies in connection with death. In fact, literature on later life individual and family development tasks tends to be organized around two major topics (e.g. Erikson, 1950; Carter & McGoldrick, 2005): reviewing and integrating life and preparing for death (one's own and that of significant others).

Older people often use the expression "in my time" to refer to their youth, denoting that this is no longer their time, that the current time is not so important and positive events belong to the past. Literature on this subject tends to reinforce this perspective by attributing development in later life to what has happened in the past. Reviewing the past is a crucial task, yet the findings in our study indicate that when the past is resolved, the elderly still have life projects that are centred on the present and the future.

Acknowledging a future for the elderly and for families in later life demands a redefinition of time. The socio-emotional selectivity theory claims that perception of time plays a fundamental role in the selection and pursuit of social goals (Carstensen, Isaacowitz & Charles, 1999; Lang & Carstensen, 2002). Perception of time is malleable, and social goals change in both younger and older people when time constraints are imposed. How individuals perceive time is associated with social and emotional adjustment.

- Individuals who perceive future time as being limited prioritise emotionally meaningful goals (e.g., generativity, emotional regulation) and therefore shift their focus towards more restricted goals.
- Individuals who perceive their futures as open-ended or future-oriented prioritise instrumental or knowledge-related goals.

The inextricable association between time left in life and chronological age ensures age-related differences in social goals. There are large individual differences in how individuals of all ages approach time, but on average one would assume that older individuals would tend to focus more on the past than on the future (in comparison with younger samples). Pennebaker & Stone (2003) observed that older individuals showed a decreasing use of past-tense verbs and an increasing use of future-tense verbs. Therefore, as people age they appear to be more anchored in the present and in the future. The authors emphasise that these time orientations were among the most consistent to be found in literature on the subject but were unexpected in terms of stereotypes of ageing.

3.2. Family Tasks

Constructing family integrity is mainly an achievement of the elderly, although it is strongly influenced by a series of family factors and competences. In Table 4 we attempt to summarise the family processes that frame the elderly person's journey towards family integrity. The older generation's construction of family integrity is crucial to family continuity and thus facilitates family integrity for the next generations.

This table needs further development, in particular with regard to compatibility between the older person's development of family integrity and the family and individual development processes of other family members. We think it would be interesting to adapt the interview used in this study for use with the family as a whole, or to interview members of the different households within the multigenerational family.

Table 4. The elderly and family life

Family integrity: outcome of older adult's development
Reviewing and integrating individual and family life: resolving the past and defining present and future projects Readjusting identity: Constructing meaning and family integrity Defining a philosophy of life: A guide for the past, present and the future

Family competencies	
Transformation of family relationships	Promoting continuity through maturity: • Renegotiating intergenerational power and attaining adult-adult relationships: mutuality and filial maturity. • Promoting (or allowing) the elderly autonomy (for instance, to explore new roles in the multigenerational family and in the community).
Resolution or acceptance of losses and conflicts	Accepting the past and living for the present and the future: • Giving time and space to help the elderly integrate past and current issues. • Anticipating needs and making decisions about the future (e.g. caregiving, living arrangements). • Involving the elderly in the current family issues.
Creation of meaning and legacy	Linking the past, present and future: • Preparing for the legacy. • Accepting transmission. • Recognizing the elderly person's contribution to family life in the past, present and future.

Based on: King & Wynne, 2004; McGoldrick & Carter, 2005; Erikson, 1997; Schaie & Willis, 2002.

3.3. Two Phases for Families in Later Life

Old age has been extended: nowadays when people reach the age of 65 (the chronological age that *officially* defines the beginning of old age) they can expect to live for at least another 20 to 30 years. Moreover, this increased life expectancy enables people to live for 30 years or more after retirement (the social mark of ageing). It is also to be expected that people will live healthier and more independent lives for much longer after retirement (e.g. Atchley, 2000).

In the family life cycle approach (Carter & McGoldrick, 2005), the last stage is termed "families in later life". In this stage of life families should develop in order to accept shifting generational roles, involving a transition in which the *penultimate* generation is prepared for and starts to assume the role of the oldest generation. To assist in this transition, the oldest generation should pass certain functions on to their descendants, whilst retaining a space for their wisdom and life experience within the family context.

However, taking into consideration some of the findings of this study in addition to other literature and research, it seems that families in later life would be better described and acknowledged in terms of two phases, particularly since, as Joan Erikson (1998) argues, old age in one's eighties and nineties brings with it new demands, reassessments   and daily difficulties. These concerns can only be adequately discussed by designating two phases to the final stage of life. Several authors support this reorganization:

- Erikson (1998) proposes two stages for the last phase of individual development, i.e., including the eighth stage (integrity vs despair) and the ninth stage (despair and disgust vs. integrity). In encounters between the syntonic (positive) and dystonic (negative), the syntonic element usually wins. However, in old age the dystonic element becomes more dominant and conflict and tension (emergencies and loss of physical ability) become sources of growth, strength and commitment.
- Borysenko, 1996 (in McGoldrick & Carter, 2005) presents the stages of individual female development, and also indentifies two stages: late middle age (approximately between 50 or 55 to the early 70s) which represents the beginning of the years of wisdom (reclaiming the wisdom of interdependence), and ageing (from 75 onwards) which centres more on grief, loss, resilience, retrospection and growth.
- Additionally, later life is being redefined in terms of the "young-old", people aged 65 to 85 who are mostly healthy and vibrant, and the "old old" or "fourth age" who are over 85, the fastest-growing segment of older people and the group that is most vulnerable to serious illness and disability (e.g. Schaie & Willis, 2002; Suzman & Riley, 1985).

According to Carter and McGoldrick (2005), the individual life cycle takes shape as it moves and evolves within the matrix of the family life cycle (embedded within the larger socio-political culture). The fact is that the two processes coexist and influence each other, and are parallel, evolving together in a very close relationship. King & Wynne (2004) also argue that the concept of family integrity cannot be located exclusively at either an individual or a family level since it involves mutually reciprocal interactions between individual subjective experiences (of self and family) and observable family processes. This strong interconnection between family and individual development explains why family researchers should take two phases into consideration when considering families in later life.

In our view, the same emotional process of transition probably unifies the two phases: building meaning and family integrity. This process involves relevant family and individual processes, particularly in terms of the transition of the generations: i) preparing the next generation to be the oldest one; ii) preparing the current older generation to develop family and ego integrity.

Included in this proposal, the first phase would involve the active (re)engagement of the older person with the extended family and the community. The period after retirement is usually characterized by strong family relationships and quality of life tends to be determined by the quality of family relationships for two reasons: older people tend to have more time to devote to the family and people may need extra support in their daily life as they age (e.g. Tongue & Ballenden, 1999). Community relations, especially the role played by friends, become important since these endure even when others are lost. The second phase would centre on the active spiritual engagement of the older person. Tornstam (1997) considerers two phases in later life that involve a shift from a materialistic and rational view to a more cosmic and transcendent view (wisdom). This also seems to operate in terms of family relations: as the elderly person evolves towards a more transcendent and spiritual way of life, family members have to adapt and readjust.

FINAL NOTE

The prevailing biomedical view pathologises later life due to its focus on disease and treatment. Moreover, the ageism and gerophobia that characterise western societies emphasise the negative aspects of old age (e.g. senility, dependence, depression) and families in later life (e.g. less cohesion and a tendency to abandon the oldest members). In this context, individuals, families and societies do not readily confront the challenges of later life or grasp the opportunities that maturity can offer. As the process of an extended later life is still recent and unknown (or still not experienced by a large number of people), ageing individuals, ageing families and ageing societies have no models for ageing. The task of aging well is therefore a challenge (Walsh, 2005) in which: i) some look for models of ageing in parents and grandparents; ii) others look to friends or even media personalities. It is essential to learn to grow old from the elderly, but society does not facilitate this process, given that old people are commonly stereotyped in negative ways. We hope that this book can contribute towards providing positive, normative and developmental models for families in later life.

ANNEX. INTERVIEW

1. Family integrity (general)
1.1. Do you feel satisfied or at peace with your family relationships?
1.2. What aspects of your family life are most satisfying? Least satisfying?
1.3. Although you may or may not see family members as much as you would like, do you feel close or connected to members of your family?
1.4. If possible, tell me about one or two of your closer relationships.
1.5. Are there family members to whom you would like to feel closer or more connected?

2. Resolution of conflicts/losses
2.1. Do you have regrets about any of your family relationships?
2.2. Do you have a sense of "unfinished business" with any of your family members? If so, have you tried to address this issue? How (if anything)?
2.3. Are there any issues or problems that you wish you could discuss with someone in the family?
2.4. If so, what do you think could help you to accept or solve those issues?

3. Creation of meaning and legacy
3.1. What aspects of family tradition, history, or values have you passed on to younger family members?
3.2. What material inheritances have you passed on to younger family members?
3.3. What would you still like to share or pass on to others (material and/or symbolic)?
3.4. Do you feel that you have a meaningful and respected place in your family?
3.5. How will you be remembered by family members after you are gone?
3.6. How would you like to be remembered?

3.7.   Are there still things you would like to do or say to influence your family's future memories of you?

4. Transformation of relationships

4.1.   How have your relationships with family members changed as you've got older?

4.2.   Are there family members whom you can count on for help or support if you need it?

4.3   Is it hard for you to ask family members for help or support?

4.4.   Are there family members who count on you for help or support?

4.5.   Is it hard for others to ask you for help or support?

Based on: King and Wynne (2004: 20/21).

REFERENCES

Atchley, R. (2000). *Social Forces and Aging* (9th Ed). Belmont, CA: Wadsworth.

Carstensen, L.; Isaacowitz, D. & Charles, S. (1999). Taking time seriously. A theory of socioemotional selectivity. *American Psychologist*, 54(3): 165-181.

Carter, E. & McGoldrick, M. (2005). Overview: The expanded life cycle: Individual, family, and social perspectives. In E. Carter & M. McGoldrick (Eds.) *The expanded life cycle: Individual, family, and social perspectives*. Boston: Allyn & Bacon.

Erikson, E.; Erikson, J. & Kivnick, H. (1986). *Vital involvement in old age: the experience of old age in our time*. New York: Norton.

Erikson, E. (1950). *Childhood and Society*. New York: Norton.

Erikson, J. (1998). The life cycle completed. New York: Norton.

Gough & Bradley, 1996.

King, D. &Wynne, L. (2004). The emergence of "Family Integrity" in later life. *Family Process*, 43(1): 7-20.

Lang, F. & Carstensen, L. (2002). Time counts: future time perspective, goals, and social relationships. *Psychology of Aging*, 17(1): 125-139.

Mitchell, B. (2006). The boomerang age from childhood to adulthood: emergent trends and issues for aging families. *Canadian Studies in Population*, 33 (2): 155-178.

Nadeau, J. (2001). Meaning making in family bereavement: a family system approach. In M. Stroebe, R. Hansson, W. Stroebe & H. Schut (Eds.), *Handbook of bereavement research: consequences, coping and care* (pp. 329-342). Washington, DC: American Psychological Association.

Pennebaker, J. & Stone, L. (2003). Words of wisdom: language use over the life span. Journal of Personality and Social Psychology, 85(2): 291-301.

Ryff, C. (1989). Happiness is everything, or is it? Explorations on the meaning of psychological well-being. *Journal of Personality and Social Psychology*, 57, 1069–1081.

Schaie, W. & Willis, S. (2002). *Adult Development and Aging* (5th ed.). New Jersey: Prentice Hall.

Suzman, R. e Riley, M. (1985). Introducing the "oldest old". *Milbank Memorial Fund Quarterly: Health and Society*, 63, 177-185.

Tongue, A. & Ballenden, N. (1999). Families and ageing in the 21st century. *Family Matters*, 52: 4-8.

Tornstam, L. (1997). Gerotranscendence: the contemplative dimension of aging. *Journal of Aging Studies*, 11(2): 143-154.

Tse, M. & Cheng, S-T (2006). Depression reduces forgiveness selectively as a function of relationship closeness and transgression. *Personality and Individual Differences*, 40(6): 1133-1141.

Vailland, G. (2002). *Aging well*. Boston: Little, Brown and Company.

Walsh, F. (2005). Families in later life: Challenges and opportunities. In E. Carter & M. McGoldrick (Eds.) *The expanded life cycle: Individual, family, and social perspectives*. Boston: Allyn & Bacon.

AUTHORS AFFILIATIONS

Ana Raquel Silva, Research assistant at the University of Aveiro (Department of Health Sciences); 3810-193 Aveiro, Portugal; Phone: +351938317292; Fax: +351234401597; E.mail:raquelgabriels@gmail.com.

Carlos F. Silva, PhD; Full Professor at the University of Aveiro (Department of Educational Sciences); 3810-193 Aveiro, Portugal; Phone: +351234370353; Fax: +351234370640; E.mail: csilva@ua.pt.

Daniela Figueiredo, PhD; Assistant at the School of Health Sciences of University of Aveiro, 3810-193 Aveiro, Portugal; Phone: +351234372457; Fax: 351 234 401 597; E.mail: daniela.figueiredo@ua.pt.

Filipa Marques, Research assistant at the Department of Health Sciences at the University of Aveiro; 3810-193 Aveiro, Portugal; Phone: 938317292; Fax: +351234401597; E.mail: filipatia@hotmail.com.

Henrique Vicente, PhD Student (Foundation for Science and Technology, Grant SFRH/BD/23545/2005), University of Aveiro (Department of Health Sciences), 3810-193 Aveiro, Portugal; Phone: +351234372445; E.mail: a37472@ua.pt.

Isabel Santos, PhD; Postdoctoral Research Fellow at the University of Aveiro (PsyLab, Department of Educational Sciences); 3810-193 Aveiro, Portugal; Phone: +351234370644; Fax: +351234370640; E.mail: isabel.santos@ua.pt.

Jorge Costa, B.A.; Clinical Neuropsychologist at the University of Aveiro (PsyLab, Department of Educational Sciences); 3810-193 Aveiro, Portugal; Phone: +351234370644; Fax: +351234370640; E.mail: jmcosta3@hotmail.com

Liliana Santos, Research assistant at the University of Aveiro (Department of Health Sciences); 3810-193 Aveiro, Portugal; Phone: +351937628391; Fax: +351234401597; E.mail:lpintosantos@gmail.com.

Liliana Sousa, PhD; Auxiliary Professor at the University of Aveiro (Department of Health Sciences); 3810-193 Aveiro, Portugal; Phone: +351234372440; Fax: +351234401597; E.mail: Lilianax@ua.pt

Margarida P. Lima, PhD; Associate Professor at the University of Coimbra (Faculty of Psychology and Educational Sciences); Rua do Colégio Novo, Apartado 6153 3001-802 Coimbra, Portugal; Phone: +351239851450; Fax: +351239 851 468; E.mail: mplima@fpce.uc.pt

Marta Patrão, PhD Student (Foundation for Science and Technology, Grant SFRH/BD/22013/2005), University of Aveiro (Department of Health Sciences), 3810-193 Aveiro, Portugal; Phone: +351234372445; E.mail: marta.patrao@cs.ua.pt

Oscar Ribeiro, PhD; Assistant at School of Health Sciences of the University of Aveiro; 3810-193 Aveiro, Portugal; Phone: +351234401558; Fax: +351234401597; E.mail: oribeiro@ua.pt

Rosa Martins, PhD; Coordinator Professor at the Polytechnic Institute of Viseu (Health Sciences School); 3510-843 Viseu, Portugal; Phone: +351232419100; Fax: +351232428343; E.mail: romymartins@sapo.pt

INDEX

A

access, 33, 42, 158
accessibility, 128, 136
accounting, 12
achievement, 171, 179
activation, 129
acute, 17
adaptability, ix, 49, 68, 70
adaptation, 3, 12, 31, 33, 101, 115, 120, 138, 156
adjustment, 16, 94, 101, 179
adolescence, 36
adolescent adjustment, 45
adolescents, 32, 47
adult, 2, 3, 8, 9, 11, 14, 15, 16, 17, 19, 20, 33, 37, 38, 47, 53, 59, 66, 69, 77, 80, 82, 97, 99, 125, 131, 144, 164, 165, 180
adult population, 11
adulthood, 27, 37, 47, 79, 112, 137, 184
adults, ix, 9, 15, 21, 23, 24, 41, 45, 46, 75, 77, 79, 80, 81, 82, 86, 131, 132
affective meaning, 57
African American, 8
age, 1, 2, 10, 11, 14, 15, 20, 23, 27, 31, 35, 37, 40, 42, 46, 52, 57, 69, 79, 80, 85, 91, 92, 98, 99, 100, 104, 106, 113, 114, 130, 138, 141, 142, 145, 150, 154, 155, 156, 158, 161, 172, 179, 180, 181, 182, 183, 184
ageing, 1, 2, 4, 9, 11, 15, 19, 20, 21, 44, 46, 87, 97, 98, 99, 100, 101, 113, 114, 118, 130, 135, 136, 159, 163, 165, 166, 179, 180, 181, 182, 184
ageing population, 98
agents, 78
aging, 23, 25, 46, 47, 54, 73, 77, 79, 80, 82, 85, 92, 93, 94, 95, 98, 99, 100, 102, 113, 115, 116, 132, 138, 159, 182, 184

aging population, 80
aging process, 54, 99, 113
aid, 151
AIDS, 32, 47
alienation, 53, 163, 164, 165, 166, 167, 168, 174, 175, 176, 177, 178
alpha, 144
alternative, 9, 143, 155
alternatives, 83, 142, 156
altruism, 20, 52
Alzheimer, 11, 12, 16, 24, 102, 106, 107, 114, 124, 131, 132, 133, 155
ambiguity, 88, 112
ambivalence, 15, 24
ambivalent, 15
American Psychological Association (APA), 93, 94, 95, 131, 184
Amsterdam, 131
Anaemia, 150
analysis of variance, 149
androgyny, 100
anger, 10, 52, 86, 90, 121, 156
anthropology, 45
anxiety, 12, 52, 80, 88, 90, 119, 125, 129, 139, 168, 175
Anxiety, 119
apathy, 168
appendix, 27, 166
application, 20
appraisals, 122
argument, 29, 106, 130, 178
arthritis, 138, 150, 156, 158
assessment, 3, 11, 13, 21, 35, 39, 77, 78, 80, 106, 126, 127, 132, 139, 141, 144, 158, 160
assets, 50, 51, 52, 55, 59, 78

F

J

K

L

M

subjective, 10, 33, 78, 86, 89, 93, 118, 123, 131, 181
subjective experience, 78, 131, 181
subjective well-being, 10, 93, 123
substance abuse, 88
substitution, 37
successful aging, 44, 161
suffering, 10, 16, 24, 109, 110, 114, 135, 136, 141, 156
superimposition, 44
superiority, 169, 176, 177
support services, 3, 9, 120, 123, 127, 139
surgeries, 77
surgery, 12
surprise, 154
survival, 38, 43, 44, 50, 51, 64, 141
survivors, 88, 133
sustainability, 85
Sweden, 120
symbiotic, 20, 43, 44
symbolic, 49, 50, 51, 52, 55, 57, 58, 59, 62, 63, 64, 65, 66, 67, 68, 69, 71, 173, 183
symbolic meanings, 62
symbols, 72
symmetry, 128
sympathy, 84, 85, 88
symptoms, 10, 25, 28, 77, 80, 110, 118, 119, 121, 122, 123, 124, 139, 156
systematic, 127
systems, 3, 5, 6, 7, 11, 13, 14, 28, 33, 34, 35, 36, 38, 44, 47, 65, 85, 121, 126, 130, 136, 139

T

tangible, 107
technology, 3
telephone, 13, 32
temporal, 128
tension, 181
theoretical, 2, 9, 14, 19, 20, 27, 36, 72, 93, 94, 104, 118, 130, 154, 163
theory, 11, 14, 21, 28, 32, 37, 41, 69, 72, 75, 93, 95, 114, 146, 179, 183
therapeutic, 28, 77, 78, 79, 80, 81, 82, 85, 86, 88, 91, 121, 128
therapeutic goal, 86
therapeutic interventions, 85
therapeutic process, 78
therapeutic relationship, 81, 82, 88, 121
therapists, 29, 78, 87, 88, 93, 122
therapy, 2, 3, 10, 25, 73, 79, 80, 94, 123, 124
thinking, 78, 82, 110, 128, 138, 163
Thomson, 131

threat, 71, 107, 110
threatening, 67
threats, 21, 71, 112, 158
threshold, 154
time, 15, 20, 27, 33, 35, 36, 38, 40, 41, 44, 52, 53, 60, 62, 63, 66, 68, 70, 71, 79, 80, 81, 84, 85, 87, 88, 89, 90, 91, 98, 100, 106, 107, 109, 110, 116, 118, 119, 122, 123, 128, 135, 136, 137, 139, 145, 156, 164, 165, 168, 171, 172, 176, 179, 180, 181, 183, 184
time constraints, 179
timing, 44, 101, 130, 142
title, 3, 36, 43
tongue, 182, 184
tracking, 136
tradition, 183
training, 10, 63, 77, 82, 122, 123, 132, 156
trajectory, 38, 111, 123
trans, 40, 66
transactions, 33, 54, 59
transcendence, 37, 69
transfer, 39, 52, 53, 62, 65, 71
transference, 82
transformation, 38, 53, 55, 58, 70, 76, 85, 164, 165
transformations, 97, 168
transgenerational, 2, 86
transgression, 184
transition, 2, 9, 52, 67, 101, 106, 113, 135, 180, 181
transitions, 16, 20, 53, 54, 73, 98, 165, 168
transmission, 8, 12, 14, 15, 21, 25, 39, 40, 49, 50, 51, 55, 65, 66, 67, 68, 69, 70, 72, 164, 169, 180
transmits, 70
transport, 18, 34
trees, 39, 167
trend, 4
trial, 166
tribal, 8, 16, 23
trust, 50, 53, 67, 89
type 2 diabetes, 138
typology, 115

U

unfolded, 156
uniform, 99
United Kingdom, 51, 120
United States, 130
urban, 55, 59, 60, 63
urbanisation, 31
users, 126, 127, 149, 166